NOTRE DAME
AND THE GAME THAT
CHANGED FOOTBALL

NOTRE DAME
AND THE GAME THAT CHANGED FOOTBALL

*How Jesse Harper Made the Forward Pass a
Weapon and Knute Rockne a Legend*

FRANK P. MAGGIO

CARROLL & GRAF PUBLISHERS
NEW YORK

NOTRE DAME AND THE GAME THAT CHANGED FOOTBALL
How Jesse Harper Made the Forward Pass a Weapon and Knute Rockne a Legend

Carroll & Graf Publishers
An Imprint of Avalon Publishing Group, Inc.
245 West 17th Street, 11th Floor
New York, NY 10011

AVALON
publishing group incorporated

First Carroll & Graf edition 2007

Library of Congress Cataloging-in-Publication Data

Maggio, Frank P.
Notre Dame and the game that changed football : how Jesse Harper made the for-
ward pass a weapon and Knute Rockne a legend / by Frank P. Maggio. — 1st ed.
p. cm.
Includes bibliographical references and index.
ISBN-13: 978-0-7867-2014-9
ISBN-10: 0-7867-2014-X
1. Harper, Jesse C., 1883-1961. 2. Rockne, Knute, 1888-1931. 3. Football
coaches—United States—Biography. 4. Notre Dame Fighting Irish (Football team)—
History. 5. University of Notre Dame—Football—History. I. Title.

GV939.H316M34 2007
796.332092—dc22
[B]
2007015489

9 8 7 6 5 4 3 2 1

Interior design by Bettina M. Wilhelm
Printed in the United States of America
Distributed by Publishers Group West

To my friend Jim Harper
and
To Christopher, Anna, Louise, Will, Rose, and Charlotte,
the next generation

"The danger to college football, as in anything else, lies in the failure to know the origins of the game and the people responsible for its growth and maturity."

Jack Whitaker (1984)

CONTENTS

Acknowledgments

Thanks to my sons, John and Mark, for their frequent support. Special thanks to my daughters, Martha Merizon and Catherine Maggio; they read and edited portions of the early manuscript and supplied frequent and needed encouragement. Martha is the only one of my children who bleeds Blue and Gold.

Thanks to my friend and legal assistant for the past thirty-plus years, Andrea Setter. Andrea worked long hours reading and editing the manuscript. Her sons, Adam and Eric, contributed needed research. Adam's research was invaluable—he can find anything.

Research assistance from Sharon Sumpter at the archives at Notre Dame (Sharon worked with me for three years), Kent Stephens at the College

Football Hall of Fame archives, and Susan Lintelmann at the archives at West Point, all were important to my book. Research assistance from Notre Dame law students Carolyn Blessing and Matthew Moberg was also valuable. Conversations with Joe Doyle were priceless—Joe has more personal knowledge of Notre Dame football than any other living human being.

Advice from author Todd Tucker was helpful and appreciated. My agent, Jodie Rhodes, and my editor, Shaun Dillon, were both passionate about my book and Harper's story from day one.

Special thanks to Keith Jackson for his Preface. It brought a tear to my eye and a smile to my face.

And of course, Jim Harper, who generously shared his family memories and mementoes to help make this book possible.

And, finally, thanks to my wife, Pamela, who has long and patiently listened to my dinner-table ramblings about some event that happened in the college football world 100 or so years ago. As this project came to an end and deadlines loomed, Pamela, wonderful as always, became an authority on *The Chicago Manual of Style* and spent untold hours helping to prepare the final manuscript for publication.

Foreword

Notre Dame 35, Army 13

Notre Dame 35, Army 13. The game that started Notre Dame on the way to its days of glory. A twenty-nine-year-old coach by the name of Jesse C. Harper, in his first year of coaching at Notre Dame, not only beat the powerhouse Army decisively but also went on to an undefeated season and set a record that still stands.

As you will read, he achieved other outstanding developments in football that set him apart as of one of the great innovators of the game. With the duo of Knute Rockne and Gus Dorais he brought innovation to the forward pass, which opened up the game to the degree that we know it today.

I was born in 1918, the year he left Notre Dame to become a cattle rancher, but Notre Dame football was a ritual on Fall Saturdays. Dad, my brother Mell, and I would turn on the Atwater Kent radio and listen to games across the nation starting on the East Coast at 8 AM and quit at 8 PM with the West Coast games. Over the years Dad related many interesting stories about football in general and Notre Dame in particular. I have given this information and a big box of pictures and newspaper clippings that my mother collected, starting with a picture of Dad with the Morgan Park Academy Team in 1901 to the author for his research.

The author has uncovered a great deal more information than I ever knew. While I admired my father greatly, this additional information has heightened my love and respect for him tremendously. He was a great father, friend, and inspiration. He taught me to respect others; to demonstrate honesty, integrity, and positive thinking; to aim for the highest; and to treat your fellow men as equals. I believe that I have passed those virtues on to my sons, Jim Junior and Chris.

—Jim Harper

Introduction

In the fifty-two seasons I covered college football for television and radio there was formed the continuing curiosity and wonder of the omnipresence of the college football team known around the world as the Fighting Irish of Notre Dame . . . even in years when the team wasn't very good.

Jesse Harper had a major role in the creation of a university and a football team that has become almost a mythical player in sports history.

Yet he remained relatively anonymous to the general football public for a very long time. As this book tells you, Coach Harper has been discovered. And though his place in this history was a long time ago, the echoes continue.

Maybe the most profound early decision came in 1913 when Coach

Harper put his nineteen-man football team on the train and headed to the U.S. Military Academy at West Point, New York, to play the mighty Black Knights of Army.

Notre Dame threw the football all over the field that day. Rockne and Dorais and their pals won big-time, 35 to 13.

Nobody could know just how big it would become.

For example, one of the New York City newspapers offered a front-page story that read something like this, "On this Saturday on the bluff of West Point the Mighty Black Knights of Army fell to the multifaceted effort of the brawny brawling lads of Notre Dame du Lac from South Bend, *Illinois.*"

It didn't take long for the whole country to learn that Notre Dame's post office was located in *Indiana.*

And more and more of those big ole brawny brawling lads were finding their way there.

A large information source for me during the years of covering Notre Dame football was Jim Harper, son of Jesse, who has been my business manager for some forty years. Jim played some football . . . at Purdue! Had something to do with a scholarship and those were pretty precious in 1936 . . . or do you remember?

Oh, the Legend was a-building as the wins on the gridiron (that was a popular term back then) accumulated, and Jesse Harper passed the coaching job on to a Norwegian chemistry student named ku-Nute Rockne. His name was not "Noot" but properly preceded by a lightly touched "kuh."

Oh, well . . . long as you're winning, baby.

The football team with all that publicity and other advantages, especially the big-city newspapers in New York and Chicago, was on its way to unprecedented acceptance.

First the team was called . . . the Catholics. Then changed to Ramblers because they traveled so much.

And then after a particularly trying game in which it was written they performed like Fighting Irish . . . the final brick for the legendary myth was in place.

Founded by a French priest as Notre Dame du Lac . . . they would be forever known as The Fighting Irish of Notre Dame. Oh, the marketing possibilities . . . wonderful, as we would come to see.

And they would build a great university along the way.

By the way . . . don't waste any valuable time looking for a Notre Dame in Ireland . . . there isn't one. I've already looked!

I really don't know nor do I really care how many football games I have announced at Notre Dame since ABC Sports got the contract for college football in 1966. Most of them were fun, some had great meaning around the country, and the Notre Dame Fighting Irish grew into a national team.

And like so many places in college football . . . no matter your concern about being fair and even in your broadcast . . . "if you weren't for 'em, you were agin 'em."

Without question provincialism is a great strength in college athletics and a great assist in keeping the campus and alumni together as a community.

Nobody has done it better than Notre Dame.

When the first step was taken toward what we now called the BCS, it became obvious Notre Dame was gonna have a special place. And when the mortar started setting, The Irish not only had their own TV network for home games, they negotiated a double fee from the BCS. Their leverage was simple and old-fashioned. They sell out stadiums and get good rating numbers on television.

The arrangement prompted me to ask more than once: is it a team, a conference, or a nation? I have yet to receive a formal reply. No need for it!

There are some wonderful stories from the days of the old Stadium. A constant sellout at 55,505 . . . I think was the number. There was always an Icon, an Idol, an All-American with whom you could share a memory or even a dram on a cool day. I don't know about the fancy new stadium. I have never been in it. We lost the TV contract before it was built.

When I retired, Notre Dame gave me a letterman's blanket with a special inscription on it. I keep it on my favorite easy chair where I like to read. When the afternoon sun leaves the western window, the blanket keeps this old-timer warm and I appreciate it.

It is a great place to ponder and wonder about people and places and especially those who were there when the seeds for future things were planted down by the Bend in the River.

—Keith Jackson

Preface

At halftime on November 1, 1913, with Notre Dame hanging on to a precarious 14–13 lead over Army, Notre Dame's head coach instructed his quarterback to start passing and keep passing. Almost one hundred years later, Harper's decision that day to use Notre Dame's newly perfected forward pass was declared to be the "greatest" single coaching decision in college football during the twentieth century.

On a fair but crisp afternoon, October 31, 1913, nineteen college football players, together with their twenty-nine-year-old coach, made their way across the campus of the United States Military Academy at West Point, New York. The young men were in awe of the dramatic grounds of the Military Academy and the grandeur of its buildings, all set high on a bluff overlooking the Hudson River. An eyewitness remembered them as "a sterling group of men, dressed as the college men of the day—few wearing hats and some dressed in sweaters of various shades, practically all carried a suitcase in which was contained articles of playing equipment." The players and their coach, Jesse C. Harper, were from the University of Notre Dame, a small and relatively unknown Catholic men's school located in South Bend, Indiana. For the moment, they were more impressed with simply being at West Point than they were with the fact that the next day they would be playing a football game against mighty Army. Though they did not know it at the time, these young men and their coach were also about to make football history.

After lunch with the cadets in the West Point mess hall, the Notre Dame men adjourned to the Army football field for a light workout. Their progress was recorded by Cadet Willet J. Baird, then the Army team mascot, and later to become a high-ranking Army officer. He observed that the awe of the Notre Dame men followed them, as they "expressed no end of amazement and joy" over the fact that the Army football field was "very smooth, well marked, and resembled the appearance of a well-kept lawn." Their own field, back in Indiana, had once been referred to as a "cow-pasture."

Ten months earlier, Harper had been hired as the athletic director and head football coach at Notre Dame. He was the first athletic director in the school's history and also the first professional football coach. Soon after his appointment, Harper wrote to several schools in an attempt to arrange Notre Dame's football schedule for the 1913 season. The custom at the time was to arrange the season's games in the preceding winter and spring. One of Harper's letters was addressed to the United

States Military Academy, a gutsy move, considering Notre Dame's then-modest status in the world of intercollegiate sports. Army, looking for a "breather," accepted.

On Saturday, November 1, 1913, on the Plains at West Point, Notre Dame upset the heavily favored Cadets in dramatic fashion. Their victory alone made it a game worth remembering. However, the game was more, much more. It was Notre Dame's national debut. It was the game that started Notre Dame on the road to becoming the most legendary program in college football. And, of even more significance, Notre Dame's victory that day was achieved through the team's daring use of the forward pass—an innovation that would change the game of football forever.

The game's significance was immediately recognized. The next day, the Sunday edition of the *New York Times* devoted three columns to the Notre Dame vs. Army contest, observing: "Football men marveled at this startling display of open football. Bill Roper, former head coach at Princeton, who was one of the officials of the game, said that he had always believed that such playing was possible under the new rules, but that he had never seen the forward pass developed to such a state of perfection."

It's fair to assume that neither the Notre Dame team nor their coach saw the *Times* account that Sunday. Harper treated his victorious team to a sightseeing tour of Niagara Falls before returning to South Bend. Harper recorded in his expense account: "Transportation to Niagara and Return, $10." They no doubt never imagined that their play that day would receive the historical recognition that eventually came its way.

Several unrelated factors converged in 1913 to lead the University of

Notre Dame through its November 1 game with Army and its history-making 1913 football season. First, the rules of the game of football, which had been steadily evolving since the dramatic changes of 1906, had progressed to the point of the game we know today, namely, rules permitting the unfettered and innovative use of the forward pass. Second, during the 1913 football season, Notre Dame had a wonderfully talented group of football players, men who would be more than able to execute the offensive plays that Harper would devise, under the new forward-passing rules. Last, but most importantly, Notre Dame had a new head football coach. He was bright and well schooled in the new rules of the game, and he possessed the vision and courage to arrange a national schedule of major opponents—a stage, if you will, for Notre Dame to display its talents. In addition, he possessed the coaching acumen to instruct his players in the use of the forward pass and to lead them to victory. Notre Dame's daunting schedule in 1913 took them 1,000 miles to the East and 1,500 miles to the Southwest. It was a national schedule, the likes of which no other college football team had ever before attempted. In the end, they were undefeated, and their victory over Army was enshrined in the history books. 1913 was a magical football season for the University of Notre Dame. It was the first of many and, in many respects, the best of them all.

1

A University Is Born on the Frontier

The Founding of the University of Notre Dame

To say that the University of Notre Dame rose from meager beginnings, and that its present stature is an example of the tall oak rising from the little acorn, would be an understatement. This great academic institution known today as the University of Notre Dame, one of the leading universities in the nation, rose from virtually nothing—nothing but the tremendous faith of its founders. In the beginning, Notre Dame was literally carved from the wooded frontier of a new nation. Then, once the first buildings of this new institution were barely completed, the school was destroyed by fire, only to be built once again.

The fathers of the Congregation of the Holy Cross, an order of

French priests, established the University of Notre Dame du Lac in 1842 on a site immediately north of South Bend, Indiana, an area that was still part of the American wilderness. The Indian wars in this part of the country had only recently ended, with the famous 1811 Battle of Tippecanoe near Lafayette, Indiana. Indiana itself was a relatively new member of the union, having attained its statehood in 1816.

In 1680, a century and a half prior to the arrival of the Holy Cross priests who would found and build Notre Dame, a mission had been established by Father Claude Allouez, a Jesuit priest, near what today is the city of Niles, Michigan, some twenty miles north of South Bend. Various wars and the eventual suppression of the Jesuits led to the decline of this mission and the eventual dismantling of the original missionary work in this area of Indiana.

In the early 1830s, Father Stephen Badin, a French priest who had lived under the terror of the Revolution in France, found his way into the region. He was a determined and outstanding missionary and was intent on making a Christian impact on the Native American children in the surrounding area. In 1831 and 1832, Father Badin began a series of land purchases, amounting to several hundred acres. His dream was to develop a school and orphanage for Native American children in the area. Father Badin's efforts, however, were unsuccessful, and eventually he deeded his land to the bishop of the Diocese of Vincennes, Indiana, on the condition that at some future date it would be used for the establishment of a school—all at such time as the means permitted.

In November 1842, Father Edward Sorin arrived. A twenty-eight-year-old priest from a newly founded French order that came to be known as the Congregation of the Holy Cross, Father Sorin had also endured the suffering and oppression that followed the French Revolution. Though Father Sorin was intent on bringing the light of the gospel into the New World, his true passion was to start a school—not just any school, but a great school, in his words, L'Université. As events unfolded, the bishop of Vincennes deeded the land he had received from Father Badin to Father Sorin, on the condition, as Badin had demanded, that a school be founded on the site.

That winter, as soon as the gift of the land had been made, Father Sorin and his party of six brothers from the Congregation of the Holy Cross set out in a blizzard to view their newly acquired property. Prior to leaving Vincennes, Father Sorin, always looking ahead, retained an architect identified as Mr. Marsile to design the main building for his new university. The party arrived in South Bend in the middle of a severe blizzard. Their first stop was the house of Alexis Coquillard, a successful French fur merchant, who had lived in the area for several years—if you drive up Notre Dame Avenue today, the main entrance to the university, the imposing tombstone of Alexis Coquillard is a prominent sight on your left. After a short introduction and the minimum social time with Coquillard, Father Sorin insisted on seeing his newly acquired land. The snow was raging and Coquillard suggested, then begged, that the party rest at his home and go to the land the next day, or even on another day, after the storm had subsided. Father Sorin replied, "I want to see my land. I want to see it now." Exasperated and defeated by Sorin's insistence, Coquillard hooked up his sleigh and drove the men to their site. It was a heavily wooded area containing two lakes, both of which were frozen. In fact, Sorin mistakenly thought there was only one lake.

In September 2005, at the inauguration Mass celebrating the appointment of Father John I. Jenkins, C.S.C., as Notre Dame's new president, President Emeritus Father Theodore M. Hesburgh, C.S.C., delivered the homily, and told the story of Father Sorin's first reaction to his site.

> He wasn't here more than a few seconds when he named the place. "Je nomme L'Universite de Notre Dame du Lac. I name you the University of Our Lady of the Lake." It didn't matter that there were two lakes actually, which came to be named St. Mary's and St. Joseph's, he was standing at St. Mary's. It didn't matter that standing before him was a broken-down log cabin, the roof broken in, the snow filling the building. It took them two days to clean it out enough to move in. It didn't matter to him that he had only 300 dollars in his pocket and that somehow he had, one might say, the gall, or perhaps, much better, the zeal, not to call this dream of his an école, which would have been normal, a school, or even a lycée, a high school, or even a college, a college. No, not for Sorin. This dream spot of his had to be called L'Universite, and indeed his dream has come true in all the years that have followed.

About two years later, on January 15, 1844, the Indiana General Assembly granted the fathers' application for a charter as the University of Notre Dame du Lac.

Father Sorin's strength and vision promptly came to the fore. Notre Dame began as a frontier school whose students were generally uneducated backwoods men, with little or no formal intellectual training. The teachers, the priests of the Congregation of the Holy Cross, were Frenchmen, who more often than not spoke little or no English. Initially, the classes were basic—the work was at the level of elementary school or high school. The Holy Cross fathers coupled their program of studies with the strong disciplinary tradition that they had brought with them from France.

Construction of the necessary university buildings began immediately, following the plans of Father Sorin's Vincennes architect. The first grand structure on the Notre Dame campus did not get under way until the spring of 1869, when, under Father Sorin's leadership, plans were made for the construction of a new church. On May 31, 1871, with six bishops present, the cornerstone of Our Lady of the Sacred Heart was laid. Five years after its inception, portions of the church were ready for occupancy. Finally, in 1887, the chapel of Our Lady was added and in it was placed a gilded Baroque altar, which Father Sorin had discovered on a trip to Rome. Though the altar was probably not an original work of Bernini, it has been said that it is almost certainly the product of one of Bernini's pupils.

Notre Dame was growing rapidly, when, on the morning of April 23, 1879, tragedy struck—the cry of "fire" rang through the small campus. The fire had started at a construction site, on a college roof approximately six stories high. Efforts to extinguish the fire and to keep it from spreading failed, and nearly the entire university, Sorin's lifework, burned to the ground. Fortunately, the new church escaped damage, and though there were serious injuries and many close calls, miraculously, there were no casualties.

Within three hours, the main college building, St. Francis' Home, the

Infirmary, and the Music Hall were in complete ruin. With the exception of Sacred Heart church, virtually the entire University was destroyed.

One of the greatest concerns for Father William Corby, then the university president, was how the news of the fire would affect Father Sorin, who was in Montreal at the time of the fire, preparing for his fifty-fifth fundraising trip to France. A university messenger was sent to Montreal to personally break the news to Sorin. A week later, upon Father Sorin's return to campus, all involved found out how the destruction would affect the sixty-five-year-old. They watched anxiously as Sorin calmly walked amid the charred ruins. An observer of the scene remembered that instead of bending, Father Sorin seemed to stiffen, and instead of a saddened expression, he took on a look of grim determination.

When Father Sorin had completed his tour of the ruins, he called the assembled Notre Dame family into Sacred Heart Church. The church was ten years old and still under some finishing construction, but though it had filled with smoke, it had not otherwise been damaged by the fire. As Father Hesburgh described the scene in his homily at Father Jenkins's inauguration mass at Sacred Heart Church in September 2005, Father Sorin "said a rather startling thing . . . 'Brothers and sisters, this fire is my fault.' And they said 'Father Sorin! You were in Montreal, how could this fire have been your fault?' He said, 'My problem was that I was thinking too small. I was not enthusiastic enough about what I should build and name after Notre Dame, Our Lady. We're going out there tomorrow and we're going to clean up the ruins and save what we can. . . . And then we're going to build a building worthy of Our Lady and crown it with Her." After that moment, there was never a doubt.

The University closed down immediately after the fire, with a promise to the students from Father Corby that it would reopen in September. The loss was estimated at $200,000, with only $45,000 covered by insurance—a devastating financial blow. Funds would have to be raised, and fast. The amount needed to rebuild Notre Dame stunned the South Bend community and the Notre Dame family. One of the first to step forward was Alexis Coquillard, who promptly contributed a gift of five hundred dollars.

And so it was, that in, 1879, while the game of football was still in its infancy in the eastern United States—the initial game between Princeton and Rutgers having been played only ten years earlier—and while Walter Camp at Yale had yet to develop the scrimmage rules and the downs rules, Notre Dame and Father Sorin had greater matters with which to contend. Under Sorin's leadership, money was raised, debts were incurred, construction forces were marshaled, and Notre Dame was rebuilt—or, perhaps more accurately, built.

2

A History of the Early Game, 1869–1905

In the early years of the twentieth century, a Wild West atmosphere permeated the game of football. The roughness that was inherent in the game was amplified by the lack of rules. In addition, at the college level there were, for the most part, no uniform or ascertainable standards for eligibility, and thus the stage was set for so-called tramp athletes. A tramp athlete was one who went from school to school, and enrolled, usually under an alias, for the sole purpose of playing football, disregarding academic requirements. Gambling, almost as a logical extension of the prevailing atmosphere, became commonplace. The gambling seemed limited, in general, to just that—gambling. Players and fans would bet on the success of their team in a particular game. Presumably, human nature being what it is, some form of cheating took place from time to time, but for the most part, cheating seemed to be the exception.

From the beginning, football fostered a rough culture, a culture that was built into the game and that is, to a certain extent, still an essential part of the game. In the early days, in addition to kicking or attempting to kick a ball in a particular direction, the object of the game was for men to knock other men around, or better yet, to knock them down. However, as the game evolved into the late nineteenth century and the early twentieth century, the inherent roughness turned to outright violence, and the violence bordered on the criminal. The consequences of this dark turn in the game threatened not only the life of the game but also the lives of the men who played it.

From 1869 to 1905 football evolved from its original soccer and rugby roots into a style of play that featured momentum-running formations and mass-running formations. Momentum-running plays were featured on kickoffs or punt returns. The players would surround the ballcarrier in a V formation—the so-called flying wedge—and run straight at the defense, building up momentum as they proceeded down the field. Mass-running formations, on the other hand, took place at the line of scrimmage. The offensive players would stand close together, sometimes literally holding on to each other, to protect the ballcarrier, and charge forward.

This early period of the game's development can be divided into two separate time periods. Between 1869 and 1880, the basics of the game—whether players could run with the ball or advance the ball only by kicking it—were determined. Between 1880 and 1905, the details and rules that would make it the game of football the game we know today were developed.

1869 to 1880

Football had its origins in the mid-1800s, at about the same time as the American Civil War. The game was attractive—running, kicking a ball, and trying to knock each other down came naturally to athletic young men. People liked to watch the game being played. And, besides baseball, football was the only game then being played across America.

The birthplace of the American game of football was in the East. The first precursors to football were played in the early and mid-1800s, under rules that were generally a derivation from the rules of soccer—a game whose origins have been traced to the ancient Greeks and Egyptians.

During these first years of football, the students at Harvard, Yale, and Princeton were the leaders, at least at the university level, in developing the rules of the game. The historian and author Mark E. Bernstein makes an accurate observation when he writes that "the Ivy League . . . created American football and . . . almost every facet of the game bears their imprint."

The first recorded intercollegiate football game took place on November 6, 1869, at College Field in New Brunswick, New Jersey, pitting Rutgers against Princeton. What rules there were had been devised by Princeton and loosely adopted from British soccer. The game was played with twenty-five players to a side, and the ball was to be kicked with the foot or butted with the head. Holding the ball and running with it was forbidden. Six goals were necessary to win the game. There were no uniforms—the players simply took off their hats and coats and played the game. Rutgers won by a score of six goals to four, using a scoring system different from the one that is in effect today. The contest was an affair, one would hardly have been recognized as the game of football that we know today, but it was typical of the games played in football's early years. A week later, Rutgers traveled to Princeton and lost, 8–0. The rubber match was never played.

Football was originally developed as a campus recreational activity. The days of its becoming a national institution were not yet even imagined. In that early era, the officials of the various institutions had little or nothing to do with how football was played, who played, or how the rules of the game themselves developed. There were no athletic departments, athletic directors, or coaches. The entire endeavor of playing football—rules, training, coaching, and the scheduling of games—was handled by the interested and participating students.

In 1874, two landmark football games were scheduled between Harvard University and McGill University of Montreal, Canada. Though not all historians agree, these two games seem to deserve the "landmark" appellation, because more than any other event or series of events they mark the adoption of the rugby style of play by Harvard—and Harvard, more than any other university involved in the early years of football, led the way. After these two games, Harvard was successful in advocating the rugby style of play for American football, a style that, in the end, made all the difference. At the time these games were played, McGill played a distinctly rugby style of football, as opposed to the soccer style that had been in vogue at Harvard and elsewhere in the United States since the Princeton–Rutgers game in 1869.

In rugby, a game developed at the famous Rugby School in England in 1823, the ball is advanced by holding the ball and running with it. Under rugby rules, players were allowed to pass the ball laterally, and defenders were allowed to tackle the player carrying the ball—but they could only tackle above the waist.

The two games between Harvard and McGill were played in a style favorable to the home team and also featured the adoption of the rugby-style scrummage as a means of putting the ball into play. McGill's rugby-style football caught the enthusiasm of the participants as well as the spectators, and Harvard, despite its inexperience with the rugby style of play, won the first game and tied the second.

1875 saw the advent of the first Harvard–Yale football game, in a series between the two schools that would grow to become an inter-collegiate football classic and be known simply as "The Game." Harvard and Yale had been competing in rowing since the 1850s and in baseball since the 1860s. It was only natural for the competitive spirit of their respective students to turn to the new and popular game of football. However, a problem arose with regard to the proposed football game—there were no set rules governing play. That October, representatives of Harvard and Yale met in Springfield, Massachusetts, to determine the rules for the game to be played in November. Harvard, drawing on its positive experience in its recent games with McGill University, came into the rules meeting stubbornly attached to the rugby style of football, while Yale favored the soccer-style rules. Harvard's position carried the day and, fortunately for the game of football, Harvard's instincts were right. Harvard successfully advocated their preference for the rugby style of play. This would not be the last time that Harvard would exert its influence to guide the game into the modern era. The rules drawn up for the upcoming Harvard–Yale game not only allowed a player to run with the ball, but also adopted the scrummage system, lateral passing, and tackling of the ballcarrier. In addition, the newly adopted rules called for fif-teen players on each side, rather than twenty-five, as had previously been the case. All in all, these innovative rules resulted in a much more interesting game for both the players and spectators, and on November 13, 1875, Harvard defeated Yale by a score of 4 goals to 0. Immediately thereafter, the rugby style of American football was adopted by every major school playing the game.

1880 to 1905

Football had evolved into rugby-style play, but, compared to today's game, it still had few rules and retained the appearance of mass confusion. Beginning in 1880, however, several changes in the rules brought the game much closer to what we know today. In the 1880s the scrimmage rule replaced the rugby scrummage as a way of putting the ball into play, and the downs rule—at the time teams had three downs to make five yards—was initiated to control abuse inherent in the scrimmage rule. By the late 1880s a new and more exciting game had been developed. Gone were the soccer rules, and gone were the rugby rules— American football had truly been born.

The innovations in the late 1800s were driven for the most part by an ingenious young Yale student and football player by the name of Walter Chauncey Camp. The son of a school principal, whose ancestors had come to America shortly after the Pilgrims, Camp was without question the single most important figure in the early history and development of American football. His vision and guidance during these early years rightly earned him the title "The Father of American Football."

Camp was born in New Haven, Connecticut, on April 7, 1859, and enrolled at Yale in 1876. He played football at Yale for seven years, a common and legitimate tenure at that time, and served as team captain for three of those years. Though he was never officially Yale's football coach, Camp served as Yale's unpaid advisory coach from his days as a player until 1906. Camp's role at Yale was unofficial, although as the dominant personality at Yale when it came to football, he was in effect the chairman of Yale's athletic program. During Camp's time, Yale was the strongest team in college football, compiling a record of 218 wins, 11 losses, and 8 ties. From 1878 until his death in 1925, Camp served on every football rules committee or commission of any significance, and his ideas dominated the politics of the early rules committees.

In 1880, at age twenty-one, Camp responded to the inefficiencies inherent in the rugby scrummage by introducing the novel idea of a scrimmage, a simple and efficient method of putting the ball into play. In the old rugby scrummage, play was started by throwing the ball between two groups of opposing players, who would then seek to kick the ball out of the crowd to one of their own players. It was somewhat similar to modern-day hockey's face-off, but much more convoluted. Camp's scrimmage procedure was simpler and more efficient. One player from the team in possession of the football—the center—would kick or pass the ball backward to one of his teammates—the quarterback. Camp's scrimmage method was immediately adopted by all of the major football schools.

However, as efficient and innovative as it was, Camp's scrimmage proposal created a new problem: one team could now maintain possession of the ball indefinitely, making no effort to score, or even to advance the ball, as there was no limit on the number of downs a team could have from a scrimmage. Under the rules in effect at this time, a tie game was awarded to the winner from the previous year, so a tie could be the equivalent of a win. In response to this dilemma, Camp, in 1882, introduced the downs system. This reform provided that a team would have three downs to advance the ball at least five yards. If the offense failed to gain the necessary yardage, the ball was to be turned over to the opposing team at the spot of the last down. The downs system had two immediate and positive effects. First, it required that lines be drawn on the field every five yards, so that the officials as well as the players could determine their progress (these line markings gave the field the nickname "gridiron") and, secondly, it stimulated creative offensive strategy.

As dramatic as Camp's changes were, the actual play of the game was still conducted in a rough and fairly lawless fashion. When interviewed years later, John W. Heisman, one of the early leaders of the game, recalled his first playing experience in 1885: "Of rules we observed few, having few. Signals we had none—needed none, wanted none. We butted the ball, punched it, elbowed it, and kicked it."

The early running plays consisted of the offense ganging into a group around the ballcarrier and running straight at the defense—wearing no protective equipment. The action was rough, and immediately injuries became commonplace. Initially the injuries were of an acceptable nature—a bloody nose, a broken tooth. In a few short years, however, the nature of the injuries would turn dramatically into the unacceptable. John Heisman described the rough aspects of the play of these early games when he recalled, years later, "We wore jerseys and shorts of great variety. We had no helmets or pads of any kind; in fact, one who wore home-made pads was regarded as a sissy." The ballcarrier was pulled and pushed by whatever means possible, and players "were permitted to grab hold of their runners anywhere they could and push, pull, or yank them along in any direction that would make the ball advance. Sometimes two enemy tacklers would be clinging to the runner's legs, and trying to hold him back, while several team-mates of the runner had hold of his arms, head, hair, or wherever they could attach themselves, and were pulling him in the other direction." To facilitate this, "some running backs had leather straps, like valise handles, sewed or riveted on the shoulders of their jackets and on the hips of their trousers, so as to offer good handholds for their team-mates."

The line play he observed was even rougher: "Nearly all linemen . . . lined up squarely against those who played the same position on the opposing team. They didn't crouch or squat or play low. They mostly stood bolt upright and fought it out with each other, hammer and tongs, tooth and nail, fist and feet. Fact is, you didn't stand much chance of making the line those days unless you were a good wrestler and fair boxer."

With Camp's changes in place, the game of football was taking on a completely new appearance. It became a much more exciting game to play and to watch, and its popularity soared. The new game soon spread to numerous colleges and universities, first in the East and then across the country. The names of these early pioneer teams fill the sports pages to this day: Brown, Cornell, Oberlin, Williams, Amherst, Virginia, Washington and Lee, Virginia Military Institute, and major Midwestern universities such as Michigan, Minnesota, Purdue, Indiana, Chicago, and Notre Dame. The 1890s saw schools in the West, such as California, Southern California, and Washington, take up the game, and in 1890 came the first Army vs. Navy game, with Navy winning 24–0.

Football's popularity with the sporting public was also reaching a new high. More and more colleges and universities were adopting the game, and attendance was booming. In 1883, some 10,000 people witnessed the Harvard vs. Yale game in New York City. In 1891, 40,000 spectators attended the game between Princeton and Yale. In 1903, in response to this newfound popularity of the game, Harvard constructed the first stadium devoted exclusively to football. Harvard Stadium's original seating capacity provided for 22,000 spectators, and it stands in use to this day, having long ago been declared a National Historical Landmark. The interest of the public translated directly into dollars for the schools playing football and the prospects of financial gain became a strong motivating factor in the game's continued development.

But the road to the top does not always run straight uphill. During the 1880s, despite Camp's revolutionary innovations of the scrimmage procedure and the downs rule, the game developed an ominous side.

In 1884, the V formation made its first appearance, and momentum play was born. The V formation, or flying wedge, was used primarily on kickoff returns. Players would form a mass in the shape of the letter V, all locking arms around one another. The halfback, who carried the ball, would stay inside the V, directly behind the man at the apex. In order to achieve this tight and hopefully impregnable formation, teams developed schemes such as clasping hands or hanging on to handles that had been sewn into their uniforms. In an attempt to break the flying wedge, the defense men would throw themselves headfirst into the onrushing players. Fractured skulls, crushed vertebrae, and broken bones, often resulting in blood poisoning or serious and lifelong injury, and in many cases death, became commonplace. Protective gear such as helmets and shoulder pads had not yet become a part of the game, and that, plus the style of play in vogue, made players of that day far more susceptible to injury than today's players.

In fact, it was a seemingly innocuous new rule, pushed forth by Camp in 1888, that permitted tackling below the waist and as low as the knee, that led to the end of open play and the rise of mass play. The repercussions of Camp's new rule were enormous. Previously, teams had formations of players stretching across the field, with the ball often being passed laterally to a runner. The game was exciting and open, with quick plays such as rugby-style reverses and end runs. However, low tackling proved to be devastating to runners in this open formation, and even the best ballcarriers could no longer consistently gain yardage. In response, teams contracted their offensive lines of scrimmage until the players stood shoulder to shoulder, and the running backs were drawn in close to the offensive linemen. Offenses and defenses concentrated their players at the point of the ballcarrier's attack.

Football had always had a rough aspect to it, and it still does, but that's part of the game's attraction. That said, there is a line between roughness and violence, and the game was starting to cross that line. One of the consequences of the violent aspects came to light in the unfortunate aftermath of the 1894 Harvard–Yale game. Despite their deep historical affinity, bitterness resulting from the game's violence caused the two schools to end their athletic relationship. They resumed in 1897.

From the mid-1880s on, serious injuries and deaths in the game increased dramatically. Momentum play, such as the flying wedge, was outlawed in 1894, but the mass-running style of play continued, as did the resulting injuries and deaths. The carnage would reach a breaking point in 1905. Injuries and deaths calculated at the close of the 1905 season literally forced the game into modifying its rules of play.

The Early Days of Football at Notre Dame

During these years of the game's development, football was entering its early stages at the University of Notre Dame. One writer recalls a casual game in 1876 when several Notre Dame students chose teams, ending up with forty-two players on each side, and played "one of the old-fashioned games of football" for the prize of "a couple of barrels of apples." In September of 1879, the fall after the fire, "a great football match was played on the campus," this time for a barrel of sweet cider. The game lasted more than three hours. Students on the victorious team were reported as "slightly unmanageable" that night, but firm words from University President Father Corby served to quell their high spirits.

Football at the University of Notre Dame had its official intercollegiate start several years later, on November 23, 1887, when the University of Michigan football team traveled to South Bend to introduce the Notre Dame men to the recently enacted rules of the game. The game ended at the half with Michigan winning 8–0. Though of little interest to the general public at the time, the game captured the interest and enthusiasm of the entire Notre Dame student body, which gathered en masse at the campus playing field, with musical support provided by the school band.

As the Notre Dame school newspaper, the *Scholastic,* reported, on November 26, 1887:

The home team had been organized only a few weeks and the Michigan boys, the champions of the West, came more to instruct . . . than to win fresh laurels . . . At first, to render our players more familiar with the game, the teams were chosen irrespective of college. After some minutes' play, the game was called and each took his position. . . . The occasion has started an enthusiastic football boom and it is hoped that coming years will witness a series of these contests. After a hearty dinner, the President of Notre Dame, Father Thomas Walsh, thanked the Ann Arbor team for their visit, and assured them that a "cordial reception that would always await them at Notre Dame."

In 1888 Notre Dame and Michigan played two games on successive days in April. Michigan won both. Both games featured arguments over the rules, which were still developing.

Though football was still in its infancy at Notre Dame, 1888 was a good year for Father Sorin. In 1888 the magnificent Sacred Heart church was completed, the church was finally free of debt, and it was the year of Father Sorin's golden jubilee of ordination. The Bishop of Fort Wayne came to the campus and solemnly consecrated the church on August 15.

How avidly the now-aging Father Sorin took to this new campus activity called football can only be guessed at. We do know, however, that he did live long enough to see the early beginnings of the game at his beloved University.

Though the football seed had been firmly planted at Notre Dame, the school's formal football program was drifting. In 1890 and 1891, the official football team of the school was completely disbanded. Play resumed, to a minor degree, in 1892.

In 1896, Francis E. Hering, who has come to be referred to as the father of Notre Dame football, arrived on the Notre Dame campus. Like Jesse Harper, who would come to Notre Dame some seventeen years later, Hering was a product of Amos Alonzo Stagg at the University of Chicago. Hering had "the jaw of a fighting man and the brooding look of a poet," and was immediately elected as the football team's coach, captain, and quarterback, positions he held through the 1898 football season. Hering's presence and guidance brought a much-needed degree of stability to Notre Dame's football program, though he took little or no money for his work with the football team and spent his time away from football teaching English and studying law.

With the turn of the century, a new person took the stage at Notre Dame. Known as Red due to his fiery red hair, Louis Salmon was an exceptional athlete, excelling in every aspect of the game, as well as at track. He punted, kicked off, and was a breakaway runner. The former Notre Dame player and historian Chet Grant writes, "At the time when it was a red-letter event for a Western Conference or a Michigan star to breach the ivy walls of Walter Camp's All-America lineup, Red Salmon of tiny Notre Dame made the third team."

As there was no coach at the beginning of the 1902 season, Salmon and some of the other regular players put together a team, with Salmon as coach. Salmon graduated with honors in civil engineering in 1903, then served as the Notre Dame head coach for 1904, leading Notre Dame to a perfect season. Salmon, who died in 1965 at the age of eighty-five, is widely regarded as Notre Dame's greatest player prior to the arrival of George Gipp in 1916.

Notre Dame's football program developed at a steady pace after Salmon's years. In 1907 Harry "Red" Miller was elected by the critics as the number-one halfback of any team in Indiana. Miller, who played from 1906 to 1909, was the first member of one of Notre Dame's most famous family football dynasties. He was followed at Notre Dame by four younger brothers, all of whom played football. Ray played for Coach Harper, backing up Rockne at end in 1913. Walter played fullback under Coach Rockne with the 1919 and 1920 teams that featured George Gipp at halfback. From 1922 to 1924, Gerald and Don played under Rockne. A member of the famous Four Horsemen backfield for Notre Dame in 1924, Don was the best of the five Miller brothers and also probably the best of the Four Horsemen. Years later, the Miller family tradition continued, when Red's son Creighton was an All-American halfback on Frank Leahy's 1943 National Championship squad.

Notre Dame's 1908 team displayed early hints of greatness. The team turned in an 8–1 record, with their only loss being to the always powerful University of Michigan by a score of 12–6.

By the start of the 1909 season, Notre Dame was gaining a reputation in the Midwest as a strong, tough football team. The pinnacle of their growing dominance came in 1909, when they notched their first win over Michigan, a landmark event in the early history of Notre Dame football. Michigan was the powerhouse of the Midwest at the time, and was looked upon as one of the most important football teams in the country. Notre Dame startled Michigan and the Midwestern football world with the 11–3 victory, and finished the season undefeated, the declared champions of the West.

The victory, however, was bittersweet. After the game, Michigan coach Fielding Yost accused Notre Dame of using ineligible players. A controversy flared, and the dispute led to one of the longest, most bitter feuds in the history of college football.

To address Yost's accusations, a group of Eastern sportswriters convened in South Bend to conduct in informal inquiry into the athletic situation at Notre Dame. The *New York Times* reported on December 5, 1909 that a "thorough investigation," including a review of academic records, pictures, and signed statements by all of the key participants revealed that the players challenged by Michigan's coach—Samuel M. Dolan, Harry "Red" Miller, Ralph Dimick, George Philbrook, Donald M. Hamilton, and Robert L. Mathews—were and had been full-time students at the University and all had excellent academic records. Notre Dame was clean, but some damage had been done, as Yost's label of unfair competition stuck, at least momentarily.

Despite the controversy, a resolution appeared to have been reached between the two universities, and they agreed to play again in 1910. However, hours before the 1910 game was to be played, and while the Notre Dame team was on the train to Ann Arbor, Yost canceled the game. Deep and bitter feelings resulted, and the two schools terminated all athletic relations. They would not meet again on the football field until 1942, when Michigan visited Notre Dame and won, 32–20. Many writers believe that another result of the feud was that Fielding Yost, an influential figure in the football world of his day, blackballed Notre Dame from admission into the Western Conference, now the Big Ten. Subsequently, the University of Michigan consistently led a group of Western Conference teams in a boycott against even scheduling games with Notre Dame.

Though disappointing to Notre Dame at the time, this exclusionary attitude, which successfully limited Notre Dame's Midwest competition, was one of the very reasons Harper, three years later, would initiate Notre Dame's policy of soliciting games on a national level.

It wasn't the last time that accusations such as Yost's would be leveled at a Notre Dame football team, and it was not completely out of line with the culture of the day. However, Notre Dame's record, though attacked from time to time, proved, upon investigation, to be clean. The complaint, however, drove one pro–Notre Dame sportswriter to attempt a response. On October 17, 1914, Paul J. Meifeld wrote in the *South Bend Tribune*:

> The best of sports writers all over the country, who have made an investigation of the Notre Dame's peculiar system, have done much to allay the once prevalent belief that the local college does not play fair. It is only the ignorant, who, not knowing the true facts, are at a loss to account for the Gold and Blue's wonderful victories. . . . At the close of the football season last year, just after Notre Dame had again been barred from the western conference, much was said by critics in the leading dailies concerning the action of that body and it was almost unanimously agreed that the organization had made a mistake. But what cares Notre Dame?
>
> In this day and age of clean sport no large university could hire its athletes and "get away with it." There must be some other reason. And in the case of Notre Dame, there is.
>
> Notre Dame, the largest boarding school in America, is peculiar. It is like no other school of any size in the west. Here the boys live and play, sleep and work, together . . . athletic sport of all

kinds is the easiest and most favorable form of recreation. On a "rec day" it is no uncommon occurrence for five or six football games to be going on simultaneously. . . .

The students reside in halls which are as little communities to themselves. The athletic rivalry between these factions is always at a high pitch and interhall championships are held annually in each line of sport. These interhall teams afford good feeders for the varsity, although that is not their primary purpose. . . .

Time given by other schools to fraternities and the like here is used to cultivate the body. . . .

And then, too, Notre Dame has a reputation. Many of her best athletes have entered because the teams are better known than many others and because bigger games are played. . . . The success of Notre Dame can be explained in no other way and needs no other explanation.

Notre Dame's student newspaper itself observed that on any given Saturday, at least eight Notre Dame teams could be seen playing football on the campus. Notre Dame was a men's boarding school, and every class and every hall or dorm had its own eleven—then, and now. It is little wonder that out of this mix of material the coaches were able to develop a representative intercollegiate varsity team.

The year 1910 saw Frank Longman, a former Michigan player, installed as Notre Dame's head football coach. More importantly, 1910 saw two young men by the name of Knute Rockne and Gus Dorais enroll at Notre Dame as freshmen students and, eventually, as football players.

John Marks from Dartmouth was Notre Dame's next head football coach. He stayed for two years, 1911 and 1912, during which Notre Dame was undefeated, albeit playing against minor competition such as St. Viator and Adrian—competition that was simply not up to challenging the stronger Notre Dame players.

At the end of the 1912 season, Notre Dame faced a crucial juncture. Having suffered serious financial losses in football during both the 1911 and 1912 seasons, the school was seriously considering curtailing its attempts to play football at a major intercollegiate level. Playing against minor and generally weaker opponents, Notre Dame had reportedly lost approximately $2,300 in 1911 and $500 in 1912. A contributing factor to those losses, of course, was Notre Dame's continuing inability to schedule major opponents. As one writer noted, "As far as Father Cavanaugh was concerned, he would have been well content to have done away with intercollegiate football." However, strong pressure from faculty, alumni, and fellow priests persuaded him otherwise. After much internal debate, Father John W. Cavanaugh determined to give football at Notre Dame a second chance.

While visiting Crawfordsville, Indiana, the home of Wabash College, Father Cavanaugh had a chance conversation with an attorney, who happened to be a Notre Dame alumnus. The attorney remarked to Father Cavanaugh that the Wabash football coach, Jesse C. Harper, was of the opinion that football could and should pay for itself. Father Cavanaugh, as well as most other Notre Dame men of that day, was well aware of Harper's competence as a football coach, as his Wabash team had nearly defeated Notre Dame when the teams met in 1911. However, it was Harper's financial sophistication that intrigued Father Cavanaugh. In

December of 1912, he hired Jesse Harper to be Notre Dame's first full-time football coach and athletic director. In addition, Harper would be the coach for basketball, baseball, and track, all for an annual salary of $2,500. Harper's tenure at Notre Dame, 1913 to 1918, marks the beginning of the modern era of Notre Dame football. In 1913, Harper brought Notre Dame into the modern era in high fashion. He immediately arranged a national schedule against major opponents and, for the first time in its history, Notre Dame's athletic program finished the year without losing money.

3

Injuries and Death Lead to a Crisis, 1906–1913

Michael Burke of Medico-Chirurgical College, dead from a "fracture of the skull" during a game against the College of Pharmacy; Harold Moore, of Union College, dead "from the effects of injuries in the football game" against New York University; Hugh Saussy, City College of New York, dead of a broken neck, "while attempting to tackle" a player from Elizabeth Athletic Club; James F. O'Brien, of Manhattan College, dead from "peritonitis," having ended up on the ground after a carry during practice, when "several players fell on top of him." On and on it went. In addition to the deaths, the papers and magazines of the day cataloged the "Details of the More Serious Injuries," such as cracked ribs; wrenched legs; concussions; broken shoulders; blood poisoning; fractured skulls; broken arms; torn ears; and so on.

By 1905, the violence resulting from the so-called mass style of play had literally brought the game to the brink of extinction. Serious injuries and even deaths were commonplace. As one commentator reported, "from 1880–1905 there were more than 325 deaths reported in college football, plus 1,149 serious injuries." In 1904 alone, 21 players were killed and the 1905 season saw another 19 men killed, all while playing college football. Different sources produced different numbers, but all added up to unacceptable totals. Despite the general outrage, in some quarters the deaths were coming to be considered a natural and an acceptable part of the game. At the close of the 1905 season, the head football coach at Columbia University casually observed: "The number of deaths from football this season was nineteen. The number last season was about the same, and I don't think there has been any increase in the death list for many years. When you consider that during the football season probably 100,000 players are engaged in the game, the death rate is wonderfully small." However, with virtual unanimity, the general public, the fans, and the university administrators were outraged with the prevailing conditions of brutality. With each new serious injury or death, their outcry against the violence increased in both volume and intensity.

A *New York Times* article from November 29, 1905, noting the nineteen football deaths during the season, remarked: "The silent protest of the nineteen graves cannot be ignored, the feeling against the homicidal pastime will not down. . . . If the truth could be fully known, might not it establish the fact that some of the nineteen fatalities would have to be

classified not as accidents but as manslaughter? . . . Football has degen-
erated into savage, brutal, bloody fight between men . . . physically dis-
abling as many of their adversaries as possible. Kick the ball or kick the
head—it is all in the game."

Reputable journals such as *Harper's* and *McClure's* and newspapers
such as the *New York Times* called for change. The game was denounced
as attracting the "depraved elements of society." Football was "a social
obsession-boy-killing, education-prostituting," according to one University of Chicago professor. "I do not know what should take its place," he
said, "but the new game should not require the services of a physician
. . . a hospital, and the celebration of funerals."

In late 1905, in direct response to the rising public outcry against the
violence, President Theodore Roosevelt inserted himself into the fray.
Having been elected for the first time in his own right—he had initially
assumed office in 1901 after the assassination of William McKinley—
Roosevelt was wrapping up a busy year. In 1905, he established the
Forest Service; gave away his niece Eleanor in marriage to a distant
cousin, Franklin Delano Roosevelt; mediated a dispute between France
and Germany over Morocco; signed both the National Monuments Act
and the Pure Food and Drug Act; and brokered the Treaty of
Portsmouth, which ended the Russo-Japanese War and earned him the
Nobel Peace Prize. Despite all of these weighty demands, Roosevelt,
known for his "bully pulpit"—using his presidency to preach on matters
outside of his constitutional authority—found time to convene a White
House conference to consider the future of college football.

His declared agenda was simple: he wanted to eliminate the violence
in football while still retaining the essence of the game. Roosevelt was an

avid football fan—he considered it a "manly sport." "We cannot," he said, "afford to turn out of college men who shrink from physical effort or from a little physical pain. In any republic courage is a prime necessity . . . physical courage no less than moral courage." Though Roosevelt's intent was to preserve the game, his attitude encouraged the conservative school of thought that championed the old running game. Changes in the way the game was to be played, if there were to be any, would be made grudgingly.

Roosevelt's conference was the sporting news of the day. In attendance were university presidents and coaches representing Yale, Harvard, and Princeton. At the conclusion of the conference, they issued the following statement: "At the meeting of the President of the United States it was agreed that we consider that an honorable obligation exists to carry out in letter and in spirit the rules of the game of football relating to roughness, holding and fair play and the active coaches of universities being present with us pledged themselves to so regard it and to do their utmost to carry out that obligation." Signing the statement for Yale was Walter Camp, for Harvard W. T. Reid Jr., and for Princeton A. R. Hildebrand.

However, besides drawing further attention to the crisis, the White House conference was without any direct effect on the game. It took a second and even more dramatic event to break the inertia. That event occurred in November of 1905, shortly after Roosevelt's conference had ended, when Columbia University dropped a bombshell by declaring that it was forthwith banning football. The front page of the *New York Times* on November 29, 1905, blared: FOOTBALL IS ABOLISHED BY COLUMBIA COMMITTEE—GAME TOO DANGEROUS AND DEMORALIZING, SAY FACULTY. The began: "So far as Columbia University is concerned, the game of football is abolished." The article continued, "The University Committee on Students' Organization . . . took final action last evening. The Committee . . . voted to discontinue the game. It ordered the Football Association which governs the sport at Columbia to disband and settle up its affairs by Dec. 31." The chairman of the committee, Columbia professor Herbert S. Lord, noted afterward, "The reasons for this action need no explanation. They must be evident to the minds of every one acquainted with the game . . . [that it] . . . has proved itself harmful to academic standards and dangerous to human life." The playing of football would not be resumed at Columbia for ten years.

The sporting world was stunned. Reaction to the announcement came swift and severe. President Eliot of Harvard, without actually abolishing football, announced: "I will never consent to intercollegiate football being resumed at Harvard until it has been demonstrated that in actual play that the objectionable features of the game have been removed." President Scott of Princeton said, "We believe in the game in spite of its evils. These we regard as capable of correction by changes in playing rules." Provost Harrison of the University of Pennsylvania declared: "We believe that changes in the game are demanded and should be made that the game may be retained."

Official statements also came from other universities throughout the country. Though the great majority were supportive of Columbia's position, none offered a solution to the game's key problem, violence—none, that is, with the exception of New York University. While declaring that they, too, intended to abolish the game, NYU coupled the announcement with an invitation for a conference of interested parties to meet forthwith in New York "to consider what course of action should be followed" to save the game. Chancellor McCracken of New York University hoped that Harvard would take the lead in calling such a conference, but President Eliot of Harvard expressly declined.

The initial New York University meeting was called to order in New York City on December 28, 1905, with representatives from sixty-eight universities and colleges from around the United States in attendance. The primary goal of the conference was to outline a course of proposed rule changes to open up the game and to establish a procedure for the purpose of enacting the agreed-upon reforms. The favored adjustment to open up the game was to permit the use of a heretofore unused tactic, the forward pass. This, it was hoped, would relieve the pressure inherent in the close, brutal physical contact associated with the mass-running play.

The consensus of the participants was that such a game would reduce the violence. "More open play would . . . change the character of the injuries . . . in open field play the injuries are usually a sprained ankle or a broken arm. That is much better than a blood clot on the brain or other injuries which occur in the heavy line plays. There the injuries are more apt to be to the head or spine." Just how to achieve a more open game would prove to be the central issue of contention at the conference and for the next several years.

At the time of the New York University conference in 1905, there was not an agreed-upon authority to issue rules for the game. Football in 1905 was under the guidance of at least three separate groups: the Intercollegiate Rules Committee; the Advisory Committee, made up of graduates from the different colleges in the Intercollegiate Association; and the University Athletic Club of New York. If any group had the respect of all and, thus, the authority, however nebulous, to promulgate rules for the game, it was the Intercollegiate Football Rules Committee. This was the group headed by Walter Camp of Yale.

The Intercollegiate Football Rules Committee, or the "old rules committee," as it was called, had as part of its bylaws a provision that required unanimous consent to make any change or alterations in the rules governing football. Camp usually got his way, but when his persuasive powers failed, he was always able to rely on the automatic veto provided by the unanimous-consent rule. In late December 1905 and early January 1906, the old rules committee met and confirmed that their unanimous consent policy would stay in force. On January 9, the *New York Times* ran a headline proclaiming CHANGES IN FOOTBALL PROMISE A DEAD-LOCK— DECISION REACHED NOT TO ABOLISH UNANIMOUS CONSENT and reported: "The trouble again is of Yale's making. It is a statement that Walter Camp is determined not to abandon the one-man veto rule, which in operation in the past meant one-man domination with Walter Camp in the position of dictator." Regarding the potential introduction of the forward pass: "to permit the forward pass behind the line of scrimmage as suggested . . . is an experimental proposition that may or may not admit of extensive development." Yale, as was noted, was among those who believed that the forward pass would "introduce little change." The article concluded: "The question of Harvard's action becomes of paramount importance in view of the developments." At the time, Harvard was clearly the leading educational institution in America and their leadership or lack of leadership on the issues facing football would be crucial. Fortunately for the game of football, Harvard chose to lead.

On January 12, the old rules committee and the new rules committee, which had been formed by the New York University conference, met at the Hotel Netherland in New York. Among those in attendance were Yale's Walter Camp; Secretary W. T. Reid Jr. of Harvard; J. B. Fine of Princeton; Amos Alonzo Stagg of the University of Chicago; and Charles D. Daly of Army, who would coach the Black Knights on the day of Notre Dame's historic victory in 1913; as well as representatives from Cornell, Haverford, Pennsylvania, Texas, Navy, Dartmouth, Nebraska, Oberlin, and Minnesota.

Harvard came to the table prepared with a power play. At the outset of the meeting, the Harvard representative, W. T. Reid Jr., resigned from the old rules committee. Then he quietly but firmly let it be known, in private discussions with various members of the two rules committees, that unless there was an amalgamation of the two committees and unless Harvard's proposed reforms were accepted, Harvard was ready to drop football, or, in the alternative, to go it alone. During the course of the discussions, President Roosevelt put some friendly pressure on Paul Dashiell, the Naval Academy representative on the rules committee, to join with Harvard. The word from Harvard was clear: if the other universities involved wanted Harvard to participate in intercollegiate football, they would have to accept Harvard's suggested reforms. In the end, Harvard's strategy was successful: the new committee was formed, and the old rules committee, minus its unanimous-consent rule, was merged with the new committee, with Reid elected secretary. A vehicle for changing the rules was now in place, though substantive reform to the rules of the game would take another six years. The new committee would change its name in 1910 and become known as the National Collegiate Athletic Association, today's NCAA.

The Rules of 1906—The Forward Pass

In April 1906, the Committee made its efforts public. Besides introducing the forward pass, the Committee enacted a rule requiring the offense to make ten yards in three tries. Whereas five yards in three downs had been an inducement for bruising line play, having to make ten yards forced the offense to gamble with big gainers like wide-end sweeps, which opened up the field. Further, a rule was adopted that required at least six men on the offensive line of scrimmage. The intent of this rule was to discourage mass-running plays and further open up the game. In addition, hurdling was banned. Previously, a ballcarrier could hurdle or attempt to hurdle a defensive player, or even a standing defensive player, which precipitated numerous serious injuries. The game was reduced from seventy minutes to sixty minutes, divided into halves of thirty minutes each.

Camp was of the opinion that the two most important changes to come into the rules in 1906 were the ten-yard rule and the rule requiring a neutral zone on the line of scrimmage. The ten-yard rule would give a team three downs to make twice the distance that was required under the old rule. This, Camp observed, would strongly "militate against mass plays" and force more open play, because ten yards would be very difficult to gain in three downs without employing an open style of play. Also of great importance to Camp was the creation of a neutral zone, which separated the teams by the length of the ball. The prior lack of such a zone was considered to have been a major factor in the violence, as "the opposing forwards took their positions on a line running through the ball, but there was no space between them. There they stood, brow to brow, foot to foot, and carnage was the order of the day. Getting linemen that close to each other was to invite fighting, and fighting there was."

Notwithstanding Camp's opinion on the importance of the ten-yard rule and the neutral zone, the consensus was that the most "radical" change in the rules was the introduction of the forward-passing play.

Though now legalized, the forward pass was burdened with draconian restrictions and it is little wonder that football people of the day, such as Camp, paid scant attention to the new rule.

Camp, of course, had led the way to seriously restricting the rule permitting a pass at all. The restrictions were formidable. First, the pass had to be thrown from at least five yards behind the line of scrimmage and had to cross the line of scrimmage five yards on either side of the center. Second, if a forward pass hit the ground before being touched by a player from either team, the ball was turned over to the defense at the point where the pass was attempted. Finally, a pass that crossed the goal line on the fly, untouched, was a touchback; and if, by chance, a pass was caught over the goal line, it resulted in a touchback. These restrictions, to Camp's design and delight, virtually doomed any widespread use of the pass. However, despite the restrictions, the more courageous coaches, especially those in the Midwest and the South, immediately began experimenting with the pass. In the East, the coaches, most of them indoctrinated by Camp, simply ignored the pass.

Little noted at the time was the addition to the rule against unsportsmanlike conduct. It provided that henceforth, unsportsmanlike conduct would include: "use of abusive or insulting language to opponents or officials." The penalty was "suspension for the remainder of the game."

The 1906 changes had a considerable effect on opening up the game.

However, the violence continued to an unacceptable degree, while the highly restricted forward pass floundered. The tradition of mass power running continued to be the offensive weapon of choice.

There was little change in the rules between 1907 and 1909. The restrictions on the forward pass remained and were somewhat increased. The scoring system was adjusted in 1909 to reduce the value of a field goal from 4 points to 3 points. Originally, a field goal had been valued at 5 points.

The Forward Pass: The Early Promoters

A number of people are credited with making the suggestion of a forward-pass play to the rules committee and in leading the fight for its adoption. The consensus seems to be that the man who first had the idea and took it to the rules committee was John W. Heisman, the namesake of today's Heisman Trophy, which is awarded annually to the college football player selected as the season's outstanding player. He was born in Cleveland on October 23, 1869, just two weeks before the November 6 Princeton–Rutgers matchup that historians have recognized as the first intercollegiate football game. Heisman's life paralleled the early years of the development of football. Heisman grew up in Titusville, Pennsylvania, where he played football for Titusville High School, entered Brown University as a seventeen-year-old freshman in 1887 and played football there until 1889. In 1889, he transferred to the University of Pennsylvania to pursue a law degree and played football until 1891. After receiving his degree in law, he coached at Oberlin College in 1893, left for the University of Akron in 1894, and returned to Oberlin the next year. In 1895, he went to Auburn University, where he stayed for five years. His combined record at all these schools included only five losses.

In 1900, he went to Clemson University, where he coached for four seasons before moving to Georgia Tech, where he coached from 1904 to 1919. He returned to Pennsylvania for one season in 1920, then to Washington and Jefferson College, before ending his career in 1927, after four seasons at Rice University. Heisman subsequently became the athletic director of the former Downtown Athletic Club in Manhattan, New York, and in 1935 the club began awarding the Heisman Trophy in his honor.

Heisman's first contact with the pass came about by happenstance. In 1895, during his first season as head coach at Auburn, Heisman traveled to Atlanta to scout a game between North Carolina and Georgia. Heisman watched the North Carolina fullback go into punt formation on his own goal line. The Georgia defense rushed the fullback, and unable to get his punt off, he threw the ball forward to one of his teammates, who proceeded to run the length of the field for a touchdown. The legendary Glenn "Pop" Warner, then the Georgia head coach, vehemently protested this clearly illegal play. However, the referee said he did not see the pass, and he allowed the touchdown to stand. Heisman never forgot the event.

The restrictions surrounding the forward pass were not the only reason it was slow to gain traction outside the Midwest and South; use of the pass was also limited by the philosophical objections of the leading universities in the East. Led by Camp, the Eastern schools simply did not like the idea of a forward pass being a part of the game. It would be seven years until the rules of the game would evolve to the point that Notre Dame would awaken the football world to the potential of the forward pass.

There seems to be general agreement that the first serious use of the forward pass after its legalization in 1906 was by Eddie Cochems, the head football coach at Saint Louis University. Cochems had been a star halfback and end for Wisconsin, where he lettered five times between 1897 and 1901. Long an advocate for the adoption of the forward-passing rules, Cochems immediately put the play to effective use in a September 5, 1906, game against Carroll College in Waukesha, Wisconsin. Despite the severe restrictions on the pass, Cochems was courageous, and prior to the start of the 1906 season he had his team "secretly practicing the art of the forward pass." As the game with Carroll College proceeded in a scoreless tie, Cochems directed his team to unleash the air attack they had been practicing. The first attempt, from Saint Louis quarterback Bradbury Robinson to end Jack Schneider, fell incomplete. By rule, Saint Louis lost possession of the ball. However, on the next offensive possession, Robinson hit Schneider with a twenty-yard pass, which Schneider ran in for a touchdown. Saint Louis passed several more times during the game, eventually beating Carroll College, 22–0.

Knute Rockne credits Cochems as a leader in the use of the pass, with Stagg and Glenn Warner close behind him. In the October 25, 1930, *Collier's* magazine, Rockne wrote,

There has been so much guessing and dispute as to where the aerial game originated, and so many have thought that Notre Dame held and holds the patent, that a little research should settle the question. The forward pass came in quietly, almost obscurely. Eddie Cochems, coach at Saint Louis circa 1907, enrolled a few boys who could toss a football just as easily and almost as far as they could throw a baseball. Saint Louis played and defeated several big teams, using the forward pass. One would have thought that so effective a play would be instantly copied and become the vogue. The East, however, had not learned much or cared much about the Midwest and Western football. . . . Old-fashioned line plunges, mass plays, and the monotonous kicking game, waiting for a break, were the stock in trade. The pass was a threat, which heavy teams disdained. Warner of Carlisle and Stagg of Chicago were just behind Cochems in evolving the open game.

Rockne's charge that the East was behind the West in taking up the forward pass was supported by Hall of Famer Bob Zuppke, the outstanding head football coach at the University of Illinois from 1913 to 1941, whose teams won four national titles and seven Big Ten Conference championships. In a letter, Zuppke wrote, "The leaders of the open game as early as 1906 were mostly in the Middle West. The East, as a rule, was slow to follow. Michigan, Wisconsin, Chicago, Minnesota, Purdue, Notre Dame, and Illinois—in fact most of the big universities and innumerable high schools—were the leaders."

Zuppke himself was an innovator and proponent of the pass. He actually developed his passing strategies while coaching at Oak Park High School in Oak Park, Illinois, from 1910 to 1912. Some credit him with the invention of the screen pass, and in 1910 he was credited as being the first coach to devise protection for his passer, dropping back two guards to block.

The forward pass had other proponents as well. William Hollenback, one of Penn's greatest players, wrote in 1954, "The 1907 Carlisle team was a very good one, and they defeated us. It was only the second year of the forward pass, and we had absolutely no defense against it. I give great credit to Pop Warner as one of the pioneers to see the possibilities of the forward pass. We were passing the ball end over end, much as you would flip a basketball; and when the Carlisle Indians came to Franklin Field they were throwing the spiral pass."

The pass was in use in the Southwest as early as 1908. Hugo Bezdek, who won fame as the Penn State coach, and also made his name in big-league baseball, went to Arkansas as coach in 1908. With the help of his friend Stagg, Bezdek's Arkansas teams used the forward pass with winning effectiveness against stronger teams that did not employ it. Having been defeated by Eddie Cochems and his pass-happy Saint Louis University team by a score of 24 to 0, Bezdek reportedly placed a call to his old coach, Stagg, to seek advice on just how to implement this new play. Stagg and his former Chicago quarterback, Walter Eckersall, traveled to Fayetteville, Arkansas, and worked with Bezdek's team until they had perfected a passing attack. Arkansas then used that attack with great success against stronger teams that did not pass.

And of course Jesse Harper, while coaching at Wabash prior to going to Notre Dame, had made his own strides with the forward pass. At Wabash, Harper had a talented quarterback by the name of Skeets Lambert. Harper devised a play where, when rushed, Skeets would simply throw the ball into the ground, to avoid a serious loss. "Wabash was the first team to use intentional grounding of the pass, also throwing the ball out of bounds instead of punting," Harper wrote to sportswriter Allison

Danzig on February 10, 1954. "At that time the ball thrown out of bounds went to the other team at the point it went out. There was no penalty for intentional grounding. It was the same as an incomplete forward pass." Intentional grounding was perfectly legal in those days.

In 1911, Wabash, then guided by Harper, came close to defeating Notre Dame with a long forward pass, but the restrictive rules of the day foiled their victory. Rockne, then playing end for Notre Dame, recalled the incident: "Wabash had beaten us on a long and perfectly executed pass from Lambert to Howard. But the officials measured it. It was thrown more than twenty yards beyond the line of scrimmage and was therefore illegal. Wabash was penalized."

Two Schools of Thought: Camp vs. Haughton

Despite the early efforts of men like Cochems, Warner, Stagg, Harper, and Zuppke, the always influential Walter Camp continued to lobby successfully against the use of the pass, and strongly urged its complete repeal. As a result, mass play, with its attending violence, continued to prevail, until two high-profile deaths shocked the football world into finally coming to grips with the problem.

Before the end of the 1909 football season, opposition to Camp's group had begun to form under the banner of Percy Haughton, the head football coach at Harvard, who would later coach at Columbia. One of the all-time great coaches, Haughton led Harvard, from 1908 to 1916, to a record of seventy-one wins, seven losses, and five ties—with only one loss to archrival Yale—a period referred to as Harvard's "Golden Era." Early on, Haughton saw the value of the forward pass, and in 1909, he competed with Camp for the leadership of the Rules

Committee. The dispute continued unabated, with Camp's group retaining control until the end of the 1909 season, when further and dramatic violence manifested itself in the game.

On October 16, 1909, in a football game between Navy and Villanova, quarterback Earl D. Wilson, who was considered to be the best all-around athlete at the Naval Academy, suffered a "twisted neck" and a "fractured spine" when he dove through two Villanova players, and with a "flying tackle stopped the play." Wilson was paralyzed from the chin down and died some weeks later.

Two weeks later, on October 30, Harvard faced Army at West Point. With only ten minutes left in the game, Harvard was running a close formation "in which sheer weight and strength predominated." Army's left tackle, twenty-two-year-old Eugene Byrne, dived into the oncoming mass, "holding his head up so as to pick out the man with the ball." Harvard's right tackle and guard both hit Byrne together, and other players piled on, leaving Byrne's neck and spine "twisted and broken." Byrne was so "badly injured as to indicate that his life was a matter of only a few moments. . . . The teammates of Byrne came off the gridiron sobbing, every man of them, as if his heart would break." The game was called. As Byrne lay on a cot on the field, his white-haired father left the cheering section and went down on the field to stand near his son. Cadet Byrne died two days later, and Army promptly canceled the remainder of its football season.

The deaths of Cadet Byrne and Midshipman Wilson shocked the nation and served as a dramatic exclamation mark on the sport's violence, which also included a litany of less-publicized deaths. Nineteen-year-old halfback Ralph Wilson of Wabash, playing under coach Jesse

Harper, was killed by a skull "fracture in three places," having dived for a Saint Louis University runner, striking his head on the player's knee. Wabash immediately canceled the remainder of its football season. Michael Burke of Philadelphia was killed playing football, prompting Archbishop Ryan of Philadelphia to remark at Burke's funeral, "Football . . . is barbarous and ought to be abolished." George Bahen of Georgetown was "feared crippled all of his days" from a fracture of the fifth cervical vertebrae. Seventeen-year-old William Hinchliffe of Fordham died from an "abscess on the brain" resulting from a football injury. And, seemingly as a natural extension of the random violence in the game, Rudoph Munk, the Captain and right halfback for West Virginia, was killed instantly in a game when Thomas McCoy of Bethany came up behind Munk and dealt him "terrific blow to the back of the head," with his fist. Munk died on the field, and "a warrant charging murder" was issued by the state of West Virginia for McCoy's arrest. West Virginia canceled the rest of its games, including its Thanksgiving date with Washington and Jefferson, its biggest annual game. And, last but not least in the litany was a child: eleven-year-old Charles Broker of Findlay, Ohio, was killed in a back-lot game when tackled by one of his young friends. In all, the 1909 season saw near-record violence—twenty-six deaths, almost double the total from the years 1907 and 1908 combined.

Clearly, the rules and reforms so optimistically adopted in 1906 and expanded upon in the Rules Committee meetings thereafter were not having the intended effect. Violence, serious injury, and death were once again on the Rules Committee's doorstep, and this time, the clamor for reform could not be denied. The attacks on the game came from all sides. Legislation was introduced in the state of Virginia that, when enacted, would simply outlaw the playing of football. The general public also had its say. Margaret E. Sangster, in a letter published in the *New York Times* on November 3, 1909, observed, "I wish . . . to put the question seriously before the minds of all thoughtful people. . . . Are we wholly civilized? . . . A few days ago it was a midshipman in the Navy who died of a fractured vertebrae, and this morning it is a cadet at West Point whose death is reported of a twisted spine. . . . Simply to die in an athletic contest that is shockingly brutal is a waste to the Nation and a stab to the home that is without excuse."

The hue and cry was heard by all. With this new and seemingly unstoppable public outcry, Camp and his supporters backed down, and, by 1910, Haughton and his followers were finally able to bring an end to Camp's lifelong supremacy on the Rules Committee.

The results were immediately manifested in the rule changes of 1910. The most important new rule required seven men on the line of scrimmage. In effect, this created a ban on mass-running plays. In addition, the penalties for an incomplete pass were eliminated. Now, instead of turning the ball over to the opposition if the ball struck the ground before touching a player from either side, such a pass was simply ruled incomplete, and the ball would be returned to the original line of scrimmage—the same as the rule we enjoy today. Furthermore, it was provided that a forward pass could cross the line of scrimmage at any point, rather than five yards to either side of the center. Finally, an interference rule was made to protect receivers. Previously, a receiver could be tackled, pushed, or prevented in virtually any way from attempting to catch a ball, before or after the ball was thrown. By the new rule, roughing up the receiver prior to the delivery of the ball was prohibited. However, in a nod to the Camp group, the Committee declared that a forward pass would be limited to a length of twenty yards from the spot where the ball was put into play, a restriction that would make a dramatic appearance a year later in the history of Jesse Harper, Wabash, and Notre Dame.

It was noted in the September 18, 1910, issue of the *New York Times* that Camp, "who did more than any other man to build up the old game, did not take a prominent part in making the changes." Though clearly not pleased with the changes, Camp appeared to be always the gentlemen and remarked in the same article that he was "heartily in sympathy" with the committee's work and the new rules. However, even with the strong and positive additions and changes to the rules in 1910, the forward pass still continued to struggle to gain any significant popularity. Coaches of the major eastern universities remained reluctant to depart from the traditional running plays: "they have stuck as close as they possibly can to old football. . . . The forward pass. . . . [has] not yet been developed into as popular or skillful a means of advancing the ball as the 'football doctors' planned to have it." The 1910 season saw little use of the forward pass. Following the 1910 Army–Navy game, the *New York Times* observed, "The Army–Navy game Saturday ended another football season, and, as in the other big matches of the year, more of the old style of football was successfully shown than the new. The forward pass . . . was not used by Army. It was seldom used by Annapolis, and then not with startling success. . . . So the season closes . . . with very little favorable display of . . . [the forward pass]."

1911 saw little change in the rules. A new and fairly innocuous rule prohibiting "concealing the ball beneath the clothing or substituting any article for the ball" was enacted and such practice was deemed to be unsportsmanlike conduct.

The Landmark Rules of 1912

By 1912, the Haughton group was in full control and they exerted their authority immediately. At long last, the rules governing the game would now allow a team to seriously utilize the forward pass as part of its offense.

Perhaps the most important change in the 1912 rules was the addition of a fourth down. This gave a team more opportunity to be creative in their effort to gain a first down or any significant yardage. The 20-yard limitation on the forward pass was removed, permitting a ball to be thrown forward for any distance beyond the line of scrimmage. The *New York Times* noted on February 14, 1912, "Many players are clever enough to thow the ball a great distance, but under the limitations of the pass had no opportunity to exhibit this talent." The field was shortened from 110 yards to 100 yards, and a 10-yard end zone was added behind each goal line. The new rules further provided that a pass caught in the end zone was now legal and constituted a touchdown; previously, when a pass was caught over the goal line, it was ruled a touchback. In addition, the kickoff was to be made from the 40 instead of the 55-yard line. Also of great but quiet import was the change of the shape of the ball from its original oval-like shape to a more aerodynamic "prolate spheroid" shape, much closer to the appearance of the football used today. And, finally, the value of the touchdown was increased from 5 points— which had been the value since 1897—to 6 points. (The field goal had already been reduced from 4 to 3 points in 1909.) The modern scoring system was in place.

Even Camp conceded that the 1912 changes were dramatic. He remarked, "There was another feature of the play still to be considered, and that was the remarkably easy way in which ground could be made on the forward pass if the passes were cleverly devised and well executed. A team would go from mid-field down to the goal line in two or three such passes, and that without any effect at all upon its endurance. It was simply a question of one or two men running 20 or 30 yards at a time with no opposition. Those who had contended that old-fashioned, straight plunging football would come to its own again, and that the forward pass would be supplanted by the line-plunging game, or that the defense to forward passes would render these latter plays ineffective, found themselves completely at sea." Despite this seemingly magnanimous observation, Camp would fight for the repeal of the forward pass until his death in 1925.

The *New York Times* of February 4, 1912, analyzed the new rules as follows: "After two long days of deliberation, the Football Rules Committee . . . finally got down to business . . . and changed the game radically. . . . Football men at the meeting . . . predict that the game has been opened up, and that next year, under this new code, the football loving public will see a faster, better, and more open game." This would prove to be a sage prediction, one that would come to dramatic fruition on the Plains at West Point on November 1, 1913.

4

Jesse Harper Before Notre Dame

Jesse Claire Harper, whose first name was pronounced "Jess," was a complex man. He was an athlete, and he loved athletics and winning, but he loved sportsmanship more; he was a learned man, having received a degree in philosophy from the University of Chicago. He firmly believed that at a university, academics came before athletics; he was a thoughtful and introspective man, known for his intelligence and sagacity; he was a congenial and gregarious man, possessing a renowned sense of humor; and, most of all, he was a teacher, not only of the intricacies of pass patterns and blocking techniques but also of how a man should live his life with character and integrity. And, with all of that, he was blessed with the gift of being able to convey his many virtues to those who came in contact with him—his family, friends, professional associates and athletes, and by so doing, to inspire those people to live better lives. After Harper's death in 1961, a close friend and a former football player at Wabash, M. E. "Doc" Elliott, wrote a letter to his Wabash classmates including the following words: "Our friend and Coach Jesse Harper received his call July 31st and responded; leaving Melville, his devoted wife, and his children plus thousands of men who as boys were coached by him and received as a bonus lasting inspiration. Great men live on in the lives of those they have touched."

Jesse Harper was born on December 10, 1883, to parents of Irish, English, and Scottish ancestry, in a farmhouse in DeKalb County, Illinois, where his ancestors had settled in 1837. When Jesse was ten years old, a fire destroyed his father's barn, where they kept their horses, and the tragedy caused the family to relocate to the town of Mason, Iowa, in Calhoun County, not far from Fort Dodge. There, Harper's father engaged himself in the business of farming and cattle feeding.

Jesse's home atmosphere always had a solid athletic bent. As a young boy, he was a strong athlete, described as "never sturdy or rugged in appearance, but rather of the wiry type, with great powers of endurance and fierce intenseness or the nervous temperament." His father, as well as his brothers Floyd and Frank, "always played on the town baseball team," and as Jesse grew up, he followed suit.

Harper's early schooling was in the local country schools. When he was sixteen, his family sent him to the Morgan Park Academy in Chicago for his last two years of high school. At the time, Morgan Park was run under the auspices of the University of Chicago, which had been founded in 1890 by the American Baptist Education Society on the strength of several large financial donations from John D. Rockefeller. Jesse graduated from Morgan Park Academy in 1902 and from there he matriculated to the University of Chicago, where, in addition to his studies, he played baseball and football.

According to Harper, his choice of schools was largely a matter of free transportation. In an interview with a newspaper reporter years later, Harper reflected on his reason for making Chicago the city where he would receive his education: "We lived in Iowa and my father was in the cattle business. I could always get a free ride into Chicago on a cattle train. For that reason, I went to Morgan Park Academy, a Chicago prep school, and then went on to the University of Chicago."

The University of Chicago: 1902–1906

Harper entered the University of Chicago in September 1902 as an eighteen-year-old freshman. Though he was always interested in athletics, at the time he suffered from rheumatism, which curtailed his athletic career at Chicago to some extent. While his rheumatism did not hinder his ability to play baseball, his true love as a player—he was elected to be the captain of the University of Chicago baseball team in 1905—it did force him to sit out the 1903 and 1904 football seasons. Harper had started out at halfback as a freshman in 1902. By 1905, his senior year at Chicago, Harper was backing up Walter Eckersall at quarterback. Chicago's first All-American, Eckersall was described by Stagg as the greatest quarterback of his time. "I played halfback and quarterback on that club," Harper once said. "And I didn't play too much at quarterback because I had a pretty good man ahead of me. You may have heard of Walter Eckersall." The University of Chicago closed out its 1905 football season undefeated and victorious over Michigan for the Western Championship. Though Harper played as a substitute in 1905, he saw enough playing time to earn a varsity letter.

Chicago's 1905 gridiron showdown with the University of Michigan for the Western Championship was, to that point, the biggest game in Harper's football career, and one of the major games in the early history of college football. The game was played on a 10-degree, windy Thanksgiving Day in Chicago. Heavily favored and undefeated, Michigan had not lost a game since 1900. It was reported that 27,000 spectators filled the stands—a crowd unheard of for that day—and even Walter Camp was in attendance. Michigan was coached by Fielding Yost and Chicago by its own legend, Amos Alonzo Stagg. Late in the game, Chicago scored a safety, which was good enough to defeat Michigan 2–0. The game was the beginning of two decades of Chicago's significance as a football team not only in the Midwest but also nationally. The game also marked the beginning of a bitter feud between Yost and Stagg, following Yost's accusation of a lack of eligibility and training rules on the Chicago team—a theme Yost would raise again, four years later, after his Michigan team was upset by Notre Dame. Eventually this and other similar concerns would result in Michigan's withdrawal from the Western Conference—now the Big Ten. Michigan did not return to the conference until 1918, by which time, Chicago had begun to curtail its football program, and the rivalry between the two schools and the two coaches dissipated. The University of Chicago, under President Robert Hutchins, then a vocal advocate for reform in college sports, deemphasized football in the mid-1930s. In 1933 Hutchins engineered Stagg's departure. Chicago dropped football completely after the 1939 season.

In addition to his athletic activities while at the University of Chicago, Harper participated in student activities and joined Phi Delta Theta fraternity. He also worked. His major enterprise, with a fellow student as a partner, was the concession stand at Marshall Field, where all of the University's home football and baseball games took place. During the historic game with Michigan in 1905, while Harper suited up for the game, his partner in the enterprise is reported to have sold 3,600 hot dogs at a cost of ten cents apiece—big money at the time.

At Chicago, Harper was a baseball star. He began as an outfielder, but when Stagg needed a catcher, Harper switched, though he would return to the outfield in 1905. In addition to his many baseball skills, Harper was a whirlwind on the bases. In one game in the spring of 1905, Harper captured the headlines on the sports page of the *Chicago Tribune.* The writer noted: "Chicago won out in the last half of the tenth, when Harper reached first base on an error after two men were gone, and stole second. He stole third a moment later, and scored on Shewbridge's overthrow of third." Harper's batting average for Chicago was over .300 in each of the three seasons he played.

While at the University of Chicago, Harper had the good fortune to come under the influence of Amos Alonzo Stagg, and though it is impossible to measure Stagg's influence on Harper's life and career with certainty, it is fair to say that it was monumental. At some point during Harper's early years as a student at Chicago, his attention turned to the technical aspects of the game of football, and it became evident that Harper was interested in following his mentor into the coaching profession. Meeting and working with Stagg was one of the high points of Harper's development. As often happens in positive human relationships, the great traits of one person somehow are transferred to the other. This transfer took place between Harper and Stagg and continued throughout their respective lifetimes. Harper, in turn, passed the qualities that he had acquired from Stagg on to those who played football for him, not the least of whom was Knute Rockne.

Unfortunately for both parties, Stagg harbored a deep bias against Notre Dame, and despite the entreaties of his protégé, Stagg steadfastly refused to schedule a football game with Notre Dame during Harper's tenure. In fact, it wasn't until the late 1930s that Stagg finally "buried the hatchet" with Notre Dame. Joe Doyle, the longtime sports editor of the *South Bend Tribune,* tells the story as it was told to him by onetime Notre Dame coach—and member of the Four Horsemen backfield—Elmer Layden. On a summer morning in 1939, Layden walked into the newly constructed Rockne Memorial on the Notre Dame campus, where he was shocked to see the Grand Old Man himself, Stagg, standing with his hand on the bronze bust of Rockne. Stagg had been driving with his wife from the West Coast to visit family in the East and stopped at Notre Dame to pay a visit, during which he made his own private peace with Rockne and Notre Dame. Layden and Stagg conversed, and their chance meeting led to the first and only football game to be played between Notre Dame and a team coached by Stagg. They agreed to play a game in 1940, and Stagg's team, then the College of the Pacific, visited Notre Dame for the Irish home opener. Notre Dame won by a score of 25 to 7. It would be Layden's final year as Notre Dame's head coach. It was fitting for all that Layden's final year at Notre Dame would feature the great Stagg himself finally striding the sidelines at Notre Dame stadium.

Stagg is often and deservedly referred to as the "Grand Old Man of Football." He was born on August 16, 1862, in West Orange, New Jersey.

Though Stagg's family had neither the financial resources nor the inclination to send him to college, his assistant high school principal at Orange
High School, a young man by the name of Alton Sherman, helped to guide
young Stagg to his alma mater, Yale. Stagg entered Yale in September of
1884 with $32 in his pocket. Tuition each term was $50. He remained at
Yale until 1890—four years as an undergrad, one year as a part-time student, and one year as a divinity student. He failed to make the football team
in 1884 and did not play regularly until 1888.

During his years at Yale, Stagg proved to be an outstanding athlete,
starring in both baseball and football. In 1889, he was selected to Walter
Camp's first All-American team as an end. But baseball was Stagg's
favorite game, and he played at Yale for six seasons. He was so outstanding on the mound that several professional baseball teams offered
him contracts, with one willing to pay him $3,000 per annum. However,
being a professional athlete was not Stagg's calling. His goal all along was
to be involved with young men as a pastor or a teacher.

After graduation from Yale, Stagg was torn between a career in athletics and a life in the pulpit. In effect, he got both. In 1892, he was hired
by the University of Chicago as Director of Athletics and Physical Education, and though he arrived as coach, by necessity he also had to
become a player, as only fourteen men had turned out for football.

Years later, Stagg reflected on his career choice. "I had studied for the
ministry and I believed I could perform as great a service in athletics as
I could in the pulpit." Prophetic words. Stagg became famous not only
for his innovations on the football field but also for his character
building. He coached at the University of Chicago from 1892 to 1932,
when Chicago forced him into retirement at age seventy. After leaving

Chicago, Stagg went to the College of the Pacific, in California, where he coached until 1946.

After leaving College of the Pacific, Stagg then served as an assistant coach to his son at Susquehanna University in Pennsylvania, finally retiring from his beloved football in 1958, at the age of 96. He lived to be 102.

Stagg made numerous innovations in the game of football. He was one of the early proponents of the forward pass as a weapon. For many years he was one of the leading proponents of open play and was one of the first coaches to have developed a spiral pass as opposed to the more common motion, throwing the ball end over end. Harper would absorb and adopt Stagg's methods and take them with him to Alma, Wabash, and, eventually, to Notre Dame. Years later, Rockne said, "Stagg brought his game from Yale. . . . Notre Dame football goes back to Stagg and to Yale."

Perhaps Stagg's greatest contribution to the game and to Harper was his ability to develop strong character in his players. Stagg was a true disciplinarian, Harper later remembered: "The old man was always awfully strict. He was a wonderful man, and a great coach who had that knack of getting men to outdo themselves for him. But, boy, he was strict, particularly when it came to the conduct and training of players. And he was death on smoking or drinking. He was always a reasonable man, but the thing you remember most about him is how stern and strict he was." The esteem in which Stagg was held by Harper and his teammates at Chicago was never more evident than at the fiftieth reunion of the 1905 Chicago team. Most of the squad members were there in 1955, and Harper remembers that even at this point in their lives, "some of those men still won't smoke or take a drink in front of Mr. Stagg." In his later years, Harper always referred to Stagg as the "great character builder."

Stagg's mentoring and teaching of Harper did not end with Harper's graduation in 1906. The two kept in close contact for several years, and on more than one occasion, Harper attended Stagg's famous summer football camps, which Stagg called "classes." Although the forward-passing rules and open-game rules came into effect after Harper's graduation from the University of Chicago, he was ever attentive to changes in the game, and at Stagg's camps in 1906 and 1907 was schooled in the new open game.

Besides attending Stagg's summer football camp in 1906, Harper also found work as a book salesman, going door-to-door in Wichita, Kansas, selling atlases for a Chicago publishing house. In the course of his sales activities he met one Ms. Melville Helen Campbell, an attractive young lady who, six years later, would become his wife.

Stagg had nothing but praise for his young disciple. In two of his many letters of recommendation on Harper's behalf for coaching positions, Stagg wrote, "he is a first class fellow and a man of excellent habits," and later, "I have no hesitancy whatever in recommending Mr. Jesse C. Harper to take charge of your athletics. Mr. Harper has been at the University of Chicago for four years, and previous to that was at Morgan Park Academy for three years. At both institutions he has been under excellent instruction and is exceedingly well trained in various sports. Mr. Harper is a fine man, has a very excellent disposition and sure to get along well with the students. He has made a great success of his work at Alma College, for which place I recommended him for this year, and they would dislike very much to have him leave."

Alma College: 1906–1908

After graduating from the University of Chicago, Harper, on the strength of Stagg's recommendation, went to Alma College, a private, four-year, liberal arts and science college that had been founded in 1886 by Presbyterians in Alma, Michigan. In addition to coaching football at Alma, Harper also coached baseball, basketball, and track; managed the entire athletic program; and taught gymnastics and history. Harper was the first football coach in Alma's history.

Reflecting on Harper's 1906 arrival in Alma, the school newspaper, the *Almanian,* wrote that October: "Alma considers that she has the best coach among the colleges of Michigan in the form of Jesse C. Harper, of U. of C. Coach Stagg of that institution could not speak too highly of him . . . [Harper] is a hustler from the drop of the hat. And when he appears, the men know they have to get down and scratch. He has all the qualifications of a successful coach, being the type to inspire the respect of the fellows. . . . Alma has set her hopes high and has her eyes on the pennant and relies on Coach Harper to bring that happy consummation to pass."

Young Harper developed his "green" team and took them to a 2–2–2 record in the 1906 season, playing twice against Ferris and twice against Michigan Agricultural College, which was commonly called M.A.C. and would later become Michigan State University, as well as against Hillsdale and Olivet. The following September, the *Almanian* noted: "Last fall Mr. Harper took the Alma squad in hand, not one man knowing the rudiments of real football. . . . Then the work began. Coach Harper has a splendid eye for placing men and they were soon placed in positions where they remained for the rest of the season. The season was a success and a hard schedule was played with only two close games lost."

A "master in handling men," as the *Almanian* hailed him that fall. In 1907, Harper scheduled seven football games for Alma: Kalamazoo, Hillsdale, Ferris, Olivet, Mt. Pleasant, Albion, and Michigan Agricultural College. The finale on November 23 against the heavily favored Michigan Agricultural College would be the highlight of his time at Alma. Though weather conditions for the game were good, Alma's Davis Field was muddy as a result of previous rains. The Alma student body spent the week prior to the game practicing new songs and cheers, and on game day every student was reported to have worn a tag reading, in red letters: "We will beat M.A.C." Prior to the game the students marched through the town and to the train station, where they gave a rousing welcome to the M.A.C. team. Perhaps a precursor to Harper's deep knowledge of the forward pass, it was noted, "M.A.C. could not gain with the forward pass, as Alma men were always on the spot to get them." The game, which ended in a 0–0 tie, "outran all hopes of the Alma supporters," and Alma senior Helmer was hailed as the star of the game, for his "line smashing, punting and running," which the *Almanian* lauded.

With that moral victory, Harper's career at Alma came to an end. During his two years at Alma, Harper had "instilled a spirit of wholesome enthusiasm into the College. . . . Every department has indirectly felt the vigor of his personality; and the infectious optimism which he dispenses is invaluable to the institution."

Even after leaving Alma, Harper's career stayed intertwined with the school. Later, when Harper was the head football coach at the University of Notre Dame, he would schedule Alma four years in a row, from 1913 through 1916. The clearly outmanned Alma eleven lost to Notre Dame during those years by scores of 62–0, 56–0, 32–0, and 46–0. It would be the 1913 game, however, that produced a historical footnote of some note, as Harper would be able to experiment freely with his Gus Dorais to Knute Rockne forward-passing combination—the same combination he would take to West Point the following weekend.

After two years of coaching at Alma to a record of 7 wins, 3 losses, and 3 ties, Harper left coaching at the request of his father and returned to Iowa to join him in the farming and cattle business. This career change did not last. Before the year was up, Harper was contacting Stagg in hopes of reentering the coaching profession, and with Stagg's guidance and strong recommendation, Harper found a position. Stagg wrote to the administration of Wabash College: "Mr. Harper left his position at Alma in order to go into business with his father, but he writes me that he is planning to get back into coaching. . . . He made a great success at Alma. . . . He is a fine man personally clean and upright and will be thoroughly respected and liked wherever he goes. . . . I consider that you will be fortunate if you secure him. . . . You will not be able to secure him unless you pay him a good salary, as I can locate him, I know, in a good position. His salary last year at Alma was $1,600." In May 1909, Wabash hired Jesse Harper as Instructor of Physical Culture.

Wabash College: 1909–1912

Wabash College, in Crawfordsville, Indiana, was founded in 1832 as an independent, nonsectarian men's liberal-arts college. From its earliest days, Wabash encouraged its young men to a life of intellectual and creative growth, and took its athletics seriously. Though Harper was to serve as the head coach for baseball and track, as well as football, it was on the gridiron where he would make his mark.

*   *   *

In 1909, Harper's first year at Wabash, he was praised for developing a team from essentially "green" material, as only four lettermen had returned. In his entire time at Wabash, in fact, Harper never had more than thirty to thirty-five men show up for football. The Wabash Little Giants tied the first game of the 1909 season, 0–0, against rival DePauw, lost their second game of the year to the "heavy" M.A.C. Aggies by a score of 28–0, and then lost to a strong Saint Louis University team by a score of 14–0. Their first win of 1909 came when they defeated Hanover, 48–0.

The highlight of the season was the matchup with Purdue, which would be described as a "fast and exciting game." The week before the game, Harper scouted the Purdue–Illinois game and "came back with a number of new ideas," which he promptly passed on to his team. The game was marked by Wabash's "long thrilling runs through a broken field, by hard, fierce line smashing and frequent forward passes," which were steadily becoming a hallmark of Harper's offensive coaching strategy. The game was also highlighted by Wabash using only one substitute while Purdue played twenty men—almost the same scenario Harper would employ against Army four years hence. The last five minutes of the game, with the score Wabash 18 and Purdue 17, were said to have been "the most desperately fought of the entire game." Purdue, using fresh substitutes, made a "terrible" but futile fight for a winning score.

Wabash finished the season with losses to Notre Dame and to Butler. Notre Dame, having beaten Michigan the previous year for the first time ever, was considered the strongest team in the West. Wabash went into the game with high but realistic hopes, understanding that beating this strong Notre Dame team would be a "most tremendous task," probably beyond the most "sanguine dreams of the most enthusiastic supporters."

Despite putting up a "nervy fight," Wabash went down 38–0. Under the circumstances, observed the *Wabash,* "Wabash was fortunate in holding Notre Dame to as low a score as she did."

The 12–0 loss to Butler the following week was unexpected, but reasonably attributed to Wabash's schedule. "The hard Purdue contest, followed by the even harder Notre Dame game, left the men badly bruised, gingerless and stale."

Harper's first year was considered a success by the Wabash student body, and they welcomed him back for more. "We wish to . . . express what we believe is the unanimous opinion of the student body—satisfaction with Coach Harper. . . . The entire student body recognizes his [Harper's] ability as a shrewd, untiring coach and appreciates the good results upon the team." Before leaving for the 1909 Christmas holiday, the Wabash administration signed Harper on for two more years.

Harper predicted that the major rule changes developed at the end of the 1909 season would prohibit all pushing, pulling, or dragging of a player, as previously permitted, with the result that the game would be opened up and mass play eliminated. He also predicted that the new rules would lift some of the current restrictions on the forward-passing play. He was correct on both counts. Football would be a different game in 1910.

Harper's 1910 squad at Wabash was said to be his strongest Wabash team. They started the season with decisive victories over Georgetown College, 57–0; Purdue, 3–0; Butler, 48–0; and Saint Louis University, 10–0. Tragedy befell the Saint Louis game, however, and ended Wabash's season.

Ralph Lee Wilson, a freshman, had just earned a starting position at halfback, and even scored a touchdown in the first half. In the third quarter, Wilson was playing defense, when a Saint Louis ballcarrier swept around right end. As the *New York Times,* on October 27, 1910, reported, Wilson "dodged the interference and dived for the runner. In diving the right side of his head struck the Saint Louis player's knee. His skull was fractured in three places." Wilson died on the operating table in a St. Louis hospital on the Sunday following the game, just three hours before his father, rushing to his side from their home in Crawfordsville, Indiana, arrived at his bedside.

The stunning impact of Wilson's death is emblematic of the aftermath of such a tragedy. Classes at the college were canceled for three days, and the remainder of the Wabash football season was also promptly canceled. The *New York Times* reported on October 27, 1910, "Members of the team declare they will not play again this season, and Captain Hopkins says he is through with the game." Crawfordsville High School, which Wilson had attended, also promptly canceled the remainder of the football season, as did the high schools in the towns of Waynetown, Waveland, and New Richmond. Butler University, greatly shocked by Wilson's death, voted to continue with their season; however, five of Butler's players turned in their uniforms and vowed never to play again. Harper was devastated. His players never forgot the death of Wilson, and never forgot the depressing impact it had on their beloved coach. A memorial to Wilson was erected near the Wabash library in 1911 and stands there to this day. It includes his last reported words: "Did Wabash win?"

The year 1911 looked bleak for Wabash. They had lost four of their top players. But Harper was at his competitive best, calling for a secret practice in preparation for the season opener against Purdue. The *Wabash* predicted: "The genius of Harper will probably fix things up all right." This proved true, as Wabash, in "one of the most bitterly contested games ever seen on Stuart Field" again defeated archrival Purdue—this time by a score of 3–0.

In their second contest of the season, Wabash secured a disappointing 0–0 tie against DePauw. After losing to Marquette University in a close game, 11–9, Wabash defeated Earlham 12–3 and Rose Poly 17–6. They ended their 1911 season with losses to Notre Dame 6–3 and to the Michigan Aggies 17–6.

The high point of the 1911 season was, strangely enough, a loss, by a score of 6 to 3, to Notre Dame. Notre Dame had an outstanding team in 1911 and had gained strong recognition as one of the best in the Midwest. The loss by such a narrow margin was rightly considered a moral victory by the heavily outmanned Wabash team. As the *Wabash* described it: "A great game! Going down on the records as the best, fastest, snappiest seen in Indiana this year. And rightly, too! . . . And it was only at the end of a long, hard game that their superior strength wore out the Wabash warriors and big [Notre Dame fullback Ray] Eichenlaub went over for a touchdown." Wabash came close to victory, but for a quirk in the rules, which would be eliminated the following season. On the controversial play, Wabash's outstanding quarterback Skeet Lambert threw a long pass for a touchdown to Wabash's Brooks Howard. According to the rules, however, a pass could not be thrown more than twenty yards in the air, and the game officials stepped the play off. Determining that the pass had indeed traveled more than twenty yards in the air, they nullified the touchdown, and Notre Dame went on to win by a score of 6–3.

Wabash came into its 1912 football season with high hopes, based primarily on the return of ten lettermen, including bigger, more physical running backs, and an outstanding guard, M. E. "Doc" Elliott, of the class of 1913, who had been class president and captain of the football team in 1911. Doc and Harper formed a relationship that lasted the rest of their lives.

New rules for the game were in effect, which, in the words of the *Wabash,* would provide the fans with a "game full of thrills, a game that will take not one brain and ten beefs, but eleven brains, all working simultaneously in offense and individually on defense."

Harper's strong 1912 team opened the season by defeating Moore's Hill College 102–0, with the game being called at the end of the third period, as the Wabash second and third teams were scoring at will. Following the Moore's Hill game, Wabash defeated archrival DePauw, 62–0, and Butler 47–0. Then came Notre Dame. The game was played on Cartier Field in South Bend. To say that Wabash was undermanned would be an understatement. Wabash had a traveling squad of twenty-two men, whereas one of the Wabash players alleged that he had counted on Notre Dame's side a "dozen full teams on the field in pre-game practice." The game gave Harper a good preview of the kind of talent that was available at Notre Dame, though, at the time, there was no inkling that Harper would be moving there. Ray Eichenlaub, Notre Dame's outstanding fullback, combined power with great speed; Joe Pliska, at halfback, was both a runner and an outstanding receiver; Gus Dorais was an outstanding quarterback and a great passer, and Knute Rockne was a talented and fighting receiver. Harper certainly had men like these in mind when he set up his aggressive and history-making schedule for Notre Dame in 1913.

The game was billed at Wabash as being for the Indiana state championship. Wabash's hopes were high for "victory and a long hoped for defeat of the Catholics." Notre Dame won, 41–6. The *Wabash* noted that Notre Dame "had an exceptionally strong team this year, one of the best in the West, and it was no disgrace to be defeated by them." Later the *Wabash* reported that Notre Dame was "far superior to us in everything that makes a good football team, except fight, for we did fight, and every man should receive credit for that."

After losing decisively to Notre Dame, Wabash was the winner over Rose Polytechnic, 39–0, and Earlham, 7–0. Wabash ended the season losing to the Michigan Aggies, 24–0.

Soon after the close of the 1912 season it became public knowledge that Harper would be leaving Wabash for Notre Dame. "Too much cannot be said in praise of Coach Harper, to whom the success of the team is largely due. It is unfortunate that we are compelled to give him up to Notre Dame, but he goes with our best wishes for success." The *Bachelor,* another Wabash newspaper, carried a story on December 14, 1912, acknowledging that Harper was leaving Wabash for Notre Dame, but noting that he would finish the school year at Wabash and coach basketball, baseball, and track.

In his Wabash years, Harper deepened his understanding of the new open game of football and continued to build on the training he had received from Stagg. By the time he left for Notre Dame in 1913, he had not only gained a reputation as a strong and innovative proponent of the forward pass, he had also developed the philosophy that academics should come before athletics, and sportsmanship should come before winning.

In a 1911 article in *Wabash* magazine, Harper urged the College to drop from its schedule teams that played "ringers and semi-pro" athletes, and argued that schools should require only two hours of practice per day, rather than the four hours a day that some schools practiced. Athletics, he contended, should be subservient to the good of the college and the athlete as a student. "At all times athletics should be held secondary to college work," he wrote. "Some schools are inclined to forget this very important point and especially some of the large universities. . . . The athlete should be required to keep up in all his studies. The percentage of men in athletics that fail is usually not as high as the percentage of failures among students not in athletics."

Harper showed his trademark commonsense disdain for the "winning is the only thing" mantra. "It will take years," he wrote, "to educate the public to the point where they will look down on the college that uses unfair means in order to win. The American spirit is that we must win. It seems we cannot play games for the sake of the games, but we have them largely to settle the dispute as to which is the better team. Seldom do we see students of one college cheering the good plays made by the other team. Instead we think of the crowd across the field as our bitter enemies. After the game, especially if we lose, instead of mingling with the supporters of the victorious team, talking over the contest from the viewpoint of good and bad plays and enjoying their good fellowship, we want to get home as soon as possible in order to avoid meeting any of the opponents. Until the time comes when we have contests for the sake of the contests, until athletics are solely for their good to the college and student body, we are bound to find colleges which will at times stray from the straight and narrow path in order to win their games."

At the end of his article, the young Harper quotes approvingly from an editorial in a Chicago paper: "The conviction is rapidly gaining strength that one of the best courses at college is the athletic course . . . it teaches men to do things for the glory of the deed—it shows them how to grow strong through trying a little harder each day—it proves that development can only be attained through application—it trains men to play fair and according to the rules—to try their level best—to vie cleanly, and to keep at it until the tape is broken and the whistle is sounded and the last batter is out."

Harper's philosophy was forming, and the influence of Amos Alonzo Stagg was clear. But Harper was not only forming his philosophy but also displaying the ability to convey it to his players. In June 1912 the *Wabash*, in reviewing the year 1911–1912, noted that the year had been successful, and that a large share of the credit belonged to Coach Harper: "Success does not necessarily mean contests won. . . . Standing for fair play, square deal, and gentlemanly sport, at all times, and in every contest, he has helped establish among Wabash men a standard of sportsmanship that is becoming recognized in the college world. This successful year . . . can be laid to Coach Harper's tireless efforts and to his energetic work."

Harper would carry this philosophy into his career at Notre Dame, both as its athletic director and head football coach from 1913 to 1918 and then as its athletic director from 1931 to 1933, and he would pass it on to his players, coaches, and all he came into contact with. It is a testament to Harper that he recognized the challenge of balancing athletics and academics so early in his career. It would not always prove to be a popular philosophy, as would become evident when he returned to Notre Dame in 1931, but it was the right philosophy, and Harper had the inner strength and conviction to know and understand that. His philosophy would find fertile ground at Notre Dame, and once planted, it would remain a hallmark of Notre Dame athletics to the present day.

5

Jesse Harper's First Year at Notre Dame, 1913

In 1912 Notre Dame's football program was in a state of crisis. The team was losing money, a situation that could not be tolerated for long by a small institution that was continually struggling to finance its academic program. Further, Notre Dame's natural rivals in the Midwest were refusing to play them. Notre Dame was being blackballed primarily by the Big Nine, now the Big Ten, on the grounds that Notre Dame's academic standards were not up to the standards of the Big Nine. The real reasons, however, seemed to have more to do with the Big Nine's latent anti-Catholicism, combined with their realistic concern that the Notre Dame team was becoming an uncomfortably strong team for the Big Nine teams to compete against. Notre Dame had always been able to attract athletic young men who loved to play football, and they were now playing the game well and winning far more than they lost. In this atmosphere, Notre Dame's president, Father John Cavanaugh, along with Notre Dame's vice president and head of the athletic program, Father Matthew Walsh, C.S.C., who would take the reins as the president of Notre Dame in 1922, set out in search of a new football coach.

First and foremost, their ideal candidate would have to be a man of high ideals and strong integrity. Second, he had to have a strong knowledge of the game of football and be an excellent coach. Third, he needed to possess a high degree of financial acumen. Finally, he had to be well connected in the football world, and he had to be a good salesman. On all counts, Jesse C. Harper was the man Notre Dame was looking for and the man Notre Dame needed. He was well known and well liked by his fellow coaches, not to mention being a protégé of one of the greatest figures in football, Amos Alonzo Stagg. In addition, Harper possessed a proven and mature philosophy of athletics and their place in an academic environment. Last but not least, Harper had a good sense of what action to take and when to take it, as well as the courage to take it.

One of the strongest virtues Harper brought to Notre Dame was his sheer love of football. Years after he had left coaching, Harper mused that he used to "hop out of bed in the wee hours with some nutty idea about a play. And gosh, some of 'em honestly worked like charms. I always believed in a lot of deception in your offense. That, plus speed, good kicking and solid fundamentals. I never cared an awful lot about beef. Rock is like that, only a much finer strategist and a better planner."

By the time Harper arrived at Notre Dame, he had also developed his own style as a teacher and a coach. Judge Norm Barry, who later played under Harper, fondly remembered his coach: "Jesse Harper was a very well-mannered man. He in no way looked like a football coach. He would come out dressed in an ordinary suit. He never had any football togs on him. He was a great tactician, he knew football. That was one of his greatest assets. Harper always had an interest in his players. When the season was over, Harper was always around to talk to his players and try to inspire them to do other things than just to play football."

In December of 1912, Harper formally signed his agreement to move to Notre Dame, and in 1913, at the age of twenty-nine, Jesse C. Harper became the head football coach and athletic director at the University of Notre Dame, not to mention the coach of the basketball, baseball, and track teams. The athletic officials at Notre Dame, understanding well their predicament, were ecstatic with the selection. As Manager of Athletics William E. Cotter promptly wrote to Harper in December 1912, "Notre Dame has been fighting against misinterpretation for the past four or five seasons, and so were denied an opportunity to meet our logical opponents. The brighter day that we have been looking for is about to dawn, we feel sure, and Notre Dame will soon come into her own . . . Mr. Harper let me congratulate you on your appointment to what I consider a very grand position. . . . My only regret is, that such a move was not taken sooner." A prophetic observation.

By the time he arrived at Notre Dame, Harper had formed his personal thinking on the place of athletics in an academic environment—it was, appropriately, to teach young men how to grow strong and train them to play fair and by the rules and to try their level best. One of his first acts was to institute academic standards for all of the school's athletes that were as high as or higher than the standards of any of the other

Midwestern schools, particularly the members of the Big Nine, or Western Conference, as it was sometimes called. "Teams may still refuse to schedule us," Harper remarked soon after his arrival at Notre Dame, "but never again will the academic eligibility of our players be a valid reason for that refusal." Now, almost a century after Harper first instituted his stringent academic standards at Notre Dame, strong remnants of those standards continue to be a proud hallmark of the Notre Dame football program—a 2006 NCAA report on football-team graduation rates noted that Notre Dame, with its rate of 95 percent, led all other teams in the top twenty-five by a wide margin.

Harper instinctively recognized that the path out of Notre Dame's football money crunch lay in the scheduling of major opponents—teams that would excite fans and bring money into the Notre Dame coffers. In his response to Cotter's letter, Harper made it clear that he was already hard at work on the scheduling. Harper wrote, "I wish you would send me some stationery at once as I am entirely out." Though he insisted on fulfilling his contract at Wabash College—an agreement that would take him to the end of the Wabash school year in the spring of 1913—Harper sent out letters to numerous colleges and universities across the country seeking to arrange games for the 1913 season. He received positive responses from several schools, including Penn State University, the University of Texas, South Dakota University, Ohio Northern University, The Christian Brothers of St. Louis, and Harper's former school, Alma College in Michigan.

But the jewel of the schedule came from a letter he wrote on December 18, 1912. "The Army game was arranged in a very simple manner," the plainspoken Harper later recalled. "I wrote the Army to see

Coach Jesse C. Harper, circa 1905.

Morgan Park 1901 football team. Jesse C. Harper in center of first row.

University of Chicago 1905 baseball team. Captain Jesse C. Harper in Center
with catcher's mitt.

Alma College 1906 football team. Coach Jesse C. Harper at far left of upper row.

Wabash College 1910 baseball team. Coach Jesse C. Harper at far right.

Jesse C. Harper, date unknown.

Jesse C. Harper, coaching baseball
at Notre Dame, circa 1914.

Jesse C. Harper, coaching baseball at Notre
Dame, circa 1914.

Ray Eichenlaub and Charles "Gus"
Dorais, 1913.

Knute Rockne and Charles "Gus" Dorais in their Notre Dame football uniforms in 1913.

Knute Rockne, circa 1913.

Knute Rockne, 1913.

Courtesy of Jim Harper.

Notre Dame's 1913 football team. Front row: Mal Elward, Alfred Bergman, Bill Cook, Art "Bunny" Larkin. Second row: Ralph "Zipper" Lathrop, Keith "Deak" Jones, Joe Pliska, Knute Rockne (captain), Charles "Gus" Dorais, Fred Gushurst, Al Fenney. Back row: Howard Edwards (assistant coach), Emmett Keefe, Ray Eichenlaub, Hollis "Hoot" King, Freeman Fitzgerald, Charles "Sam" Finegan, Coach Jesse C. Harper.

Army's 1913 football team. Front row: Jouett, '14, (F.B.); Hobbs, '15, (H.B.); Capt. Hoge, B.F., '14, (H.B.); Wynne '14, (R.T.); Goodman, '15, (C.). Middle Row: Merillat, '15, (R.E.); Benedict, '15, (H.B.); Prichard, '15, (Q.B.); Ford, '17, (H.B.); Hodgson, P.A., '15, (F.B.); Jones, W.G., '14, (L.G.). Back Row: Woodruff, '15, (H.B.); Huston, '14, (R.G.); McEwan, '17, (C.); Weyand, '16, (L.T.); Markoe, '14, (L.E.).

"Getting ready for the Football season of 1913. Our future Generals 'Making a Kick,' April 5, 1913," signed S. Ellis Heath, Peekskill, NY.

*The completion of one of the start!
"Dorais to Rockne" passes which b
the Army in 1913 and modified the
tire game of football. Here's Kn
making a touchdown.*

Rockne scoring Notre Dame's first touchdown against Army on a forty-yard pass from Dorais, 1913.

if they had an opening on their schedule, and if so would they give us a game. No outside person knew anything about it until the game was arranged and contracts signed."

Harper's timing was fortunate. "My letter to West Point had arrived at a time when the Army–Yale series had ended somewhat abruptly," he said. "And the Cadets had an open date.

"You can imagine my surprise and delight when I received a reply from West Point officials to the effect that they had an open date on Nov. 1, 1913, which we could have. They guaranteed us $1,000 for the game, too." In his initial contacts, Army had offered $400—the well-heeled Eastern colleges always paid their own way to the Point—but Harper had explained that Notre Dame could not afford to travel to West Point for that amount. Finally they settled on $1,000, which was an unheard-of amount of money for that day, and Harper immediately conveyed the news to Notre Dame president Father John Cavanaugh and vice president Father Matthew Walsh. They promptly instructed him to accept.

Dan I. Sultan, a student football manager at West Point who was in charge of arranging Army's football schedule, later remembered the rationale for scheduling Notre Dame: "We needed a 'breather' before our annual meeting with Navy."

Army, as it turned out, was also having trouble filling its schedule. "After the 1912 season Yale discontinued its annual game with Army, giving Army an open date on Nov. 1, 1913. Army at the time was becoming a pariah in intercollegiate sports because it was flouting accepted eligibility rules, witness Elmer Olpihant, who went to West Point after attaining All-American honors at Purdue for his playing there from 1911 thru 1913."

But none of this bothered Harper; he needed games, big games, and Army fit the bill. Harper had managed to put together a full schedule for his first season as coach:

Oct. 4	Ohio Northern	87–0	Home
Oct. 18	South Dakota	20–7	Home
Oct. 25	Alma	62–0	Home
Nov. 1	Army	35–13	Away
Nov. 7	Penn State	14–7	Away
Nov. 22	Christian Brothers	20–7	Away
Nov. 27	Texas	30–7	Away

Although Harper himself would not see all the financial fruits of his scheduling strategy during his initial tenure at Notre Dame, he had during that time stabilized the school's program, and he clearly set the table for those that followed him. Harper's expense report for the Army game on November 1, 1913, shows that Notre Dame made a grand total of $154.50 from the game. In 1914 Notre Dame would end the season $1,408 to the good, despite showing a deficit of $404 for its trip to New Haven to play Yale, the only game ever played between the two universities, which the Bulldogs won, 28–0. Even being able to schedule Yale was evidence of how far Notre Dame had come and how much credibility Harper had brought to the program.

By 1915, Harper's strategy would begin to show positive financial results, and Notre Dame turned a handsome profit of $6,120. Its major income came from a trip to Lincoln to play the University of Nebraska— a net profit of $4,688. Its trip into the Southwest to play the University of Texas on November 25, 1915, and Rice University on November 27, 1915, netted receipts totaling $4,311. In 1916 Notre Dame netted $5,376 for the season with the major income coming from its game with the University of Nebraska, again in Lincoln, in the amount of $5,221. The finances, to be sure, would come a long way from the deficit years of 1911 and 1912. From that point on, the financial outlook for Notre Dame football would be bright. By the time Rockne was coach, the Army game alone would eventually move from the Plains at West Point to New York City, and the returns to Notre Dame in those games would exceed a quarter of a million dollars each.

Harper and Rockne Meet

In 2006, Kent Stephens, an author and historian at the College Football Hall of Fame, wrote: "Jesse Harper is . . . an important figure. For without Harper there may have never been a Knute Rockne." It was on the Notre Dame practice field that Harper first encountered a senior student and player by the name of Knute Rockne. Born on March 4, 1888, in Voss, Norway, Knute Kenneth Rockne was the son of a carriage maker, whose family immigrated to the United States while he was a child. After completing his secondary education in Chicago's rough Logan Square area, Rockne worked as a dispatcher in the Chicago post office. After three years of working and saving, he enrolled at Notre Dame.

Harper immediately perceived something unique in Rockne. Upon first watching Rockne on the practice field, he knew that in all of his years in football he had never seen any fight like Rockne's. Rockne never quit, and that stark impression stayed with Harper forever. Equally important, Harper observed that Rockne, even as a young player, had the ability to lead and inspire his teammates to a level of performance that was beyond their natural capabilities.

In Harper's words, "he was one of those natural fighting football players that a coach finds once in a blue moon. He was a little light and inexperienced, but my how that boy would battle 'em. . . . That everlasting fight of his, was his dominating trait. How his eyes would light up and blaze, when he was stirred! His personality was attractive too, and I consider him one of the headiest football players who ever wore a suit. The combination was ideal to make a coach."

Harper and Rockne's coach-player relationship soon developed into a close, lifelong friendship. Through the years that followed, the friendship between Harper and Rockne grew, to the point that Harper's youngest son, Jim, would later observe, "I have never seen two brothers any closer than Dad and Uncle Rock." After Rockne's death, the *South Bend Tribune* wrote, "It was from Harper that Rockne received his greatest training as a player and later as an assistant coach." Harper would have taken mild offense at the remark. When asked, he contended, "No man made Rockne a coach, but Rockne himself. I just happened to be there while the process was under way."

Harper also discovered that Rockne had a "terrible temper," one that could impede his development as a player and as a man. Harper worked long hours with Rockne, successfully counseling Rockne not only on how to understand his temper but also, more importantly, on how to channel and control it.

And channel it he did. As Harper would relate in the late 1920s, Rockne was "the greatest of all football teachers. There's many a star of football who cannot impart the game to others, but that is where Rock shines. He's got the stuff and he knows how to instruct. He's a great teacher of the game and second only to Stagg as a builder of character."

The First Games of the 1913 Season

It takes a variety of attributes to make up a winning football team. Having skilled, smart players who possess a fair degree of brawn, brains, and a strong level of football instincts, ranks at the top. As Harper had observed the previous year when Notre Dame routed his Wabash squad by a score of 41–6, Notre Dame had such a group of players.

The returning veterans on the 1913 team included their captain and undisputed team leader, Rockne, at end. Then came Notre Dame's outstanding quarterback, Gus Dorais, whom Harper called one of the finest passers he had ever seen. At 5-foot-7 and 145 pounds, the native of Chippewa Falls, Wisconsin, was a fast, elusive runner and dangerous kick returner as well as an accurate passer, and would become Notre Dame's first consensus All-American, finishing his three years as a starter with a record of twenty wins, no losses, and two ties. Though Dorais and Rockne, his roommate, would come to be known as one of the finest passing tandems of all time, it would in fact be as a coach that Dorais would gain election into the Football Hall of Fame in 1954, after a distinguished career at Loras, Gonzaga, and Detroit University, with stints as a Notre Dame assistant under Rockne and head coach of the NFL's Detroit Lions.

The team's fullback, Ray Eichenlaub, who stood 6 feet, 210 pounds, and possessed great speed, vied with Rockne and Dorais for the honor of being the best player on the squad. As the Notre Dame yearbook, the

Dome, described Eichenlaub: "His terrific speed, his bull-dog courage, and his ability to hit the line for a gain when everything else fails, has made him one of the greatest players of his day." Eichenlaub was inducted into the College Football Hall of Fame, as a player, in 1972, the only player from the 1913 team so honored—Rockne, like Dorais, was inducted as a coach. Closely following the big three was halfback Joseph S. Pliska, always one of Harper's favorite players. According to the *Scholastic,* "Pliska struck his real stride in the Army game of 1913. He picked passes out of the clouds, hit the Cadet line for long gains, and skirted the ends like the wind." In the Army game, he caught two passes and scored two touchdowns. The rest of the starting eleven for Notre Dame in 1913 included Lathrop, Berger, Fitzgerald, Finegan, Gushurst, Fenney, and Jones, a lineup that, at season's end, would be declared by the *Scholastic* "the greatest eleven that ever did honor to the Gold and Blue." Their monumental efforts that season would give Notre Dame its first national recognition and start Notre Dame on the road to legendary status in the annals of college football, while also changing the game of football forever by demonstrating the dramatic effect that the forward pass, when properly executed under the new rules, could have on the game.

Ohio Northern

Notre Dame's first game in 1913 was at home, against Ohio Northern, a team that all understood was seriously outmanned by the Notre Dame squad. The preparations for the game were a harbinger of things to come. At a scrimmage against the freshmen on the Friday before the game, a reporter observed, "Dorais, following Harper's directions, used the forward pass continually. The peculiar danger and value of this play was strikingly brought out in to-day's play. Dorais shot three forward passes in quick success. All three were intercepted. Then, with three downs and 10 yards to make, he tried a fourth. Elward, the varsity right end, caught the ball and dashed down the field for 30 yards." In pregame preparations, Harper made it clear that this team would engage in open play and heavily utilize the forward pass. Notre Dame won handily, as one paper described it, "Featured by brilliant forward passing and machine precision in the execution of their plays, the Notre Dame eleven swamped Ohio Northern Saturday by a score of 87–0."

South Dakota

Notre Dame's second game of the 1913 season, also at home, was against a much more formidable opponent, the Coyotes of the University of South Dakota, who would prove to be a good test for evaluating this Notre Dame team.

Anticipation for the game was high. Ticket sales were heavy; Notre Dame alumni were coming in from Chicago, Indianapolis, Fort Wayne, Elkhart, and Michigan City. Cheering was being practiced in the Notre Dame gymnasium.

Though South Dakota had a physical advantage—their line out-weighed the Notre Dame line by thirty-five pounds per man—both coaches were cautious and respectful in their remarks about the other team. The South Dakota coach said, "I rank Notre Dame as one of the strongest teams in the west. In fact, I think that Notre Dame has as good a team as Wisconsin last year. If we win we will consider the victory a high achievement: if we lose we will consider the defeat far from a disgrace." Knute Rockne was injured and would not play in the game. However, giving early evidence of his later famous ability as a coach to inspire, he said, "The Dakotans are a husky looking bunch . . . and are out for the game, but, although I probably won't be able to get in the game, I know the other fellows will fight just as hard as ever and put on a battle that will make the westerners go some to carry away their scalps."

In a hard-fought battle, described as the "hardest football game played on Cartier field in many years," Notre Dame won by a score of 20–7. There was concern about Notre Dame's light line, as it was observed that the "line will have to improve greatly if it succeeds in holding against the heavy Penn State and Army lines." It was noted that Notre Dame's last touchdown of the game was scored by Dorais's long forward pass. The other scores were all on the ground.

Alma

Notre Dame's third victory of the 1913 season was on October 25 against Alma College. It would be the last home game of the year for Notre Dame. The next four games would be played on the road, as Notre Dame would travel east to Army and Penn State, then west to St. Louis and Austin, Texas. The 62–0 outcome against Alma revealed that once again, Notre Dame was playing a completely outmanned opponent. The game, however, was a healthy warm-up for what lay ahead, and the Notre Dame coaches were definitely looking ahead. Harper was said to be educating the team with a number of new and "fancy" formations, designed specially to counteract the heavy lines of Penn State and Army.

During the week preceding the Alma game, Notre Dame was looking ahead to the Army game the following weekend. "The military men are working just as hard as the locals to get in shape for the game and the battle promises to narrow down to a battle between east and west. The Army has a strong team and so far the soldiers have not met defeat this year. Notre Dame has the same reputation with the addition that it lost no games last year."

Even in 1913, despite the dramatic changes in the rules of the game, the specter of death still lingered. Ralph Dimick, who had starred for the Notre Dame football team from 1908 through 1910, had been killed two years earlier while playing in an alumni game. In attempting a tackle, Dimick had broken a rib, which in turn punctured a lung. He died within days. On the weekend of the Alma game, the University of Notre Dame was finalizing plans for a memorial to be placed on Dimick's grave.

With Dimick on their minds, Notre Dame completely dominated Alma, riding a passing attack that complemented their strong running game. Defensively, Notre Dame was as solid as a rock—literally, Rockne. He was back, and his strong defensive play was noted as one reason for Notre Dame's domination. This play would hold true in the Army game as well. As it was said of Notre Dame's offensive prowess, "Time after time Dorais pegged swift forward passes to Gushurst and Rockne for big gains and four of the touchdowns were effected, by neat forward passes near the goal line." Furthermore, "Pilska showed up strong at pulling down forward passes and the little touch of baseball introduced by Dorais, Pilska, Rockne and Gushurst netted some splendid gains for the varsity." The running game was also featured against Alma, just as it would be against Army. "Eichenlaub, Pilska and Finegan pierced the visitor's line time after time for gains varying from three to twenty yards."

Once the three consecutive home games were out of the way, Notre Dame was ready to go on the road to face the heart of their history-making schedule.

First up would be the United States Military Academy, at West Point, New York. Six days later Notre Dame would travel to College Station, Pennsylvania, to meet Penn State, and then on to St. Louis, Missouri, to play a strong Christian Brothers team. Finally, Notre Dame would travel to Austin to play the powerful University of Texas.

6

The Game That Changed Football: Notre Dame vs. Army, November 1, 1913

That Army considered Notre Dame a "breather" may have been true when the game was scheduled in the final weeks of 1912. However, as game day approached in 1913, it was clear that Army understood full well the strength of the Notre Dame team and was taking exceptional steps in their preparation, bringing in extra coaches the week before the game to assist. Lieutenant Boyers, captain of the 1902 Army team and one of the greatest centers in Army history, was called in to work with Army's centers; Ham Fisher from the 1909 Harvard team came in to work with the forwards; and "Germany" Schultz, described as the best center ever developed by Fielding Yost at Michigan, was also on hand. The Cadets were serious and prepared to the fullest.

As one eastern paper reported, "The Army eleven is preparing for the hardest game of its season by long practice hours and hard work. They have some dubious forebodings regarding the outcome of the game and the appearance of the South Bend huskies (on the grounds at West Point) didn't brighten the outlook. Coach Daly has put his men in excellent fighting trim . . . but the strength of the Notre Dame team is an unknown factor to him and he is unable to bank on the result."

Notre Dame's preparation for West Point was also at the highest level. Harper, in an unusual adjustment to his standard coaching methods, scheduled an additional practice each day of the week before the game. "No prospects for rest are in view for the Notre Dame squad before the team leaves for West Point," it was said before the game. During the afternoon practices, the team scrimmaged and worked on new plays that Harper had devised specifically for the Army game. Harper drove his team until darkness forced them from the field. After supper the team was given signal drills and blackboard exercises. By Wednesday before the game day it was observed that Harper had succeeded in instilling a fighting spirit in his men.

Neither Notre Dame nor Army had any real handle on the strengths or weaknesses of the other, but both knew they were in for a battle. "It is impossible to get a line on the respective strength of the two teams," it was said. "The only thing which is an absolute certainty is that both teams are of the first class and that both are going in for a life and death fight in the contest."

Dorais to Rockne

The sophisticated passing attack that Harper installed at Notre Dame had been long in the making—after being introduced to the weapon by

Stagg, Harper perfected the scheme during his years at Alma and Wabash. Harper, having played Notre Dame twice while at Wabash, knew he was inheriting talented players, particularly the duo of Rockne and Dorais, who had the ability to take his offense to new heights.

From the start, Rockne and Dorais were close. They were thrown together as roommates at the start of their freshman year and they had naturally common interests; both were young, poor, and exceptionally talented athletes. And neither of them was an altar boy.

In later years, while Gus was visiting his son Tom, who was then a student at Notre Dame, the two walked over to the famed Grotto on campus to light candles and make an offering. As Tom recalls, his father had just given him about $3 in spending money, but put an entire $20 bill in the offertory box. Tom asked his father why he had made such an offering without even lighting a candle. Tom was surprised by the unusually generous act, especially given the fact that he had only received $3. Gus explained that during his years at Notre Dame, the campus policy was lights-out at 9:00 PM. Because this interfered with their nightly poker games, he and Rock occasionally "borrowed" candles from the Grotto. With the twenty, he was just trying to even things up.

During the summer of 1913, the two Notre Dame seniors-to-be worked as restaurant clerks at Cedar Point, a resort on the Ohio shores of Lake Erie, and brought a football to the beach with them to practice during their free time. Harper had devised a more effective way to throw and catch the football. Harper's son Jim recalls that his father had innovated, or at least advocated, the overhanded throwing motion and the method of throwing to a receiver with the receiver catching the ball over his shoulder, while on a dead run. Both had carried over from Harper's days as a baseball player at the University of Chicago. Harper also understood, from his baseball-playing days, that the best way to catch a ball was to keep your hands open and relaxed. He often referred to this as "soft hands."

That summer Dorais perfected an overhanded technique for throwing a spiral pass. "I worked hard to increase the accuracy and length of my passes," he later recalled. Rockne, meanwhile, learned to catch the ball with "soft" hands, rather than the stiff-handed method he had previously used, and he worked on running routes. As Dorais put it, "Rockne continued to develop his deceptive, stop-and-go style of going down the field for a pass, a style used by nearly all good pass receivers."

"Perfection of the forward pass came to us only through daily, tedious practice," Rockne later observed. "I'd run along the beach, Dorais would throw from all angles. People who didn't know we were two college seniors making painstaking preparations for our final season probably thought we were crazy. Once a bearded old gentleman took off his shoes to get in the fun, seizing the ball and kicking it merrily, with bare feet, too, until a friendly keeper came along to take him back where he belonged."

As Chet Grant wrote in the *South Bend Tribune,* "Certainly it was Harper who encouraged, if he did not initiate, the highly publicized forward passing drills by Dorais and Rockne on the beach at Sandusky, Ohio, during the summer vacations. Certainly he provided the football and the football shoes and the end results were fabulous." Later, at Harper's urging, Grant would leave his employment as a sportswriter for the *South Bend Tribune,* matriculate to Notre Dame, and end up playing football for both Harper and Rockne.

In early 1951, while Harper was in San Francisco for the national convention of cattlemen, he was interviewed at the Palace Hotel by Prescott Sullivan, a sportswriter for the *San Francisco Examiner*. Sullivan took the opportunity to revisit a few of the old Notre Dame legends, and check the myths against the facts. "Another tale we've long accepted as fact has to do with the Notre Dame–Army game of '13," he wrote. "The victory was gained largely through the effectiveness of the Dorais to Rockne pass combination and, according to the historians, Dorais and Rockne developed the bewildering aerial patterns by daily practice during the summer vacation period."

Harper confirmed the truth of that "old legend" but explained to Sullivan that regular and rigorous team practice sessions had been the key to the perfection of Notre Dame's 1913 passing attack. "We worked on those pass plays that beat Army as a team and during the regular practice season. It is true, Dorais and Rockne did a little of it on their own. Rockne, an end, wasn't much of a pass receiver to start with. His style, fashioned after that of the day, was to catch the ball with his arms and stomach and I told him he'd never be a good receiver until he learned to catch the ball with his hands. So, Rockne got Dorais to throw him a few. Together they spent perhaps a couple of afternoons at it. The pass plays were rehearsed for weeks by the entire squad."

Notre Dame Travels to West Point

On Thursday, October 30, 1913, the entire Notre Dame student body, along with priests, faculty, and friends, gathered on campus to see the team—"a band of nineteen gold and blue warriors," as the *Scholastic* put it—off to West Point, "where for the first time in the history of Notre

Dame football, the Varsity will meet the Army eleven. We are putting our full strength in the field this afternoon against the soldiers, and are ready to put forward all our substitutes in case of accident." Before departing, Harper stopped and spoke to the assembled crowd: "We are going for victory, but of course I am not going to make any forecast of the result. Chances seem about even, but with chances even, Notre Dame always wins. I consider this the hardest game on our schedule and the men are going to fight a battle of their lives. The strength of the cadets is a mystery to me so I have trained my men to put up the bitterest fight of their lives in Saturday's game."

In 1913, Army was one of the strongest teams in the East—if not the strongest—the following year, they would go undefeated and be declared national champions. "The Army has a team somewhat heavier than ours," the *Scholastic* opined, "and should the field be heavy, this fact will militate against our chances." The opponent was formidable. This was clear, even if the paper did offer Notre Dame some hope: "On a dry field, there is no reason to suppose that the Varsity is inferior to the cadets. The Army enjoys a clean slate thus far this year, having won from Stevens by a 34-to-0 score, from Colgate, 7–6, and from Tufts, 2–0. The last two scores indicate a weakness, but both games were played on heavy fields, and are no criteria for just appraisement. It is safe to say that the Military Academy has one of the strongest teams in the East, and should the Varsity prove superior to them, we can rank ourselves as among the best in the country."

Not only were the cadets a strong team in 1913, but, in addition, they would have the home-field advantage. With the exception of their annual game with Navy, West Point had a policy of playing all of its games at home. This not only gave them the confidence of having a loyal group of supporters, it meant, at least in Notre Dame's case, that the opposition would have to travel 1,000 miles to arrive at the West Point playing field.

Years later, to the great financial advantage of both institutions, Rockne would coax West Point into playing their annual game with Notre Dame in New York, a move Harper had suggested upon his departure from Notre Dame in 1918. Eventually the annual Notre Dame–Army game would be played at Yankee Stadium each year, and each school would realize profits from that game alone in excess of a quarter of a million dollars—in 1946, preceding the Game of the Century, when both teams entered the game undefeated and fought to a scoreless tie, $500,000 in ticket applications had to be returned for lack of additional seating.

But New York and the big time were all in the future. In the fall of 1913, not only was Notre Dame a small and relatively unknown institution, but it was also in poor financial condition. Harper had to bargain hard with the officials at the Army to obtain a game payment of $1,000, after an original offer of $400. As Harper's final expense report revealed, even the $1,000 payment barely covered expenses, despite the fact that West Point provided room and board. Notre Dame would return home with a profit of $154.50.

In keeping with the austere circumstances of the day, the Notre Dame traveling team, which consisted of nineteen players, was only able to round up fourteen pairs of cleats. Most of the players had dual-purpose shoes, Fred "Gus" Gushurst, who started at end opposite Rockne, later said: "We would wear our shoes without cleats, of course, while on the train and then, just before game time, screw the cleats into the soles of the shoes." For their meals on the trip, the Notre Dame players carried sandwiches that had been packed by the nuns in the school cafeteria. Each player carried his own gear and equipment.

"We were permitted few luxuries on this trip from Indiana," Harper later said. "The boys carried their uniforms in satchels—some wearing their jerseys under their coats to conserve space." As Rockne would put it: "The morning we left for West Point the entire student body of the university got up long before breakfast to see us to the day coach that carried the squad to Buffalo—a dreary, all-day trip. From Buffalo we enjoyed the luxury of sleeping-car accommodations—regulars in lowers, substitutes in uppers. There was no pampering in those days. We wanted none of it. Our only extra equipment was a roll of tape, a jug of liniment and a bottle of iodine. To cut expenses, we traveled by coach as far as Buffalo before changing to sleepers."

The uncomfortable travel conditions were not the only challenge the team would face on their trip east. The evening before the team departed an incident in the dorm occurred that exemplified Harper's integrity as a coach, as well as the loyalty of his young player and captain, Rockne. As Harper remembered, he walked into the room of one of the team's best players, who remained unidentified, though he was also one of Rock's best friends. The young man was smoking, a violation of team rules. Harper said, "I told the young man we wouldn't need him on the Army trip." The player's response was "All right, sir." Harper was somewhat concerned, given the circumstances, about what Rockne would say about the incident. But when Harper informed Rockne of the suspension, Rockne simply said, "That's all right; it was the thing to do." Harper always appreciated Rockne's support in the matter and never forgot Rockne's quick loyalty to him and to the team.

Though they would be playing this important game 1,000 miles from home and in front of a hostile crowd, Notre Dame would not be completely alone. Even in its infancy, the Notre Dame spirit was alive and strong. It was reported before the game that, "The Notre Dame club of New York has chartered a train to West Point for the event and there will be a section among the spectators that will give the old N.D. yells and encourage the team from Indiana." In addition, a small contingent of fans from South Bend—five to be exact—had accompanied the team on the trip.

Notre Dame arrived in West Point on Friday, October 31, at 1:30 PM. The Cadets, of course, were curious to get a "take" on their visitors from the Midwest. "I was in the Cadet locker room on a Thursday afternoon following practice when I first heard of the Indiana institution called Notre Dame," said Willet J. Baird, the Army mascot, who would later become a high-ranking military officer. "The players, as usual, were asking questions about this Indiana team and no one present seemed to know a great deal about it. Everyone, however, was convinced that Saturday would bring a 'breather.'"

Baird had also been on the train platform when the Notre Dame contingent arrived. Like others, he had come out of curiosity to see what a Midwestern football team looked like: "They presented the usual appearance of a small college team which considered itself lucky to have so many players," he said.

They had a small trunk with some equipment and the men seemed to carry the rest. They came without the usual large trunks of baggage which were carried in those days by many leading eastern teams. They were more impressed at having arrived at West Point and more concerned with the appearance of the academy than they were with the game that would take place. Jesse Harper was their guiding light and all arrangements were left to him. The players themselves were particularly concerned with the size of the institution, the buildings of the academy, and, above all, could not wait to take a look at the football field. Most of the players visiting the playing field expressed no end of amazement and joy over the fact that the field itself was very smooth, well marked, and resembled the appearance of a well-kept lawn. This to them was most remarkable.

Though the Notre Dame contingent was small in number, it still attracted some South Bend fans. As John Voelkers, Notre Dame's backup center, told the *Chicago Daily Tribune* in 1955: "I was one of eight substitutes, so we must have had 19 players in all, plus the coach. And, oh yes, we brought along our own rooting section—five fans from South Bend," which included a pair well known as "Hullie and Mike": George Hull and Mike Calnon.

The starting lineup for Notre Dame on that historic Saturday, according to the *Scholastic,* featured Captain Knute Rockne and Fred Gushurst at end, Keith Jones and Emmett Keefe at tackles, Ralph Lathrop and Freeman Fitzgerald at guard, Al Fenney at center; Joe Pliska and Charles Finegan at halfback, Ray Eichenlaub at fullback, and Gus

Dorais at quarterback. The substitutes included Elward and Nowers at end, Cook at tackle, King at guard, Voelkers at center, Berger and Art "Bunny" Larkin at halfbacks, and Duggan at fullback.

A further, but surmountable, challenge for the men from Notre Dame that day was that they were poorly equipped. "I remember being asked by many of the players, who were in the process of dressing before the game, if they could obtain some ankle wraps, knee guards, supporters, extra shoe strings, several pairs of shoes and two extra pairs of football pants," Baird recalled.

> A man by the name of Blanchard, who was the storekeeper at that time, was able to supply them with everything needed and his kindness was most appreciated.
>
> It was in the dressing room that I first became acquainted with Knute Rockne. After bringing several articles of equipment to other players, Rock asked me if I could obtain some adhesive tape and handed me a dime in order to purchase it. I told Rock that the dime was not necessary; that he could have all he wanted, and proceeded to get him a large roll which was readily used not only by Rock but by a group of players nearby.

Though far from home and settled in a foreign environment, the mood of the Notre Dame team was positive. "We were a confident crew," Voelkers said. "We knew we were going to win because we had worked hard on a series of forward pass plays. The pass hadn't been used much until then, probably because no coach until Harper saw the possibilities of it. He developed it even more later."

At 3:00 that first afternoon, after the Notre Dame team and Harper had been entertained and fed by the Cadets in the Cadet mess hall, Harper took his men out to the football field for a light workout, which included limbering up their legs and arms with long forward passes. As the *Scholastic* would put it the next day, "They have had a good rest and are prepared for the battle."

Game Day—The First Quarter

The game conditions were severe. "It was a cold, raw day," Voelkers remembered, "and a sky full of clouds put blinders on the sun most of the afternoon. Army didn't have a stadium at the time, just a field flanked by none too sturdy wooden bleachers." As the nineteen Notre Dame players and their young coach entered Cullum Hall Field on the Plains at West Point for the kickoff, they were greeted by a crowd of 3,000 to 5,000 spectators—one newspaper estimated the crowd to be 10,000. Whatever the number, admission was free, and 99 percent of the spectators were West Point Cadets or Army fans. No Notre Dame marching band, no Notre Dame cheerleaders, and a minor contingent of Notre Dame fans in the crowd.

As the game got under way, the Cadets would initially be impressed at the excellent all-around caliber of the Notre Dame team. However, the big surprise for the Cadets was the high degree of sophistication to which Notre Dame had developed the forward pass. That would come later.

After the team captains, Benny Hoge of Army and Knute Rockne of Notre Dame, shook hands at midfield, the referee flipped the coin. Notre Dame won the toss and elected to receive. The ball was set up on a mud tee at the Army forty-yard line, and McEwan signaled to the referees that he was ready to kick off. As the *New York Times* put it, "McEwan kicked off for the Army and Dorais had taken only a few steps when he was buried under a pile of men. Eichenlaub tried the Army line, but it would not yield, and then the Cadets let out a yell when the Army got the ball on a fumble." The Midwesterners, or the "Catholics," as they were called, had begun their historic day on a down note. For a moment, the Cadets had to be feeling that perhaps this game was going to be just the breather they had bargained for.

The next few series of plays saw a seesaw battle, with the game going back and forth between the two teams. "Both sides were penalized 15 yards for holding," the *New York Times* wrote. "Hodgson and Captain Hoge jammed through the forward for big gains, but Hodgson was finally forced to kick. He booted the ball to Dorais on the five yard line and the quarterback wiggled his way back to the 35 yard line before he was brought down. Pliska got around the end for five yards and then Dorais tried his first forward pass, and it failed, so the quarter back punted to midfield."

Rockne recalled that during the opening minutes of the game, the Army line, which outweighed Notre Dame by some fifteen pounds to the man, "pushed us all over the place. . . . After we had stood terrific pounding by the Army line and a trio of backs that charged in like locomotives, we held them on downs."

"The teams," the *Times* continued, "exchanged punts with both Notre Dame and Army emphasizing their respective running games. Dorais attempted his second forward pass and it too failed." After some vicious line play by Notre Dame's outstanding fullback, Eichenlaub, Pliska carried the ball to the thirty-five-yard line.

As play continued into the first quarter, Harper discerned that Army was using what was then a conventional defense, with the backs up close to the line. It was normal in that day, because the offensive play of choice was almost always a running play. With Army's use of the conventional defense in his mind, Harper instructed Dorais to start probing Army with Notre Dame's passing attack—the very offensive strategy they had been perfecting in practice.

Dorais responded, and near the middle of the first quarter, in a dramatic harbinger of the events to come, he stepped back and threw a perfect forty-yard forward pass to Knute Rockne, which Rockne caught on the run at the two-yard line and took in for a touchdown. Dorais kicked the extra point. The crowd and the Army team were both in shock. A pass of that length to a receiver on the dead run was simply unheard of in 1913. Notre Dame had the lead, 7–0.

Rockne loved to talk about that first touchdown, which he called a "successful deception" ploy: "After one fierce scrimmage I emerged limping as if hurt," he said.

On the next three plays Dorais threw three successful passes in a row to Pliska, our right halfback, for short gains. On each of these three plays I limped down the field, acting as if the thing farthest from my mind was to receive a forward pass. After the third play the Army halfback covering me figured I wasn't worth watching. Even as a decoy he figured I was harmless.

Finally Dorais called my number, meaning that he was to throw a long forward pass to me as I ran down the field and out toward the sideline. I started limping down the field and the

Army halfback covering me almost yawned in my face, he was that bored. I put on full speed and left him standing there flat-footed. I raced across the Army goal line as Dorais whipped the ball, and the grandstands roared at the completion of a 40-yard pass. Everybody seemed astonished. There had been no hurdling, no tackling, no plunging, no crushing of fiber and sinew. Just a long-distance touchdown by rapid transit.

As Harper remembered, "We knew not what to expect from Army—except it would be tough. But we had confidence on our side and a few tricks in our bags. We showed one of them early in the game, when Rockne caught a long pass from Dorais on the dead run and scored the first touchdown."

Even through one quarter, the effect of Notre Dame's passing attack was startling. Dorais ended the quarter having completed six passes in a row, including the long touchdown pass to Rockne—a good number even by today's standards.

The Second Quarter

In the second period, Army attempted to mount a passing game, but it was no match for Notre Dame's. As the second period began, a successful forward pass by Prichard, the Army quarterback, to Lovett carried the ball to Notre Dame's fifteen-yard line. From there, Hodgson and Hobbs drove their way toward the goal line, with Hodgson taking the ball in for the score. Woodruff was rushed in as a pinch kicker, and he booted the ball over the crossbar to tie the score: Notre Dame 7, Army 7.

Army soon regained possession, and Prichard drove the team to the five-yard line. Three times Hodgson and Hobbs tried to batter their way across the goal line, but got only as far as the one-yard line. Here, Notre Dame was penalized for holding, and Army got a first down. Notre Dame made a desperate stand with the ball only six inches from the goal line. Hodgson slammed himself into the line twice, only to be turned back. On the fourth try, however, Prichard hurled his way over for a touchdown. Hoge missed the goal, but Army now had the lead, 13 to 7.

"The Cadets went wild with joy, but their happiness was short lived, because Dorais then executed a string of forward passes which put the Army team up in the air."

Starting from their own fifteen-yard line, Notre Dame rolled down the field with ease, primarily on the strength of Dorais's arm. "Dorais fell back and the Notre Dame team spread out across the field," the *New York Times* reported. "Dorais hurled the ball far and straight for twenty-five yards and Rockne on the dead run, grabbed the ball out of the air and was downed in midfield." Dorais then passed to Pliska for a thirty-five-yard gain. "The ball went high and straight and Pliska was far out of Army's reach when he caught it. The partisan Army crowd forgot for the moment that the Army was being defeated, and burst forth in a sincere cheer for the marvelous little quarterback Dorais and his record toss of thirty-five yards. The ball again shot up into the air and was grabbed by Finegan and few yards from the Army goal line. Pliska, behind compact interference, skirted the Army tackle for the touchdown." Dorais kicked the extra point and put Notre Dame in the lead, 14 to 13.

"Notre Dame had West Point on the run," the *New York Times* reported, "and there was no stopping their wild, reckless advance." Notre Dame soon got the ball back, and

Dorais kept at his great work and had his ends and half backs dashing madly around the field chasing his long throws. Just before the end of the second period, Notre Dame had the ball on the Army's forty-five-yard line close to the east side of the gridiron.

Dorais barked out a signal and the whole western backfield and ends rushed across to the west side of the field. Dorais received the ball from his center and ran back several yards before he tossed the ball. He set himself and waited just a second too long. His throw was a wonder. It sailed far and straight through the air for nearly 40 yards, soaring toward the outstretched arms of Rockne. If this pass had been executed, it would have been a dazzling trick, but just as Rockne was about to grab the ball Prichard hurled himself high over the Notre Dame Captain's head and caught the ball.

With that play, Dorais's first and only interception of the day, the first half came to an end. In the second quarter, Dorais had completed six out of eight passes, and at the half, Notre Dame clung to a precarious 14–13 lead.

Halftime

There is no transcript as to what transpired in the Army dressing room at the half, but one can well imagine that the Cadets, in case they had missed the point, were made fully aware of the fact that they were in a battle. Notre Dame was not the breather they had anticipated. Army came out after the half inspired.

From Notre Dame's side, Harper has the following halftime recollection: "At the half we were ahead by 14 to 13, but I was afraid it couldn't last . . . I told Gus to keep throwing. We figured it was the best chance we had. Gus could throw the football as well as any man who ever lived, and I think he proved it in that game." Voelkers recalls that at halftime, "Harper told us to open up with the forward pass and get a few more points."

The Third Quarter

Despite Harper's halftime entreaties, Notre Dame played conservative football in the third period, and Army played the same. That Dorais attempted only one pass in the third quarter, an incompletion, was likely a result of the highly charged play of the Cadets. They came out after the half rejuvenated and fighting, and Notre Dame had all it could handle to keep Army from scoring in the third period. The highlight of the third quarter for Notre Dame was its defensive play. "The teams fought stubbornly in the third period, the ball see-sawing up and down the field from one team to the other," the *New York Times* reported. "The Army was fighting hard and stubbornly and threw back the Notre Dame charge." Near the end of the third quarter, Notre Dame was penalized for holding, and Army had the ball on the Notre Dame two-yard line. Army's Hodgson threw himself into the line. He was lifted bodily by Rockne, who hurled him back for a loss. Milburn had a carry, but he too was forced back for a loss by the Notre Dame line. Finally, Prichard, as a last resort, attempted a short forward pass over the goal line. The ever-resourceful Dorais intercepted, ending Army's drive and the third period.

The final period would begin with Notre Dame hanging on to its slim 14–13 lead. The game had been a hard and evenly fought battle, with both teams excelling in their running games and in their defenses, but the die was cast.

The Fourth Quarter

It was in the fourth quarter that the physical conditioning that Harper had demanded of his team began to pay dividends. Years later Harper often remarked how proud he was that Notre Dame did not call one time-out in the game and had only one substitution, as opposed to twelve for Army. And that one substitution was a fluke. Late in the game, Finegan broke his shoelace, and because Notre Dame did not have extra football shoes, Harper ordered Al "Bunny" Larkin to take off his shoes and give them to Finegan. Larkin refused, apparently having decided that he had not come 1,000 miles merely to sit on the bench. So Harper had no choice but to put Larkin into the game to play at right halfback during the closing minutes.

Harper of course was, among his other duties, the team trainer, and Notre Dame players were known to be "iron men," in great condition. "That iron man stuff was no accident," Voelkers remembered. "Training and the game itself were different from the way it is now. Harper was a stickler on condition. We had two, sometimes three scrimmages every week—rough ones. They often lasted until it was too dark to see, and always ended with wind sprints and a run to the locker room. The scrimmages were harder than the game, and longer. We were always glad when the day of the game arrived because it meant a respite from scrimmages."

As the fourth and final period began, Notre Dame's Finegan ran for twenty-five yards around the right end. After several rushes by Notre Dame's bull-like fullback, Eichenlaub, Notre Dame scored and Dorais kicked the extra point. Notre Dame 21, Army 13.

Then, Notre Dame opened the game up with its devastating passing attack, and history was made. In short order, Dorais had passed his team deep into Army territory. Before Army could get its bearings, Pliska ran to the Army five-yard line. From there, Dorais hit Pliska with a short pass in the back of the end zone for a touchdown. Dorais again kicked the extra point and Notre Dame led 28 to 13. The Army team was befuddled. One of the Army linemen even asked his Notre Dame counterpart to tell him when they were going to pass so that he would not have to exert himself charging in foolishly to stop a running play.

"There was no stopping Notre Dame now," the *New York Times* reported. "They had a score thirst which would not be quenched." Finegan caught a pass, taking the ball to the thirty-yard line, and Army was penalized fifteen yards for going offsides. With the Cadet defenders spread out to cover the receivers, Dorais sent Eichenlaub, the big fullback, thundering through the line. Notre Dame's passing was mixed in with its strong running game, led by the powerful fullback Eichenlaub. Harper was employing the very type of balanced attack that many college teams seek to implement today—spread the defense out with the pass, then hit them with the run, and so on.

"From here," the *Times* wrote, "the Notre Dame scoring machine got together and began to hammer and hammer relentlessly at the tiring line of the stubborn soldiers. Yard by yard they fell back before the rushing Westerners. Notre Dame, through the fierce plunges of Finegan and Eichenlaub, slowly but surely decreased the distance which separated them from another score. The Notre Dame fullback pounded his way along without check until he was thrown over the line exhausted and as limp as a sack of meal." The final: Notre Dame 35, Army 13.

1913 predated radio, let alone television. The main method of communication was the printed word, the newspaper. The most current news a person could receive was by telegraph, and that is exactly how the Notre Dame students followed the progress of their team that historical afternoon. Game day, bulletins detailing the action were posted in the window at the headquarters of the *South Bend News-Times* in downtown South Bend. The Notre Dame students and fans crowded around the window, anxiously awaiting word, but for a time, all they knew was the halftime score, Notre Dame's slim 14–13 lead. Finally the fourth quarter results were posted. "As the bulletin for the fourth quarter went up, announcing that Notre Dame had torn loose and had scored 21 more points," the *News-Times* reported that

pandemonium broke loose among the students. With wild shrieks of delight they turned into Main Street and in a few moments 300 had gathered to celebrate the overwhelming victory. A snake dance was quickly formed and the men invaded Michigan Street winding from curb to curb and yelling like demons. At frequent intervals, Cheer Leader . . . Kane called a halt and the varsity yells were given with a view to proclaiming the splendid achievement of the Notre Dame football machine. After the demonstration on Michigan Street, the crowd returned to the Oliver hotel, where, after cheering individual members of the team, the students dispersed.

The Aftermath

Years later, Jesse Harper recalled: "Army had its usual great team, but the passes demoralized them completely. By the time it ended, we could do anything we pleased, running or passing. They didn't know what to expect, or what to do about it. We just kicked hell out of 'em. We played a helluva game."

On the Army bench sat a frustrated and injured halfback, Dwight David Eisenhower, with his roommate, Omar Bradley, both of whom on another day, in a much more critical setting, would see success in a truly historical battle—D-Day, June 6, 1944. Both were members of the West Point class of 1915, "The Class the Stars Fell Upon," which ultimately included fifty-nine generals, and both would achieve the highest rank, five stars. While Eisenhower and Bradley sat on the Army bench, Coach Charley Daly paced in front of it. "Daly paraded up and down the sidelines nervously as he watched the depressing spectacle," said one newspaper. But he learned from it, and later in the season, Army used the forward pass almost exclusively while beating Navy, 22–9.

Gus Dorais was hailed as the hero of the game. As the *Brooklyn Eagle* put it the next day, "Dorais is a little fellow who weighs about 145 pounds," yet he "astonished the spectators. . . . Some of his passes traveled more than forty yards and all were wonderfully accurate. The forward pass was responsible for every score made against Army today." Regarding Notre Dame, the paper continued, "They were the most wonderful collection of football players that have been seen on the Plains in years, and the fact that they defeated Army by 35 to 13, did not prevent them from being exceedingly popular with both the Cadets and the spectators that crowded the little stands."

As another historian wrote, "The feature of the game that most amazed the sports fans in the East was the length of Dorais's passes. Some of the spiral throws traveled 35 to 40 yards to the receiver, an unheard-of distance in those days." Dorais also threw a large number of passes. By game's end, he had completed fourteen passes for 243 yards, extraordinary statistics at the time.

Though the forward pass was the hallmark of Notre Dame's victory, Notre Dame won the game on the basis of a balanced attack—which included a strong running game to complement the passing attack, together with a solid defense. The next day, the *South Bend News-Times* attributed the victory to three factors, all of which still delineate a championship football team. First, "Notre Dame's long forward passing . . . was spectacular and a revelation to eastern football enthusiasts." All of Notre Dame's touchdowns in the game were either scored on a forward pass or set up by one. Second, Eichenlaub, Notre Dame's powerful fullback, "was a demon on the offense, plowing through the Army line for good gains and bowling over the interference in slashing style." And third, the Notre Dame defense, with the exception of its play in the second quarter, held Army to a standstill, including a goal-line stand near the end of the third quarter with Army in control of the ball on the Notre Dame one-yard line. As one South Bend reporter noted, "In a word, the entire Notre Dame team played like a unit, a condition for which the coaching of Jesse Harper is held responsible."

The Return Trip to Notre Dame

Notre Dame left West Point immediately after the game, arriving in Buffalo, New York, on Sunday morning. There the players were treated to a day of rest and relaxation including a sightseeing trip to Niagara Falls. The team returned to South Bend on the morning of Monday, November 3, 1913, to a heroes' welcome.

"When we got out of our day coach at the South Bend railroad station, we found most of the town waiting for us," Dorais remembered.

"There was a parade with several bands and plenty of red fire, and, of course, captain Knute Rockne was called on for a speech. He made one, but he was so nervous and embarrassed that he twisted most of the buttons off his coat while he was doing it; and no one in the audience could understand a word of what he said."

As Notre Dame historian Arch Ward described the team's arrival in South Bend, "The homecoming was one of Rockne's fondest memories. The entire populace of South Bend turned out to greet the boys who had upheld Western football against the East. There were brass bands and a torchlight parade and speeches. The players themselves had the most enjoyable trip of their lives."

"The pleasure of victory is heightened not only because the Army is one of the hardest fighting teams in the East but also because it is one of the most sportsmanlike," the *Scholastic* reported. "Our players, on their return, one and all, declared that it was a pleasure to play in the game; that hard, clean football was played throughout; and that the vast crowd of spectators, although Army partisans for the most part, was fair at all times, refusing to try to drown our signals, and giving generous applause when a brilliant play was executed by our boys."

And so it had begun. The heretofore obscure Catholic men's school in the Midwest had made its dramatic debut on the national stage. In the process, it had awakened the football world to the true potential of the forward pass.

That December, the *Scholastic* quoted *Collier's Weekly*, noting that the powerful Yale team considered it a good hard day's work if it could score one touchdown against Army in a game. In the 1913 game alone, Notre Dame scored more touchdowns against Army than Yale had scored against them in the previous six years combined.

In an interview with sportswriter John M. Ross, in 1957, Harper said,

It has been recorded in some places that this game marked the birth of the forward pass. That is not true. Some teams, including Army, had been using it since 1906, when it was legalized. However, the pass till then was usually thrown to a stationary receiver. In our new scheme, the receiver took the pass on the run. It opened up the game considerably and many schools copied it. The passing itself didn't baffle Army in 1913, what baffled them was the length of Dorais's passes, some traveling thirty-five or forty yards.

Because of this ringing success in our Eastern debut, Army immediately became the big game on Notre Dame's schedule. And the Cadets, thirsting for revenge, awaited each succeeding game eagerly. And so the rivalry blossomed. In 1918, when I turned over the coach reins to Knute Rockne, I told him: "Rock, keep this Army game on your schedule. One day it might be big enough to play in New York City."

One newspaper reporter observed, "The Cadets were completely routed and outclassed by the Westerners. Beautifully executed forward passes were largely responsible for the Army's undoing. Every one of the Hoosiers' touchdowns was brought about by their great success with this style of attack. Fourteen times during the game they tried it and twelve times it was good for long distance gains. Dorais, one of the best quarterbacks ever seen here, did the throwing with either Rockne, Pliska, or Finegan on the receiving end. All were equally good."

The writer continued: "Eichenlaub smashed his way through the

Army line time and time again," and, "The Western linemen played hard and charged fast. Their tackling was unerring and deadly."

Dorais was promptly touted for All-America honors. "The showing of quarterback Dorais of the Notre Dame football team in Saturday's game at West Point is expected to gain for him recognition as a player of all-American caliber."

In 1956, Allison Danzig, a prominent football historian and long-time sportswriter for the *New York Times,* wrote, "In 1913 came the greatest impetus of all to the use of the forward pass. This was the sensational victory of Notre Dame over Army at West Point, achieved largely through the passes of Gus Dorais to Knute Rockne and other receivers. That was the game that brought Notre Dame from obscurity to national fame. And it did more to make coaches pass conscious than anything that had happened since the pass was put into the game in 1906."

In 2006, Kent Stephens, a historian and archivist at the College Football Hall of Fame, wrote, "the 1913 Notre Dame–Army football game was one of the most important games in college football history. The play of this game was crucial to the development of the forward pass."

7

The Final Games of 1913

Penn State

Notre Dame's victory over Army was dramatic. But for all of the excitement created by the Army win, Notre Dame's victory against Penn State on Friday, November 7, just six days later, would be even more telling of the depth of Notre Dame's talent and Harper's newly instituted "open" style of play. Despite the historical implications of the Army game, Penn State would be Notre Dame's toughest game of the 1913 season.

The game would be played at Penn State, in front of an "unusually large crowd" gathered both for the game and for the university's homecoming festivities. Penn State had not been scored upon on their home field in five years.

Both teams were in top physical condition. Harper worked his team hard in the days leading up to the game and cautioned them to stay in shape. "Go to bed early boys and get plenty of sleep," he instructed his players, "and don't spend too much time at the table. Keep in the best of condition for this is the hardest game of the season."

As one paper put it, "Confirmed in his conviction of the worth of the forward pass by the demonstration in the east last week, Harper is coaching his men steadily at this play. It was the perfect handling of the ball over the heads of the husky cadets that won the last game and the men are getting ready to pull a few new stunts along this line in Friday's contest."

Penn State was well aware what Notre Dame had accomplished the week before against Army, particularly Notre Dame's ability to execute the forward pass. But Penn State was not to be outdone. They had been developing their own forward-passing skills. They, too, had an outstanding quarterback, "one Miller," who was reportedly able to "put the ball just where he wants it." And their defense had spent the entire week before the showdown practicing against all of the plays that Notre Dame had run against Army, particularly Notre Dame's passing attack. Penn State was reminded, however, that just a week earlier, Coach Charles Daly of Army had received advance word of Gus Dorais's skill at dropkicking, and made sure his team practiced hard to defend against it. But when the Cadets put in their dropkick defense, Dorais surprised them by throwing a forty-yard pass to Rockne.

The Notre Dame team arrived at State College, Pennsylvania, on the afternoon before the game and immediately went out to the field for a light workout. Dorais went through a forward-passing exercise that "caused a lot of comment among the Penn State fans," Then the teams took the field. Penn State's coach, Bill Hollenbeck, sent his team out with instructions to "tear them to pieces and show the east and west that we have got a team."

Notre Dame's first score came in the second period. Dorais ran for thirty-five yards and then, on the next play, threw a forty-yard pass to Rockne for the game's first touchdown—the first touchdown against Penn State on their home field in five years. Notre Dame's final score came in the third period on a long run by the fullback, Eichenlaub, and the score stood at 14 to 0. As in the previous week, Notre Dame's strong running game was crucial to the success of their now-famous passing attack. Penn State scored late in the third quarter on a pass play from Miller to Lamb, but it wouldn't be enough. The game ended with Notre Dame bringing home a 14–7 victory, and Dorais being praised in the game reports as "the phenomenal little quarterback . . . the brightest star on the field."

The Notre Dame team returned to South Bend to find half a foot of snow on Cartier Field and the news that Wabash College had canceled their matchup with Notre Dame, which had been scheduled for November 17. The snow and the cancellation were taken by the Notre Dame coaches with some relief. They knew Wabash would not have been up to giving them a competitive game, and the extra week would give Notre Dame time to recover from the bruising physical battles the team had just gone through against Army and Penn State. The extra week also gave them time to recuperate and prepare for their upcoming 1,500-mile trip southwest to play Christian Brothers in St. Louis and the University of Texas, in Austin. Harper gave his tired team five days off.

Fresh from his two major victories in the East and more confident than ever in his team's open style of play and the perfection of his innovative forward-pass offense, Harper sent out a challenge to the University of Nebraska to play a postseason game at a neutral site, preferably Chicago. With their recent victory over a powerful University of Minnesota team, one of the strongest teams in the Big Nine, Nebraska had emerged as the strongest team in the West, and would be one of three teams to go undefeated in 1913, along with Chicago and Notre Dame. This was another telling example of Notre Dame's aggressive attitude toward scheduling. The Notre Dame Club of Chicago immediately organized a committee to assist in the preparations for the game. The *Chicago Tribune*, on November 6, 1913, wrote that Harper and "his charges are clamoring for more action." Harper and Notre Dame were quickly developing a reputation for going anywhere to play the best, a scheduling philosophy that would carry down through Notre Dame's history and would come to distinguish Notre Dame from all of the other college and university football teams in the country. In these very early years in its football history Notre Dame was already being recognized for its willingness, even eagerness, to go up against the strongest intersectional competition it could find. Harper's scheduling strategy, perhaps more than anything else in Notre Dame's football history, contributed to the emergence of Notre Dame's fame and resulting legendary status. On November 15, 1913, the *South Bend Tribune* perceptively observed: "No other team in the country has played intersectional battles which are equal to those on Notre Dame's schedule."

Though the idea of a postseason contest was a brilliant stroke by Harper, logistics would work against him. Notre Dame's final game of the season would be on Thanksgiving Day in Austin, Texas, and returning to South Bend and getting in shape for a hard game the following week, combined with the players' academic obligations, would prove to be a bridge too far. Nebraska appeared eager to accept, and as late as November 25, 1913, both teams were still attempting to work out the details. Nebraska, which was then a member of the Missouri Valley Conference, had to work through conference rules that stipulated that its members play a maximum of eight games and that there be no games after Thanksgiving. In the end, the game would not be played, but it was a bold idea initiated by Harper and the seeds for such contests in the future had been planted. As one paper reported, "That Harper is going to put Notre Dame athletics on a higher plane seems certain."

With some extra time on his hands after the Penn State game, Harper visited coaching friends at Indiana University and then visited with his former coach, Stagg, at the University of Chicago. In both instances, Harper watched their respective teams in practice and picked up "some new points to work into the gold and blue system of attack." The visit also provided Harper, ever the relentless salesman, an opportunity to spread some Notre Dame goodwill and build relationships for future games.

Meanwhile, Notre Dame's quest to be declared national champions immediately ensued. Notre Dame's argument, as put forth in the *South Bend Tribune,* was that if Notre Dame had defeated Army decisively, and Army had defeated Colgate, which in turn had decisively defeated a powerful Yale team, then Notre Dame was the best team. However, there is no evidence that Notre Dame's victories were taken seriously in the East, and crowning the newcomer on the national stage as the "best" was not going to happen in its first year.

At the same time, Dorais was being highly touted for All-American honors, but that too was not yet to be. However, at least one Eastern writer, Billy Morice of Philadelphia, who had watched both the Army game and the Penn State game, had Dorais as his number-one pick for All-American honors at quarterback. "The Western man may not be chosen by all critics to fill this position," Morice wrote of Dorais, "but it will be because they have not seen him in action."

Christian Brothers

After a short layoff the team went to work in preparation for the game against Christian Brothers in St. Louis on Saturday, November 22. Notre Dame would continue its emphasis on the forward pass. "Coach Harper has always been a strong advocate of this style of game," one South Bend sportswriter noted that week, "and this season he has done wonders. In Dorais he found a quarterback with a swift accurate pass and cool head that could be depended on in the most exciting moment of the hottest fight. On the receiving end he found that Gushurst and Rockne were able to get down the field and catch the ball with almost unfailing success. . . . It is this style of game that the gold and blue eleven has especially used against any team that has met them and in which they are probably superior to any team in the east or west."

By mid-November 1913, it was becoming clear to the football world that Harper had developed a forward-passing attack at Notre Dame that was second to none. One sportswriter observed that this new, so-called open style had been perfected by Harper to a "greater extent than it has been by any other coach in the country."

The Christian Brothers in St. Louis, coached by former Notre Dame player "Luke" Kelly, entered the game against Notre Dame undefeated, and proved to be a stronger opponent than anticipated. Encouraged by the high scores they had piled up against their opponents already that season, the Christian Brothers hoped to "spring a surprise by taking a game from the Notre Dame eleven." Coach Kelly was "straining every nerve to put his men into shape to beat the gold and blue delegation and the St. Louis men are confident of turning the trick on the South Bend eleven."

Notre Dame's preparation hit a snag during practice on November 18. Dorais was carrying the ball over the center when he was hit with a jarring tackle and temporarily laid out. After some nervous moments, it was determined that their leader would be in shape for the upcoming game, but Harper immediately relegated Dorais to the sidelines for rest.

The battle was hard-fought, especially because Harper kept three of his key men, Dorais, Eichenlaub, and Feeney, on the bench at the beginning of the game. He was conserving his troops for Texas. Toward the end of the second quarter, however, with Notre Dame still scoreless, he put the trio in, and Dorais and Eichenlaub scored three quick rushing touchdowns. Notre Dame's 20–7 win dealt the Christian Brothers their first loss in two years.

Texas

Notre Dame left for Austin, Texas, on the Sunday after their game with the Christian Brothers and stayed and practiced at St. Edwards College, which was also run by the fathers of the Holy Cross. Upon their arrival, Notre Dame received a welcome, Texas-style. "They were notified by the president of the Texas Athletic Association that the town was theirs till they left. Tuesday night the men were entertained at a theater party and invitations have been given to the whole squad to attend the Thanksgiving ball after the game."

Harper was highly concerned about the depth of talent at the University of Texas. Their most recent victory had come over a strong Kansas A & M team by a 48-point margin. Earlier in the season Texas had registered a commanding victory over their archrival, the University of Oklahoma. The Longhorns were clearly the champion of the Southwest and their fans excitedly claimed to "have the best team ever produced in the southwest." In addition, and of special concern to Harper, was the fact Texas was gaining a reputation as a strong advocate of the new open style of play. Harper would now be faced with defending against his own attack.

Ever the master of all details, Harper determined that Notre Dame would carry its own water supply to Austin. The water supply in the Austin vicinity had a reputation for a heavy sulfur and mineral content, and Harper wanted to take no chances on his players being adversely affected. They would drink only South Bend water, at least until after their Thanksgiving Day battle with the University of Texas.

It had rained in Austin for several days before the game, so the contest would be on a muddy, slow field. The Notre Dame line, which all year long had been one of the secrets of the team's success, battered the Texas line until the Longhorns were exhausted. In addition to Notre Dame's smashing ground game, Dorais scored 17 of Notre Dame's 29 points himself. He completed ten out of twenty-one passes for two hundred yards and one touchdown, and ran for another. By game's end, Notre Dame was completely dominating, and left the wet and muddy field with a 29–7 victory.

It was a great season for the Notre Dame team, the greatest yet, and much of the credit was bestowed on Harper. At season's end, the *South Bend Tribune* noted that "Harper started in to place athletics at the university on a higher plane than they had ever been before. . . . Harper worked hard every minute of the time and no coach has ever been more successful with a squad than he has. Notre Dame is fortunate in securing the services of a man of Harper's calibre."

At the close of the season, the 1914 edition of the Notre Dame yearbook, *The Dome,* commemorated Harper's first year with these words:

The past year has seen an entire revolution in the conduct of athletics at Notre Dame. The student manager is abolished; Freshmen are barred from the 'Varsity teams and have organized teams of their own; and we have one coach for all the 'Varsity sports. The man upon whom the duties of all-around coach, manager and trainer rest is Jesse C. Harper. . . . During his one short year at Notre Dame he has arranged . . . (the best schedule) ever attempted by Gold and Blue. . . . In football, for the first time in history, Army, South Dakota, and Texas were met, and now Yale, Carlisle and Syracuse are lined up for next year. . . . And when we remember that Coach Harper is coach, trainer and manager we see that it is difficult to overestimate his value to the teams. With a brain for new plays and a knack for maintaining harmony in his teams, with an Irishman's fight and a gentleman's honor, he is a gold mine for Notre Dame. May his success be ever greater.

8

1914: Mighty Yale Is on the Schedule

1914

Oct. 3	Alma	56–0	Home
Oct. 10	Rose Polytechnic	103–0	Home
Oct. 17	Yale	0–28	Away
Oct. 24	South Dakota	33–0	Neutral
Oct. 31	Haskell	21–7	Home
Nov. 7	Army	7–20	Away
Nov. 14	Carlisle	48–6	Neutral
Nov. 26	Syracuse	20–0	Away

Notre Dame's goals for the 1914 season were lofty. The *Scholastic,* the Notre Dame student newspaper, in its season preview, predicted that

1914 would be "the greatest football season in Notre Dame history."
Harper had outdone himself in scheduling. He had arranged games with
Army and the popular Carlisle Indian School, the latter game to be
played on a neutral field in Chicago. The highlight of the season, and
one of the biggest scheduling accomplishments of Harper's career, would
be Notre Dame's mid-October game against Yale, to be played on Yale's
home field in New Haven, Connecticut. If Yale wasn't the number-
one team of the era, it certainly was in the top two or three, and being
able to schedule Yale brought great credibility to Harper and to the
Notre Dame football program. The *Scholastic* noted with a touch of
pride that Walter Camp had finally "seen fit to acknowledge that (Notre
Dame) had a football team" when Camp, in an interview published in
the *Chicago Examiner*, said that in 1913, "Notre Dame had a wonderful
team . . . which simply swept West Point off its feet."

Before the 1914 season, Harper had hired as an assistant football
coach his former player Knute Rockne. It would prove to be a landmark
decision for both of their careers.

From the outset, the two men worked closely together, with Harper, at
least in the early years of their association, often in the role of teacher. A
story involving their early relationship that Harper liked to tell was one of
his first attempts at taming Rockne's enormous intensity. Early in the 1914
season, just after Rockne had joined Harper's football staff, which in those
days meant only the two of them, Harper felt that the team needed
improvement at the end position. Since this had been Rockne's position as
a player, Harper logically put Rockne to work developing the team's ends.

"Rock was a very intense man," Harper later recalled. "He was a tireless worker who lost himself in any job. He went to work on those ends

like it was life and death. He pleaded, threatened, and did about every-thing trying to improve those guys in a hurry." However, Rockne's efforts, as sincere as they certainly were, were to no avail. "A few days later" Harper recalled, "we had a scrimmage, and the ends were terrible. Riding home after practice, Rock talked about it, and said he'd have to work even harder with them. I had a different idea. I told him to forget the ends for a while, and work with guards and tackles.

"A week later, we had another scrimmage, and the ends looked pretty good. Rock commented on it right away, so I laughed and told him, 'Yeah, and if you'll leave 'em alone for another week, we might have a pretty fair pair of ends.' Rock was pretty upset by that, so I explained what I was getting at. I told him that his mistake was trying to teach those ends all he knew in a hurry. He thought he could make 'em as good as he was practically overnight. It's just as bad you see, to over-coach a boy as it is to under-coach him." In later years, Rock often said that was one of the most valuable lessons he ever learned.

Alma, Rose Poly, and Yale

The first two games of the 1914 season, against Alma College and Rose Polytechnic Institute of Terre Haute, Indiana, were no more than warm-ups for the big game with Yale. Against Alma and even more so against Rose Poly, Harper used mostly his second- and third-string players and kept his best offensive plays under wraps.

From the season's beginning, Harper was driving his team hard, all with an eye toward Yale on October 17. On the Tuesday before the Yale game, Harper ran his practice for four hours. Special emphasis was put on the forward pass. With the graduation of Gus Dorais, a new quarterback,

Stan Cofall, had taken over, and was reportedly throwing excellent passes in practice to Mills and Elward.

Though rumored to have an unusually strong team, Alma proved to be easy pickings. The Notre Dame squad played straight football, passing only once or twice, in order not to divulge secrets to the suspected representative said to be scouting the game for Yale. The final score was Notre Dame 56, Alma 0. Harper turned the team over to Rockne for the Alma game and he traveled to New Haven to personally scout Yale University in their game against the University of Virginia. He came away from New Haven impressed.

As preparations got under way for the Rose Poly game, the practices became even more intense, and Harper made no secret of the fact that he was looking ahead to Yale. He abruptly closed practices on the rumor that a Yale man was on the Notre Dame campus scouting for the game and took the drastic step of scheduling night practices to more thoroughly prepare. On October 13, Harper scheduled an unprecedented three practices, the last being an evening session starting at 6:30 PM and ending at 8:00 PM. Behind closed doors, Harper was having the freshmen run Yale plays against the varsity.

Yale understood the challenge that Notre Dame would present and the formidable group that Harper had assembled. They, too, were taking the game seriously. The *South Bend News-Times* reported that the Yale coaches were pushing their players through "fast" scrimmages, making an "aggressive start toward whipping their football team in shape" for their upcoming battle with Notre Dame.

On October 10, in a game on Cartier Field, Notre Dame swamped Rose Poly by a score of 102 to 0. Everyone on the Notre Dame team got into the game, and Notre Dame carefully concealed its big plays. No passes were thrown.

Anticipation for the Yale game was running at a fever pitch. Around New Haven, interest in the game was said to be exceeded only by interest in Yale's annual clash with Harvard. Advance demand for tickets generated reports that as many as 15,000 people would be in attendance. And they were. The game would be Notre Dame's "supreme test" of the 1914 season and students, alumni, and fans by the thousands were looking forward to the contest.

The game was billed as a classic East vs. West contest. Notre Dame would be the first Western team in fifteen years to play at Yale, the last being the University of Wisconsin, which was defeated by Yale 6–0 in 1899. Speculation ran high on whether or not Yale would be able to control Notre Dame's excellence in executing the forward pass. Notre Dame was coming into the contest with two easy early-season victories under its belt, and had not lost a game since the 1910 season, when the team was defeated 17–0 by Michigan State. By game day, Yale themselves had scored three victories, over Maine, Virginia, and Lehigh.

For reporting on the game, the gymnasium on the Notre Dame campus was set up with a direct wire to the Yale field. Each individual dormitory made its own preparations for cheering before and during the game and for meeting the players when they returned to South Bend. Every evening, the students' procedure was the same. First, a student speaker would call attention to the great national importance of the upcoming game, then a series of school cheers would be given by the assembled crowd.

The Notre Dame traveling team, consisting of the coaches and twenty-three players, along with thirty fans from South Bend, left for

New Haven on the morning of Thursday, October 15, with a tumultuous send-off. An estimated 500 Notre Dame students defied University officials and marched four abreast down Notre Dame Avenue to the train station, pausing intermittently for impromptu snake dances and cheers. "The send off this morning will no doubt increase materially the confidence which the team already possesses," declared the *South Bend Tribune* reporter on October 14, 1914.

Notre Dame's arrival in New Haven garnered a front-page headline in the *South Bend Tribune,* second only to the headline announcing a major German advance into Belgium. The team arrived that Friday to a drizzly and disappointing rainfall—rain and a muddy field were not conducive to Notre Dame's passing attack. In addition, Notre Dame's star player and top runner, fullback Ray Eichenlaub, was playing at less than full strength. "I believe Yale is stronger than in years and is playing progressive football," Harper told one paper. "The field will be muddy, the worst conditions we could have for our specialty, the forward pass. . . . Three of our best players, Eichenlaub, Backman, and Lathrop, have not fully recovered from recent injuries, but we will have no excuses to offer after the game." Injured or not, Eichenlaub would play an excellent game against Yale, with the *South Bend News-Times* reporting "he ploughed through the line for forty yard gains."

But this time, almost one year after Notre Dame's stunning victory against Army, Cinderella's glass slipper cracked. Yale, under first-year coach Frank Hinkey, came out with a highly polished open game and literally ran the Notre Dame squad off the field. In addition to mixing running and forward-passing plays, Yale introduced lateral-passing formations that at times had two, three, and sometimes all four of their backs running toward the goal and passing off to each other when attacked by the Notre Dame defense. The *South Bend Tribune,* on October 19, 1914, observed that Hinkey had "introduced a new method," into the game by combining extensive lateral passing with forward passing. It was an offense "capable of so many variations as to make the attack almost unsolvable." This time, Notre Dame, as well as its coach, Harper, was the bewildered team.

The first half ended with Notre Dame on Yale's two-yard line. However, at that point there was confusion among the Notre Dame players and coaches and they let the clock run out, losing their best opportunity to score. At the half, Yale led, 7–0. However, Notre Dame had gained 100 yards in the first half and had made eight first downs to five for Yale. The second half was a different story. Both teams used the forward pass extensively in the third period, but Yale completely outplayed Notre Dame, scoring two more touchdowns, and one more in the fourth.

Notre Dame's winning margin in the statistical battle, having outgained Yale 408 yards to 287, was of little solace to the defeated squad. In what would be the only football meeting between the two schools, Yale upended Notre Dame by a score of 28 to 0, though the game reports noted that Notre Dame fought to the end, with the game being called for time when Notre Dame again had the ball on the Yale 2-yard line.

The Notre Dame team returned to South Bend that Monday afternoon to a welcome that was even greater than the send-off. The entire student body, together with the university band, gathered at the Lake Shore station in South Bend to greet the returning warriors—this type of welcome after a disappointing defeat would become a trademark of the Notre Dame tradition. "Everyone was on hand with hardy handshake and an encouraging pat on the back for the men who had shown the special Notre Dame fighting spirit against a team that is declared by football experts to be the best that has ever worn the blue."

Several years later, in the midst of Rockne's great successes of the mid-1920s, Harper reflected with pride on the fact that he had been able to schedule Yale, especially in light of being turned away by the Big Nine teams, but he also acknowledged that he had been outcoached by Yale's Frank Hinkey, and that Notre Dame had been outplayed by Yale. "When we first started out to get ourselves into the front ranks, the Big Ten laughed at us. Then started those stories about 'ringers' and no requirements—oh, you know—that same old stuff they handed out about a fellow on the upgrade. Big Ten wouldn't let us in; but now they couldn't get us in. And Notre Dame today is welcomed all over the land by all comers. Say, didn't I get a chuckle when Yale consented to play us! And Yale showed us we hadn't much football that day we played 'em."

South Dakota

All eyes immediately turned to the next foe, South Dakota, a game that would be played in Sioux Falls, South Dakota. It was back on the road for the Notre Dame players. The buildup for the South Dakota game was headlined by the news that Notre Dame's star fullback, Ray Eichenlaub, had not recovered from his early-season injury and not only would not play against South Dakota, but would probably be out for the remainder of the season. According to Harper, Eichenlaub had reinjured his leg during the first five minutes of the Yale game and was not himself during the remainder of the contest, although he made several spectacular runs. As usual, Harper's game preparations were intense. A stern contest was anticipated in view of the fact that South Dakota had given the University of Minnesota a tough battle in a close loss the previous week. The game started slowly for Notre Dame and at the half the teams were tied, 0–0. Then, Notre Dame exploded, scoring five touchdowns in the second half on the way to an easier-than-expected 33-to-0 victory.

Haskell

On Saturday, October 31, 1914, the Haskell Indians traveled to South Bend to meet Notre Dame. The Haskell Institute, located in Lawrence, Kansas, was formed in 1884 as an industrial training school for Indians. Like Carlisle and other such Indian schools, Haskell was part of the U.S. government's effort to assimilate the Indians into the greater population. Football had always been Haskell's main sport, and in the early years of the twentieth century Haskell competed against several major colleges and universities in the Midwest and in the South. Harper had been advised that this was the strongest team in Haskell history, and he was wary. The fact that several of his key players were injured gave him further concern. He drove his team hard in practice, again, Instituting nighttime practice sessions.

Game day in South Bend was warm and sunny. A large crowd was expected, and the paper noted that parking for thirty automobiles had been arranged—latecomers would be "unable to get parking room." The Notre Dame band was in full military uniform. Notre Dame's 21-to-7 victory was credited to the strength of "Brilliant runs by 'Dutch' Bergman, Notre Dame's speedy little quarterback." Bergman was said to be able to run the 100-yard dash in ten seconds flat; whatever the reality, he was fast. Haskell's only score came in the fourth period on the strength of a successful thirty-yard forward pass.

Army

Next up was Notre Dame's the much-anticipated rematch with Army. By game day, Army was one of only five undefeated football teams in the east. As one paper reported, "Notre Dame defeated Army last year and awoke the east with a start. Since Notre Dame's 1913 invasion however, the eastern teams have adopted the open style of play." Anticipation was high, and the news early in the week that fullback Eichenlaub would be ready to play was greeted with great cheer.

On the eve of departure, however, gloom struck the Notre Dame team. Eichenlaub's leg was not healing, and Harper said he would not start and likely not play at all. In addition, Sam Finegan, the team's star halfback, was injured in practice and declared unable to play against the Cadets. In the end, Finegan did not even make the trip to West Point. Army was without four of its key players. Assistant coach Rockne took the team through signal drills on Thursday morning, and coach Harper scheduled a light workout for the team on the Army field after their arrival that Friday afternoon.

Army dominated the game from the start. "The soldiers scored their first touchdown right off the bat when Cofall muffed the kick off and Goodman fell on it on the fifteen-yard line. Three plays took it over, Hodgson scoring the touchdown." Notre Dame's only touchdown came in the third period, and was set up by a long run by Pliska.

The Cadets had taken their revenge by a score of 20 to 7, and the great rivalry, though still in its infancy, was now tied at one game apiece.

For the 1914 season, the Army football team would be named national champions by the Helms Athletic Foundation.

Carlisle

With no time to waste, Notre Dame entered preparations for their next opponent, the Carlisle Indian School. Though the highlights of the 1914 schedule in terms of prestigious opponents were clearly Yale and Army, Harper's primary financial effort for the year was the game with Carlisle, a game that he had planned, with great effort and some personal disappointment, to be played on November 14, 1914. Finances were paramount, and Harper, looking to arrange a good payday, wanted to see the game played in Chicago. Harper had originally contacted his former coach, friend, and mentor, Stagg, in hopes of being able to schedule the Notre Dame–Carlisle game at the University of Chicago's home football field. But, in a stark manifestation of his continuing prejudice against Notre Dame, Stagg turned his former player down, replying to Harper that the Board of Trustees of the University of Chicago opposed the idea, with no reason given. The turndown was yet another reflection of Stagg's, Chicago's, and the Big Nine's general aversion to Notre Dame. Years in the future, Stagg would make his peace with the University of Notre Dame, and, in of all places, it would occur in The Rockne Memorial. The scene would have been worthy of portraying in a movie, and no one would have thought it could have happened as it did. However, at this stage in the history of football, Stagg remained adamant in his opposition, even when the request came from his friend Harper.

Undaunted, as usual, Harper turned to the Notre Dame backer and fan Charles Comiskey and succeeded in scheduling the Carlisle game for

Comiskey Park in Chicago, then the home of the Chicago White Stockings baseball team. In addition, Harper solicited his old friend and former teammate at the University of Chicago, Walter Eckersall. At the time, Eckersall was a prominent sportswriter for the *Chicago Tribune,* and also, as was the practice in those days, a paid official in numerous college football games. In a letter to Eckersall dated November 9, 1914, just days before the game, Harper asked his old friend for a plug. "I would appreciate very much if you could give us a boost in your paper for the Carlisle game," Harper wrote. Eckersall complied.

The Carlisle Indian School in Carlisle, Pennsylvania, had a short but sometimes brilliant life span in big-time intercollegiate football. The school had been founded in 1879 for the express purpose of solving the "Indian problem," by a policy of forced acculturation, with the educational system designed to play a pivotal role in that process. In 1893 more than three dozen young Carlisle students petitioned the school requesting the right to form a football team. The superintendent relented, and so began the Carlisle Indians' short but historic saga on the college gridiron.

The legendary Jim Thorpe had played at Carlisle off and on from 1905 to 1912, under coach Glenn "Pop" Warner. Though a controversial figure, Warner was one of the early leaders in the game, and was considered by the historian Ivan N. Kaye to be one of the two greatest innovators, the other being Amos Alonzo Stagg. Kaye argued that Warner might have been a greater innovator than even Stagg.

Thorpe first gained national attention in 1911, when Carlisle upset Harvard by a score of 18 to 13, with Thorpe scoring all of Carlisle's points.

In 1912 many considered Carlisle the number one team in the nation, the highlight of their 1912 season being their 27–6 victory over Army, with Thorpe starring. During that game, in fact, the future president Dwight Eisenhower injured his knee while trying to tackle Thorpe, an injury that would sideline him for the historic 1913 contest between Army and Notre Dame. Against Army, Thorpe scored a touchdown on a ninety-two-yard run, only to have the play nullified by a penalty. On the very next play, Thorpe scored again, the time carrying the ball ninety-seven yards. The touchdown stood. Many football historians would vote Thorpe one of the two or three greatest players in the history of the game, and his true sport was track and field. He had won two gold medals in the 1912 Olympic games, only for them to be stripped in one of the great injustices in sports history. In any event, by the time of the 1914 football game with Notre Dame, Thorpe had moved on. By 1914, Carlisle, which was more of a trade school than a college, had become somewhat of an outcast in inter-collegiate sports. But they were still considered a force to be reckoned with.

There were many freewheeling personalities in the early days of football, but none took second chair to Pop Warner. Born in 1871 in Springfield, New York, Warner attended Cornell University, and after graduating with a law degree in 1894, immediately embarked on a football coaching career, beginning at the University of Georgia in 1895 and 1896 before returning to his alma mater. Warner spent the next ten years between coaching stints at Cornell and Carlisle, where he coached from 1907, the year that Thorpe arrived, until 1914.

Warner left Carlisle after the 1914 football season, spurred on by a congressional investigation of his allegedly corrupt practices. Not to be dissuaded, he moved on to the University of Pittsburgh, and then to Stanford, where he would coach against Rockne and Notre Dame in the 1925 Rose Bowl game. Author and historian Murray Sperber described Warner as "one of the great buccaneer coaches of the early era, openly paying and lavishly housing" his players. . . . "He scheduled long money-making tours for his team, personally pocketing part of the game receipts and betting heavily on his own and other games." In Carlisle's 1914 game with Notre Dame, the teams had agreed to split the $10,000 gate. The settlement statement listing Carlisle's share specifically provided "Paid to Glenn Warner."

With the announcement that both Eichenlaub and Finegan would be ready for the game, hopes for victory ran high. Between 300 and 400 Notre Dame students were planning on making the trip, as were Notre Dame's enthusiastic Chicago alumni. The Reverend Joseph Burke, the prefect of discipline at the university, announced that a special train for the game would depart from the South Bend train station at 8:15 on Saturday morning, returning to South Bend at 8:00 PM. "On arriving in South Bend," he noted, "everyone is expected to report to the university by 10:30 PM." Discipline at Notre Dame had no holidays, then, or now.

Rockne took charge of Friday's final workout while Harper traveled to Chicago to make final arrangements for the game. The *South Bend News-Times,* on November 15, 1914, reported that the Indians "are determined to take Notre Dame's scalp and have been working hard with that end in view." Despite a stubborn and valiant effort by the Carlisle defense, Notre Dame routed the Indians, 48 to 6. Notre Dame played "straight" football until the final period, when they "opened up and by a succession of wonderfully placed forward passes completely demoralized the defense of the Indians." The game would be the only football game ever played between the two schools. Harper put on a strong promotional effort, and the game, as he had planned, was a great financial success, drawing an estimated twelve thousand spectators and generating a gate of $10,175, which was split between the two schools.

Syracuse

Back in South Bend, the team was given a three-day rest and the preparations began for the season's final game at Syracuse University on November 26, Thanksgiving Day. It would be the final game for some of the men who had distinguished themselves at Notre Dame for the past several years, including Eichenlaub, Finegan, and Pliska, three stars of the Army game of 1913.

School spirit, as always, was high, but there was tension in the air, as Syracuse had just defeated the University of Michigan by a score of 20 to 0. Furthermore, the Syracuse team was said to be much heavier than the Notre Dame squad. It was generally thought that if Notre Dame were to have a chance, it would have to rely on its passing attack. But there was snow on the ground in South Bend. That, or a wet field, could hamper the Notre Dame passing game. With only one exception, all workouts for the game were conducted in the Notre Dame gymnasium.

The Notre Dame team arrived in Syracuse amid heavy kudos for the fine season and the strong schedule they had endured. "The game at Syracuse will be the last intersectional battle of the season and will wind up the hardest schedule ever attempted by a Notre Dame eleven and perhaps the hardest ever attempted by any team in football history."

Pundits were building the game into a comparison with Michigan, whom Syracuse had defeated earlier in the season. Accordingly, if Notre Dame were to defeat Syracuse, it would give them an edge over Michigan and have the effect of ranking Notre Dame the top team in the west.

To the delight of the Notre Dame fans, especially those in the crowd following the play-by-play action of the game on the wire at the Anderson and Welch cigar store in downtown South Bend, Notre Dame overwhelmed Syracuse. The final score was 20 to 0, the same margin by which Syracuse had defeated Michigan. Notre Dame's senior fullback, Eichenlaub, now fully recovered from earlier season injuries, was the star of the game. Following the game a "large number" of local alumni and fans entertained the team at the Welch–Brown boxing match and then treated them to a Thanksgiving banquet.

Walter Eckersall, one of the top sports commentators of the day and Harper's teammate on the 1905 Chicago team, wrote: "Although Notre Dame was beaten by Army and Yale, Harper's eleven has met and defeated such strong teams as the Haskell Indians and South Dakota, and its victory over the New York eleven, the team which decisively beat Michigan, entitles it to recognition." Notre Dame's decisive victory over Syracuse, he argued, gave them "an equal claim to the western championship with Illinois and Nebraska." It was flattering, to be sure, but Eckersall was a close friend of Harper's and often wrote more than favorably about Notre Dame's achievements on the football field. With the Syracuse victory, the 1914 season came to a close.

1914 saw the first clouds of World War I. As the *Scholastic* noted in its November 28, 1914, issue, with the specter of war looming, fifteen thousand people knelt at the Cathedral of Notre Dame in Paris and prayed for the deliverance of France.

At the conclusion of the 1914 football season, in a small ceremony held in the Oliver Hotel in downtown South Bend, the team, its fans and supporters gathered for an evening of "music, banqueting and good fellowship." Coach Harper was the master of ceremonies, and in his introductory remarks, he "sounded the chords of comradeship and regard that grows in men who have fought together, shoulder to shoulder, in many hard battles." In closing, the *Scholastic* remarked, "Coach Harper this year gave Notre Dame a schedule second to none in the country; he worked untiringly to produce the best results, and these results speak of him. He had a tremendous amount of work on his shoulders and to the students and those who know him, his ability needs no remark."

The 1914 season proved to be another watershed year in the early history of college football. The forward pass had now been universally adopted and was given as the cause for "spectacular playing that featured nearly every game in which evenly matched teams figured." The new open style was credited with changing football from a game that was "rather uninteresting" into a game "replete with open and spectacular plays." An immediate result was felt by the dramatic impact this style of play had on the spectator attendance and the economic aspects of the game. The Harvard–Princeton game in 1914 drew 40,000 people, the Yale–Princeton game 42,000, and the Harvard-Yale game a heretofore unheard-of 72,000 fans. At $2 per ticket, profits from these three games alone were reported to exceed $300,000.

The new style of play also had an impact on the coaches. It was now recognized that a professional coach, as opposed to an interested student or alumnus, was preferred, and that this coach had to be well compensated. It was said that Percy Haughton of Harvard was being paid $7,000 for three months' work.

9

1915: The University of Nebraska Makes Its Notre Dame Debut

1915

Oct. 2	Alma	32–0	Home
Oct. 9	Haskell	34–0	Home
Oct. 23	Nebraska	19–20	Away
Oct. 30	South Dakota	6–0	Home
Nov. 6	Army	7–0	Away
Nov. 13	Creighton	41–0	Away
Nov. 25	Texas	36–7	Away
Nov. 27	Rice	55–2	Awy

Prospects for the 1915 season were bleak. Harper had lost several of his star players to graduation, particularly his standout fullback Eichenlaub, and he was concerned about the quality and strength of his squad. Nevertheless, Harper had arranged another strong schedule for the 1915 season. Rose Poly was gone as an opponent, never to return. Alma was still on the schedule, but, soon they too would be left to a footnote in Notre Dame's early football history. The new highlight of the 1915 schedule was the University of Nebraska, a game that would be another landmark in Harper's quest to bring a schedule of top-ranked opponents to Notre Dame football. A perennial power in the West, Nebraska was known nationwide as one of the stronger football teams in the country. At the start of the 1915 season, it was noted that the University of Nebraska had not lost a football game since 1912. The 1915 game with Notre Dame would be played in Lincoln, on the University of Nebraska's home field. The *South Bend New-Times* observed before the game: "These teams had equal claim to the western title last year, and they will attempt to settle the long standing question of supremacy."

The new series between Notre Dame and the University of Nebraska was an important one for both schools. It set up a Midwest contest between two teams that were now annually ranked as the best in the Midwest, and among the best in the country. It was not only competitive, it was also profitable. The series would run for eleven consecutive years, until 1925, when Notre Dame canceled the series due to insistent anti-Irish and anti-Catholic bigotry demonstrated by the Nebraska fans and student body. In earlier years, Notre Dame's administration and its coaching staff had quietly suffered the anti-Irish and anti-Catholic insults—such as newspaper headlines that read HORRIBLE HIBERNIANS INVADE TODAY and crowd chants of "Mackerel Snappers Go Home," But, in 1925, after

Notre Dame had "turned the other cheek" for ten years, Notre Dame's patience had come to an end. In 1925, Nebraska fans and students outdid themselves and Notre Dame, by then a national attraction in its own right, had had enough. That year, the Nebraska students put on a halftime show insulting not just the Four Horsemen, but Irish Catholics in general. The stunt is well described by Murray Sperber: "four boys, each carrying a brickmason's hod and astride make-believe horses, sought to perpetrate a little fun at the expense of the Four Horsemen of Notre Dame." The stunt outraged the Notre Dame students, fans, and administration. The implications were that the Four Horsemen were not really college students, but ignorant, hired laborers, and that Irish Catholics were good for only menial tasks. Whatever the true intentions of the Nebraska students, deeply felt prejudice or simply misguided insensitivity by a group of overzealous college students, the damage had been done. Rockne, like Harper before him, seemed to have a tough skin when it came to ethnic or religious slights. Though neither approved of such behavior, in the long run they couldn't have cared less. They were football men. They had heard taunts of all sorts before, and they simply were not bothered by them. Their interest was clear—they just wanted to play football. Rockne was upset by the series being canceled and fought as best he could to prevent the cancellation. But, the matter was out of his hands, and Notre Dame's administration voted to end further athletic competition with the University of Nebraska. Rockne never reconciled himself to the fact that the series was ended, but ended it was. Under Harper, Notre Dame had won one and lost two; under Rockne they had won four, lost three, and tied one. Nine of the eleven games had been played in Lincoln. The series would not resume until the reign of coach Frank Leahy in 1947 and 1948. Notre Dame won both of those home contests.

Alma, Haskell, and Nebraska

From the initial practice sessions in the fall of 1915, Notre Dame was clearly looking past its first two opponents to the Nebraska game. The season's first game, at home against Alma on October 2, proved to be an easy but uneventful 32–0 triumph. Alma was reported to have the best team in their school's history, and their defense proved stubborn and strong against Notre Dame. Notre Dame did not attempt a forward pass until the third quarter, and in the end, as was expected, their strength and depth proved too much for Alma.

Stiffer competition was expected from the Haskell Indians the following week. Haskell was said to be the start of Notre Dame's real season. Harper's team preparations for the Haskell game were held in secret. The Notre Dame students openly prepared their cheering support, however. Each evening, students met to practice their cheers "in concert," and a "mass assembly" of students was held literally every night. It was observed, "No university in the country possesses the school spirit more deeply than Notre Dame." That statement holds true to this day. The quality and longevity of the Notre Dame spirit is second to none.

Football weather with a "wintry edge" greeted a capacity crowd at Cartier Field. New bleachers had been installed at the field's north end, while the south end had been reserved for automobiles. "The university band furnished musical selections during the game while the cheering and singing of the rooters under the leadership of Yell Master Gargen was a feature of the game." Running and straight football were featured with only three forward passes being thrown, and Notre Dame's "Dutch" Bergman, who had been shifted from quarterback to halfback, was the star of the game. Despite Harper's concern about the strength of Haskell, Notre Dame rode to an easy 34–0 victory.

After the victory over Haskell, Notre Dame had a week off, giving it time to prepare for Nebraska. Notre Dame's practice sessions were long and strenuous. Assistant Coach Knute Rockne, it was reported, "pound[ed] away steadily at the fundamentals of the game," a hands-on, stress-the-basics trait that would become one of the trademarks of Rockne's future coaching techniques.

Harper sent Rockne to Lincoln on Saturday, October 9, to scout Nebraska's game against Kansas A & M. Nebraska was victorious, and Rockne returned to Notre Dame impressed. "According to Coach Rockne," the local paper reported, "the Cornhuskers have a powerful offense and a strong defense and are full of aggressiveness, and the locals will have a battle on their hands when they clash with the husky west-erners." Harper directed Rockne to instruct the Notre Dame freshmen on how to run the Nebraska plays. The varsity immediately thereafter began scrimmaging against Rockne's "Nebraska" freshmen. The initial results were depressing. By Friday, October 15, the freshmen were scoring big gains against the varsity. It was reported that the freshmen "used the Nebraska plays with such convincing effect that the coaches were plunged in gloom."

The next day, Harper had his team concentrating on the kicking game, and he praised Hugh O'Donnell, the varsity center, who was also the team's kicker. As one newspaper noted: "The speedy center is showing good form in his kicking and will be worked steadily at it until the Nebraska game." O'Donnell, who became Harper's lifelong friend, joined the Congregation of the Holy Cross after graduation, he was ordained, and eventually served as president of the University of Notre Dame from 1940 to 1946.

On Monday, October 18, "a stranger appeared on Cartier Field during the practice and was ordered off the lot by Coach Harper." It was reported that the stranger was a spy from Lincoln. Harper announced that practices would be closed indefinitely. Before this, even in closed sessions, Harper had permitted newspapermen on the field, but this time he instituted the most rigid privacy yet. Everyone, including the newsmen, was barred during the final three days of practice.

As game day approached, tensions on the Notre Dame campus were running high. The oddsmakers favored the more experienced Nebraska squad over the relatively inexperienced Notre Dame team. Furthermore, Nebraska was said to outweigh Notre Dame by an average of eleven pounds per man. On the Wednesday before the team's Thursday departure for Lincoln, Coach Harper lifted his "closed practice" policy and threw the gates open to allow the students to attend a practice session. The result was loud and continuous cheering by the students.

Confidence in Lincoln was running high. "The Cornhuskers claim the best team in their football history," one paper wrote, "and the betting odds they are offering testify that they are sincere in their claim. Despite the fact the Notre Dame is looked on as representative of the best in the middle-west, the Nebraskans are offering to wager that their eleven will win by at least 15 points." Harper was unmoved by such reports. Though he was cautious, he was confident as well. In an interview before leaving South Bend, he stated: "We simply must win, and I believe we will. Nebraska man for man probably has a better team, but when the old Irish fighting spirit begins to rise nothing can stop the boys, I think. It will surely be the hardest fight in the west this year, and I do not believe I have ever had a team on keener edge for a football game."

The game would be relayed by wire to the Notre Dame gymnasium, and Notre Dame cheerleader Joe Gargan would be reading the play-by-play to the students and fans assembled in the Notre Dame gymnasium. There would be cheering and, during intermissions, a ten-piece string orchestra would furnish music. Downtown, "Goat" Anderson would be performing a like duty from the second-story window of Jimmy and Goat's cigar store on North Michigan Street.

The final score, Nebraska 20, Notre Dame 19, though disappointing, told only part of the story. For one thing, with two minutes left in the game, Notre Dame scored and missed the point after, which would have given them a hard-fought tie. Notre Dame's strength on this day lay in its running game, but they were battling far from home in front of 8,000 hostile fans, and had four runs of fifty yards or more called back on penalties. Nebraska's strength, ironically, was found in its strong forward-passing attack, together with the strong running of its star, Chamberlain. Harper exclaimed upon the team's return that his men had played "consistently and brilliantly on both offense and defense, clearly outclassing the Cornhuskers in all departments." One Lincoln sportswriter observed: "The Cornhuskers concede that Coach

Harper brought the most powerful eleven to Lincoln that ever stepped on the Nebraska field."

The Notre Dame *Scholastic* was similarly impressed: "[We] again congratulate Coaches Harper and Rockne upon the splendid showing of our team. We knew that our men would do their best, but we had no idea that their best was so good."

Next up would be a strong South Dakota team, at home. Afterward, Notre Dame would finish the season with four games on the road: Army in the east, then Creighton, Texas, and Rice in the west. It was a travel schedule that did not bode well for the team's physical and mental health, but despite the trying schedule, Harper's men would finish strong.

South Dakota

With Army looming on the immediate horizon, Harper readied his team for what he correctly anticipated to be a strong fight with South Dakota. The previous Saturday, South Dakota had given the University of Minnesota, the team favored to win the Big Nine conference title that year, a scare, succumbing by the same 20-to-19 score that Notre Dame left behind in Lincoln. Adding to speculation were concerns about the strength of the Notre Dame team. They came away from their game with Nebraska with bruises, cuts, and sprains, so beat up that Harper determined to rest the varsity for the entire week. There would be no contact scrimmages for the first team. With the lone exception of their star center, O'Donnell, Notre Dame would nonetheless be physically ready for South Dakota. South Dakota arrived on Friday and went straight to Cartier Field for a practice that lasted from 3:00 to 4:30 PM. Notre Dame then took the field and worked out until 5:20.

South Dakota proved to be a stubborn opponent. Understanding that his varsity was still recovering from Nebraska, and also anticipating the next week's contest against Army, Harper played his second team for most of the first half. It was a defensive battle, and the half ended with the teams tied at zero. In the third quarter, however, Harper put in his regulars, and Notre Dame promptly scored on a run by "Dutch" Bergman, the only score of the game. The final was 6–0.

Army

Preparations for Army began immediately after the South Dakota game. It was only the third game in the series between the Cadets of West Point and the men from Notre Dame. The series stood at one game apiece, and it was already being hailed as "America's great intersectional football classic." Harper was intent on winning the rubber match.

Notre Dame boarded the New York Central at noon on Thursday, November 4, and began the journey to West Point. Harper, as was his custom, would not predict the outcome. He would only note: "The Notre Dame team is only in fair shape, but we expect to put up a hard fight." The team arrived at West Point on Friday at 1:30 PM. and went directly to their rooms at Cullum Hall. After a lunch in the cadet mess, Harper took them out to the Plains for a light workout. Although the trip to the U.S. Military Academy, which had been so awe-inspiring just two years earlier, was now becoming routine for Notre Dame, the intensity of this great series was growing. "With the exception of the annual contest with Navy," it was reported, "it is perhaps only the truth to say that the soldiers would rather beat Notre Dame than any other aggregation which they meet. The taste of that first defeat . . . still hangs heavy before the West Pointers." The students and local fans continued to follow their traveling Notre Dame team by telegraph reports, with Gargen and "Goat," as was becoming the custom, again announcing the play-by-play.

The first three quarters saw a defensive battle end in a 0–0 tie. With little more than three minutes remaining in the fourth quarter, Army's Elmer Oliphant attempted a forty-seven-yard field goal. The ball hit the crossbar. Notre Dame took over on its own twenty-yard line. Cofall ran for twenty-five yards. Then, after two more running plays, Cofall threw a pass twenty yards on the fly to the speedy halfback Bergman, who ran the remaining twenty-five yards for a touchdown. It would be the game's only score. Though Notre Dame's forward-passing attack won the game, the sophistication of their passing was said to be "not of the same degree" as in the 1913 game.

Starring for Army was Oliphant, who would go down as one of West Point's all-time greats. Oliphant had already played for four years at Purdue, attaining All-American status, but for him to continue to play with Army was not unusual at the time. Halfbacks Cofall and Bergman stood out for Notre Dame, as did "Mel" Elward at end. Years later, Elward would serve as an assistant football coach at Purdue, at the same time that Harper's youngest son, Jim, who played at Purdue from 1936 to 1939, was a backup quarterback.

Creighton

Preparations for Creighton began on Monday, with Harper starting the week by giving his first-string players a day of rest. Then, on Saturday, November 13, in Omaha, Notre Dame handily dismissed

Creighton by a score of 41 to 0. For Notre Dame's part, the game featured a revised forward-passing attack. The only Notre Dame player injured in the Creighton game was their backup quarterback, Joe Dorais, the younger brother of 1913 star Gus Dorais. Notre Dame would be at virtually full strength for their upcoming trip to the Southwest.

The team returned to South Bend on Sunday morning and began preparations for their final two games of the season, which would be at the University of Texas on Thanksgiving Day and then, two days later, at Rice Institute in Houston, Texas. A two-day period between games would be unheard of in today's competitive atmosphere, but transporting a football team 1,500 miles in 1914 was no easy matter, and the most had to be made out of such a trip. Rice was expected to be a win, but the Longhorns, said to be strong and seeking revenge for their loss to Notre Dame at the end of the 1913 season, were another matter. Notre Dame and Texas had not met during the 1914 season, and the 1915 game would be the last in their series until 1934, when Texas made its first trip to South Bend for Notre Dame's home opener, Coach Elmer Layden's first game.

Texas and Rice

Notre Dame's final road trip of the 1915 season promised to be a long one. The Monday before the trip, the team worked out on Cartier Field in a light snow. With the exception of Joe Dorais, the team was in top shape, and Harper was especially pleased with the team's effort. As the men practiced in the cold, mud, and snow, Harper smiled and said to the reporters, "Here are these men, despite the weather, and with the season nearly over, working just as hard as ever and doing their utmost for the team. . . . The men have been showing the proper pepper and spirit."

The team left South Bend on Saturday, November 20, traveling by train through Chicago, where they were guests of the Notre Dame Club of Chicago at the Illinois vs. Chicago football game, and on through St. Louis, finally arriving in Austin on Tuesday. Harper had workouts scheduled on the Texas playing field in Austin for Tuesday and Wednesday.

The Texas team was said to be strong and confident of a victory. Harper said: "Texas is represented by its strongest team in years and the southwesterners have been pointing toward the Notre Dame game all season."

Notre Dame jumped out to a 16–0 lead, but Texas scored in the third quarter, narrowing the gap to 16–7. It wasn't long until Notre Dame broke loose, however, eventually leaving the field with a 36–7 victory. Only one forward pass was completed in the game, and that was a five-yard pass executed by Texas. Otherwise, all of the offensive activity was on the ground. Notre Dame's two outstanding halfbacks literally carried the load for Notre Dame, with Cofall gaining 201 yards and Bergman gaining 177. Texas was hampered by the illness of their starting quarterback, who was hospitalized prior to the game with typhoid fever.

Two days after the Texas game Notre Dame traveled to Houston and, as expected, had little trouble downing Rice Institute by a score of 55 to 2. Harper played his second team for most of the game.

Against another strong schedule arranged by Harper, Notre Dame finished the 1915 season with seven wins and one loss, the loss being by one point to Nebraska at Lincoln. By any measure, it was a successful year. In their season review, the student editors of the *Dome* said of Harper:

To the man behind the guns in time of war is credit due, not to the guns alone . . . credit [must] be given to the man who plans and directs from a position on the sidelines. Such a director is necessary . . . and the man who guides the destinies of Notre Dame is Jesse C. Harper. Harper is well supplied with knowledge . . . and he demands the respect and confidence of all Notre Dame men; these factors have combined to make him a remarkable success at Notre Dame. . . . Possessing a firm, business-like attitude at all times and playing no favorites, the Coach is himself a model for the men in his charge. Since Harper took charge of Notre Dame athletics three years ago, the prowess of the Gold and Blue has been heralded throughout the country and success has been hers in the far East, South, and West.

10

1916: Undefeated and Never Scored Upon Until Army Turns the Tables

1916

Sept. 30	Case Tech	48–0	Home
Oct. 7	Western Reserve	48–0	Away
Oct. 14	Haskell	26–0	Home
Oct. 28	Wabash	60–0	Home
Nov. 4	Army	10–30	Away
Nov. 11	South Dakota	21–0	Neutral
Nov. 18	Michigan State	14–0	Away
Nov. 25	Alma	46–0	Home
Nov. 30	Nebraska	20–0	Away

Clouds of war hung over the country as the 1916 college football season got under way. World War I was now being carried on with full force in Europe. Though not yet a participant in the war, the United States was well on its way to formally entering the conflict in April 1917 by officially declaring war on Germany. Despite the war, football prospects for the 1916 season at the University of Notre Dame were bright. For one thing, Notre Dame had lost only three regulars from 1915, so virtually the entire team was back. Harper had arranged another strong schedule, with anxiously anticipated newcomers such as Michigan State, Case Tech, and Western Reserve being added to the mix. Repeat games against Army and Nebraska would be the centerpieces of the 1916 season.

Case Tech and Western Reserve

Playing their opening game of the season at home on September 30, 1916, Notre Dame had little trouble is disposing of Case Tech, 48 to 0. Only one Notre Dame forward pass was attempted—and completed. Otherwise, Notre Dame relied on its running game. "Chet" Grant started the game at quarterback and brought the home crowd to its feet with runs of eighty-five and ninety-five yards. Case would play Notre Dame only one more time, in Rockne's first season, 1918. The following Saturday Notre Dame traveled to Cleveland, Ohio, to face Western Reserve. For Western Reserve, it would be their first and last meeting with Notre Dame. Turning in an easy 48 to 0 victory, Harper and Notre Dame were on a quest for bigger games.

Haskell

On October 14 the Haskell Indians visited South Bend for Notre Dame's first real test of the season. So said Harper and Rockne, anyway.

Despite the stated concerns of the Notre Dame coaching staff, Haskell again was no match for Notre Dame. Haskell would appear twice more on Notre Dame's schedule, but after losing 72–0 in 1932, mercifully, Haskell would appear no more.

As war raged in Europe, ethnic stereotypes were common on the sports pages in 1916, in a way that would be unacceptable in today's environment. For example, the *South Bend Tribune,* on October 14, 1916, referred to Haskell as the "Indians" or the "red men"; Notre Dame, on the other hand, was described as a hodgepodge of nationalities resembling more closely an "Allied attack than a college football eleven." The writer went on to identify selected Notre Dame players as follows: Cofell of English descent; Bergman, German; Miller and Fitzpatrick, Irish; Grant, Scottish; Morales, Mexican; Baujan, French Canadian; Ronchetti, Italian; and Rydzewski, the "magnetic pole"—all guided, as he wrote, by an assistant coach who was a "Swede." The reporter had not yet figured out that Rockne was from Norway. This combination, he noted, mindful of World War I exploding across the sea, "would send the jayhawk Germany . . . tribe back to their little village . . . sans scalps, sans scores, sans anything." Though his commentary was offensive and unprintable by today's standards, his prediction nevertheless was right. The final was Notre Dame 26 to Haskell 0. Notre Dame played "straight" football most of the way, and its strong running game proved to be sufficient to defeat the stubborn resistance put up by the team the reporter dubbed, in racist terms, the "aborigines."

Wabash

Next up was Wabash College, in a game that would be close to their final appearance on Notre Dame's schedule. Preparations were intense, as usual.

On Saturday, October 21, an off day for Notre Dame's football team, Harper traveled to Ann Arbor to watch Michigan State play Michigan. On the same day, Rockne traveled to West Point to scout the Army when they faced off against Trinity College.

The Wabash game went true to form, with Notre Dame completely dominating play in a 60–0 victory. The crowd, said to be the largest in the history of Cartier Field, included Charles A. Comiskey of Chicago, owner of the Chicago White Sox. Comiskey was in town to visit his grandson, a student at Notre Dame, and his granddaughter, a student at St. Mary's Academy. Also reported in the crowd was Gus Dorais, now coaching at St. Joseph's College in Dubuque, Iowa. The highlight of the game was a ninety-yard touchdown run by Notre Dame's Chet Grant, a product of South Bend High School.

Harper, forever cognizant of the need to schedule major games, was reported to be working on a postseason game in Boston, against, Tufts, Dartmouth, or Brown. The game did not come about, but the effort to even attempt such a postseason schedule was another manifestation of Harper's continuing quest to market Notre Dame by scheduling major games throughout the country.

Army

Notre Dame played nine games in 1916, and the only opponent to score against them was Army. The first four games were little more than organized scrimmages for Notre Dame, which outscored its opponents 182–0. Among the major schools, Notre Dame was the only one at that point in the season that had not been scored against. But Army would be the first real test of the season.

From the beginning of the season, Harper had regarded Army, led by its two "giant" halfbacks, Elmer Oliphant and Eugene Vidal—the father of author Gore Vidal—to be the strongest team on the schedule. Rockne's scouting reports were sobering, and on the Saturday on which Notre Dame was handily defeating Wabash, Army was overwhelming Villanova by a score of 69 to 7, with Army great Oliphant scoring six touchdowns.

The "eyes of the football world" were on the game, as it was described as a clash between one of the best of the west and most likely the best of the east. The game, again played at West Point, was to be witnessed by "three car loads of Notre Dame alumni" who made the trip up from New York.

Through three quarters, it was a game of straight football and mutually strong defenses. Army held a 13 to 10 lead. Much was written, however, about problems with the officiating. In the third period, with Notre Dame leading by a score of 10 to 6, Army had the ball on its own thirty-five-yard line, when Notre Dame was charged with pass interference. Instead of assessing a fifteen-yard penalty, the referee, lacking "knowledge of one of the most important new rules," wrongfully assessed a thirty-yard penalty against Notre Dame. Army promptly scored.

The Cadets "were outplayed in the line until the last quarter," when, as the "dusky twilight" set in, Army opened up with their forward-passing attack, which, ironically, would prove to be Army's lethal weapon in this game. Oliphant, Army's Mr. Everything, promptly completed three "long passes to Vidal" for touchdowns, putting the game out of reach. The timing and the excellence of the attack bore an eerie resemblance to Notre Dame's timing in the landmark 1913 game between the two schools. The final score was Army 30, Notre Dame 10, and the great rivalry, still in its infancy, now stood even, at two games apiece.

But it was time for the game with South Dakota, and looming on the near horizon were major games against Michigan State and the season finale against Nebraska.

South Dakota

The sixth game of Notre Dame's 1916 season would be played in Sioux Falls, South Dakota, where Notre Dame would once again meet and defeat a strong South Dakota contingent. The final score was Notre Dame 21, South Dakota 0. Harper had no comment on the victory, but was reported to have been pleased with his team's performance, especially in their ability to stop South Dakota's forward-passing attack.

Michigan Aggies (Michigan State)

The game against Michigan State, then known as the Michigan Aggies, would serve as a benchmark for Notre Dame's standing against the best teams in the West. Michigan State had recently been defeated by the University of Michigan by a score of 9 to 3, and had tied South Dakota, 3–3. The Notre Dame score against the Aggies would be compared to the Michigan and South Dakota scores. It was homecoming at Michigan State and the game crowd was said to be the largest in the school's history. The "Farmers" fell to the "Catholics" by a score of 14 to 0, the credit being given to Notre Dame's backfield combination of Cofall, Bergman, and Grant.

Alma

Alma was next on the schedule and rightfully was looked upon as no more than a scrimmage. Harper's practices and attention were clearly focused on the season final game against the University of Nebraska. On a wintry day, Notre Dame's last home game of the season, Harper's second- and third-stringers defeated Alma by a score of 46 to 0. Harper was saving the varsity for Nebraska on Thanksgiving Day.

Nebraska

Notre Dame arrived in Lincoln on Wednesday, November 29, in time to hold a light scrimmage and signal drill on the Nebraska field. As was his custom, Harper would make no prediction as to the outcome of the game. In play that was described as a "variety of attacks and display of speed," Notre Dame succeeded in overwhelming Nebraska by a score of 20 to 0. Notre Dame's first score was on a forty-four-yard run, the second was on a seventy-eight-yard fumble return, and the final touchdown came on a forward pass from Miller to Bergman. It was Notre Dame's eighth shutout of the season.

During the 1916 season, Harper was approached about the possibility of coming to Nebraska as their head football coach. His response was a telling example of his personal character: "No, because I am . . . still under contract at Notre Dame . . . hence it would be impossible for me to consider Nebraska even if you should want me." At the close of the 1916 season the Notre Dame school newspaper reported that Harper "has signed a contract to supervise athletics at Notre Dame for three more years after his present contract expires in June [which] was received joyfully by students and alumni of the university." As it would turn out, at the end of the 1917 season Harper would ask to be released from his contract so that he might join with his father-in-law in the ranching business. The university would accommodate him.

11

1917: Harper's Final Season

1917

Oct. 6	Kalamazoo	55–0	Home
Oct. 13	Wisconsin	0–0	Away
Oct. 20	Nebraska	0–7	Away
Oct. 27	South Dakota	40–0	Away
Nov. 3	Army	7–2	Away
Nov. 10	Morningside	13–0	Away
Nov. 17	Michigan State	23–0	Home
Nov. 24	Washington and Jefferson	3–0	Away

1917 would be Harper's last season as the head football coach at Notre Dame. The country was at war, and along with most other coaches,

Harper found himself with a substantially depleted squad. The heart of the Notre Dame team, including Bergman, Grant, Fitzpatrick, and Murphy, had gone into the service. Of Notre Dame's eight scheduled games in 1917, three would be at home: Kalamazoo College in the opener, South Dakota on October 27, and Michigan State in the middle of November. The remaining five would be on the road.

Kalamazoo and Wisconsin

Making frequent substitutions, Notre Dame buried Kalamazoo College by a score of 55 to 0. On the first play of the game, Pete Bahan ran seventy-six yards for a touchdown. Kalamazoo never threatened.

Next, Notre Dame traveled to Madison for its first-ever meeting with the University of Wisconsin, Notre Dame's first game against a Western Conference team since 1908. The Wisconsin coach announced in the local papers that he considered Notre Dame to be a weak opponent and thought the game would be no more than a good scrimmage, as his team outweighed Notre Dame by at least ten pounds per man. Notre Dame outplayed Wisconsin, but both teams were unsuccessful on several scoring opportunities and the game ended in a 0-to-0 tie. It was a feather in Harper's cap, however, because Wisconsin was the first Big Nine team since 1908 to break ranks and put Notre Dame on its schedule—all due to Harper's never-ending efforts at selling Notre Dame football.

Nebraska

While Notre Dame was battling Wisconsin in Madison, assistant coach Rockne was scouting Nebraska's one-sided victory over the University of Iowa. Rockne reported that Nebraska had the best team in its history, and the papers gave Notre Dame little chance in the game. Nevertheless, the team traveled to Lincoln in high spirits.

Both teams put up strong defenses. The game's only score was made by Nebraska on a twelve-yard run late in the second quarter, for a 7–0 victory. Not only would it be Notre Dame's only loss of the 1917 season, it was also the only touchdown that would be scored against Notre Dame all year. Notre Dame was gaining attention for its "fighting spirit," and one writer praised Notre Dame's "story of undiluted gameness that is even greater in defeat than in victory." One of the new "shining lights" to appear for Notre Dame was a sophomore by the name of George Gipp.

Born February 18, 1895, in tiny Laurium, Michigan, near Calumet on the Upper Peninsula, Gipp was the seventh of eight children of Isabella and Matthew, a Baptist preacher. Gipp was bright, and he was a phenomenal athlete. He was 6 feet tall and weighed 180 pounds. He could run the 100-yard dash in 10.1 seconds, throw the old oblong football 50 yards with accuracy, and drop-kick it 60 yards through the goalposts—stats that might even land him in the NFL today. His niece, Lillian Gipp Pritty, the daughter of his eldest brother Alexander, remembers her dad saying that Uncle George could do anything—and he could do it better than the other guy: "Uncle George could throw a ball from his knees at home plate with just his wrist all the way to second base, and the second baseman would say, 'Hey, Gipp, not so hard!'" But despite Gipp's talents, he was also considered lazy, and dropped out of Calumet High School in 1913. He worked construction and drove a cab until 1916, when three of his friends left for Notre Dame.

Harper had recruited Gipp early in 1916. On May 16 of that year, he wrote, "Dear Mr. Gipp: I wish to formally welcome you to Notre Dame and look forward to coaching you this coming season. The University of Notre Dame, in recognition of your fine play at Calumet High School, is offering you a scholarship for baseball. Please visit my office when you arrive in the fall. Sincerely yours, Jesse C. Harper, Head Coach."

Gipp responded in longhand, writing: "I read your letter of the 16th and look forward to playing baseball at Notre Dame. It is my hope that someday I will be able to play professional baseball after I graduate. Yours sincerely, George Gipp."

In 1916, Gipp entered Notre Dame as a freshman, but because of university policy, he would not be eligible to play football until his sophomore year. His years at Notre Dame would be remarkable, yet filled with highs and lows. Not long after his arrival, Gipp moved out of the dormitory and into the Oliver Hotel, which at the time was South Bend's most luxurious. The hotel was often the unofficial host to gatherings of high-stakes gamblers, and Gipp was a hustler in every sense of the word. His success at pool, billiards, craps, poker, and bridge was phenomenal. And he was generous with his winnings, often using them to buy meals for destitute families or to help teammates with their tuition or other college expenses.

In 1917, Gipp became a member of the varsity football squad, playing the halfback position. However, he did not report to campus until mid-October, missing his first two games. That November he would suffer an injury against Morningside and drop out of Notre Dame, after spending only a month on campus, to enroll briefly at the University of Wisconsin. Rockne understood full well what a great talent Gipp was—even in that limited time Gipp had made his mark, particularly in the game against

Army, and Rockne would later proclaim him "superior to Jim Thorpe and Red Grange on the football field." So Rockne went after the halfback to convince him to return to Notre Dame. In his junior year, Gipp would be expelled from Notre Dame for failing to attend class, and it would be rumored that he was headed for the University of Michigan. Rockne would again chase him down and bring him back to Notre Dame, exerting all possible pressure on the university administration to have Gipp reinstated. Rockne clearly went out of his way to make Gipp happy at Notre Dame.

Gipp, of course, would become "one for the ages." The 1940 movie *Knute Rockne, All-American* portrayed Gipp as a great natural athlete and a clean-living young man. They got the first part right—Gipp was indeed a great natural athlete, one of the greatest—but they clearly didn't understand him when they portrayed him as clean-living college boy. Though he was generally considered to be honest and considerate of others, he was also an avid gambler who enjoyed an open and freewheeling lifestyle. He was seen as a wonderful guy, but he was a maverick.

It was after Harper's departure from Notre Dame that Gipp would finally realize his potential as an athlete, but from the early stages of Gipp's career, Harper saw his greatness. "Even in his first year he was the smartest player I ever saw," Harper said. "He beat Army for us in 1917 with his head."

Gipp's play would be nothing less than brilliant through Notre Dame's unbeaten 1920 football season, when, just before the last game of the season, he would become ill with pneumonia and strep throat, requiring hospitalization. Today, penicillin would have cured him of both. Gipp died on December 14, 1920, at the age of twenty-five.

Years later in 1928, while trailing a far superior Army team 6–0 at the half, Rockne gathered his players for a pep talk. "Boys, I want to tell you a story," Rockne said. "I never thought I'd have to tell it, but the time has come." He then recounted his final conversation with Gipp. "I've got to go, Rock," Gipp said. "It's all right. I'm not afraid. Sometime, Rock, when the team is up against it, when things are wrong and the breaks are beating the boys—tell them to go in there with all they've got and win just one for the Gipper. I don't know where I'll be then, Rock. But I'll know about it, and I'll be happy." The team responded in the second half, upsetting Army, 12–6.

Some challenge that Gipp ever made such a request or that Rockne ever made such a speech, but the weight of opinion says it's true, something Rockne insisted upon until his dying day. Whatever the case, the story and Gipp are firmly woven into the tradition and legend of Notre Dame football.

Just an hour after the Nebraska game, Jim Phelan, Notre Dame's Captain, reported for duty at the local army camp. The specter of World War I loomed over the country and Notre Dame. Notre Dame professor Frank Miller reported for duty at a military camp in Missouri and former Notre Dame Yell Master Joe Gargan, "now with the American Expeditionary Force in France," sent his regards to the team.

South Dakota

Next, the University of South Dakota would travel to South Bend for what the press was describing as a "battle royal." Both Harper and Rockne were driving the men "feverishly" in preparation for the game.

As it turned out, South Dakota had a fairly weak team. On the second play of the game, Gipp skirted around right end for forty yards. With an eye on the Army game the next week, Harper soon put his regulars on the bench, and using mostly substitutes, Notre Dame recorded an easy 40–0 victory.

Army

Faced with snow three to four inches deep on Cartier Field, Harper took his practices in preparation for Army into the school gymnasium. This would be Notre Dame's fifth trip to West Point, and Harper's last. Army had grown to be Harper's favorite series, and in later years Harper would look back at the 1917 edition as one of the most enjoyable games of his coaching career. The rivalry between the two schools was now well developed. "The game had come to be a classic in the east, and it is recognized by followers of both in the east and in the west as the most important intersectional contest of the season." Army once again was strong, led by Elmer Oliphant, whom some considered, with the possible exception of Thorpe and Mahan, to be "the greatest backfield man of all time."

It would be a tight and hard-fought contest. Harper and his team were well prepared, and their game plan was flawless. The Associated Press report noted: "Notre Dame executed her plays faster and cleaner than the Army and with better judgment. The Army line, with the fear of the forward pass always hanging over its head, was inclined to play wide and loose." As a result, Notre Dame made most of its gains on the ground.

The crowd, which included a "famous French General," saw another display of George Gipp's brilliance. As one paper wrote, "It was at West

Point that the agile Michigander really made a name for himself. There he advanced the ball more than any other Notre Dame man. His forward passing and his punting left nothing to be desired."

As the game progressed, Harper's strategy was to send his running backs to the opposite side of Oliphant and Army's outstanding tackle, Jones. "We had a small team since most of our boys were in the war," Harper later recalled. "Army was big and tough. We couldn't crack the right side of the Army line so we kept running the other way."

This thinking worked, and near the game's end, with Army leading 2 to 0, Notre Dame found itself on Army's seven-yard line. Harper recalled, "I was wondering what we could do when Gipp first showed me what kind of a head he had. All during his career, you know, he had a habit of making up plays to fit the situation. He did it this time. He told our quarterback to fake a play the way we'd been going away from Oliphant, and let our halfback, Joseph Brandy run right at Jones and Oliphant. It worked. The Army was so surprised by the maneuver that Brandy ran right past them and scored a touchdown." The final was 7–2. "We won the game," Harper said. "Nothing else ever gave me quite as big a kick."

As the *New York Times* reported on November 4, 1917, "the Army football team crumpled up before the persistent attack of a lighter but scrappier eleven from Notre Dame this afternoon, the soldiers meeting their first defeat in two years . . . a shocking defeat to a team which was being hailed as one of the greatest the Point has seen in years."

Evidence of the importance the game was gaining in the eyes of West Point could be found in Army's tradition of "dipping the colors." This distinctive tradition had been reserved for the annual game against Navy, but in 1917 it was initiated for the Notre Dame series as well. *The Scholastic,* on November 11, 1917, described this ceremony. The cadets,

> in full dress march from their barracks to "the Plains." Midway in line of parade are borne the Stars and Stripes and the flag of the Army corps. When the football field is reached the color-bearers accompanied by the cadet band proceed to the center of the gridiron . . . (after the band and songs) the colors are then dipped solemnly three times to the cadet stands. A cheer for Notre Dame follows, and the colors are dipped once more. The simple but striking ceremony is over, and 'the Plains' awaits the great battle between the men of West Point and the men of Notre Dame.

Morningside

After Army came Morningside College, a small liberal-arts school founded in 1894, in Sioux City, Iowa, by the Methodist Episcopal Church. Shortly after its founding, Morningside had developed a competitive intercollegiate football team.

Harper was disappointed with his team's midweek scrimmages in preparation for the game, and Rockne didn't even attend, having been sent east to scout Washington and Jefferson, Notre Dame's final opponent for the season. Notre Dame played listlessly, yet emerged victorious by a score of 13 to 0. Early in the game, misfortune struck. George Gipp was "tackled severely outside the sidelines and thrown severely against a post," breaking his leg near the ankle. He would be unable to play in Notre Dame's final two games of the season, Michigan State in South Bend and on the road against Washington and Jefferson.

While recuperating back at his home in Laurium, Michigan, Gipp received the following letter, dated December 4, 1917, from Rockne: "Dear George: I hope that you are recuperating from the broken leg that you received in the last game. Your teammates and I want you to know that we look forward to seeing you this coming year and need you for our football team. If there is anything that I can do for you, please do not hesitate to ask. Sincerely yours, Knute Rockne."

That week, a Notre Dame sophomore by the name of Norman Barry was inserted at left end during practice and was projected to get into Saturday's game with Morningside. Barry was a "lifer" at Notre Dame, having attended grammar and secondary school at Notre Dame, as well as college, and would later play left halfback next to Gipp, on Rockne's early teams. He would go on to graduate from law school at Notre Dame as well.

"I played right half and Gipp played left half," Barry later said, referring to his senior year, 1920, when Notre Dame went 9–0, and Gipp died. Barry is a legend in his own right. After graduating from Notre Dame, Barry coached for thirteen years in Chicago, for the professional Chicago Cardinals, and at DeLaSalle High School, where he sent his player to Notre Dame to play for Rockne—Ed "Moose" Krause, one of the finest athletes ever to wear the blue and gold. When his coaching career was over, Barry would spend thirteen years in the Illinois legislature, and then serve as a judge, while his son, Norman J. Barry, would play football at Notre Dame for Frank Leahy, and his grandson, also Norman J. Barry, would play for Ara Parseghian.

Notre Dame's 1916 team.

Jesse C. Harper at the family ranch in Sitka, Kansas.

The ranch house at the family ranch in Sitka, Kansas, winter, 1940.

George Gipp, circa 1920.

George Gipp, circa 1920.

Jesse C. Harper and Knute Rockne standing in Harper's
front yard in Wichita, Kansas, in 1928.

Jesse C. Harper and Heartley "Hunk" Anderson on the sidelines, circa 1931.

College Football Coaches Conference at Universal in California, August 1, 1932. Left to right: Jesse C. Harper (Notre Dame Athletic Director), Amos Alonzo Stagg (University of Chicago Coach), W. A. Alexander (Georgia Tech Coach), Glenn S. "Pop" Warner (Stanford Coach), Heartley "Hunk" Anderson (Notre Dame Coach).

Jim Harper with his father, Jesse, in Los Angeles, 1947.

Mr. and Mrs. Jesse C. (Melville) Harper, c. 1950.

Fiftieth Anniversary of the University of Chicago 1905 Football team. Jesse C. Harper, seated left, talking with Coach Amos Alonzo Stagg, standing center, and other players.

Jesse C. Harper; Knute Rockne Jr.; Charles "Gus" Dorais, in 1958.

Presentation of Jesse C. Harper's Hall of Fame plaque to Mrs. Harper and Jim Harper at Notre Dame Stadium, October 16, 1971. Left to right: Mrs. Paula Salmon, widow of "Red" Salmon; Mr. Edward "Moose" Krause; Mrs. Jesse (Melville) Harper; Mr. Jim Harper.

Jesse C. Harper, date unknown.

Michigan State

Michigan State traveled to South Bend for Notre Dame's final home game of the 1917 season. Notre Dame's passing attack "failed," but its running game proved successful, and Notre Dame prevailed by a score of 23 to 0. Barry was active in the game and credited with at least one run of fifty yards.

Washington and Jefferson

The final game of the season, and of Harper's career as Notre Dame coach, was to be played against Washington and Jefferson College, in Washington, Pennsylvania, just south of Pittsburgh. Washington and Jefferson was established as a private liberal-arts college in 1787, and the team was said to have one of the strongest defensive teams in the country. Their play against Notre Dame proved that assessment to be correct. Notre Dame entered the game with both of its regular quarterbacks on the injured list, along with several other starters, most notably, Gipp. The game was a defensive battle from the start. "Slip" Madigan, a second-string junior, was put into the game in the middle of the second period to replace starter Frank Rydzewski, who was thrown out for "slugging," a charge protested by Notre Dame, but to no avail. Madigan was suffering from pneumonia at the time, and played against the advice of his physician. "He couldn't talk and after the game could scarcely walk," but fought like a tiger. Joe Brandy kicked a forty-five-yard field goal in the fourth quarter for the game's only score and Notre Dame came away with a hard-fought 3–0 victory. Years later, Madigan would be one of six Harper prodigies inducted into the College Football Hall of Fame for their success in coaching college football.

*   *   *

In 1916 Harper's father-in-law Melville C. Campbell had been experiencing poor health and asked Harper if he would consider returning to the Kansas cattle ranch to assist him. He agreed to match Harper's salary from Notre Dame. At the time Harper appeared to be tiring from the pressure that was pouring in from many fans and alumni, whose goal as he described it "was winning at all cost." Harper had other priorities—academics and sportsmanship—and he felt the pace of the intercollegiate game was starting to encroach on those priorities. Whatever his reasoning, Harper resigned at the conclusion of the 1917 football season to join his father-in-law, and took over the active management of the ranch.

Joe Doyle speculates that there may have been another reason for Harper's departure from Notre Dame. While acknowledging the foregoing reasons, Doyle notes that Father Matthew Walsh, then the vice president of Notre Dame and the man in charge of athletics at Notre Dame, had volunteered for duty in World War I as a military chaplain. Harper and Walsh were, as Doyle had personally observed in later years, very close, and Doyle believes Walsh's departure also spurred Harper's decision to leave.

At this point, Rockne's considerable talents had become apparent to other universities, and Harper found himself frequently writing strong letters of recommendation for Rockne, though he felt that Rockne should remain at Notre Dame. During the 1916 season, Harper in effect promised Rockne that if he would stay on as assistant, he would be in a position to be the head football coach at Notre Dame.

But Harper discovered some resistance to this plan. "To hear Harper tell it, there was some doubt that Rockne would have been hired as the head coach," Joe Doyle recalled in a column in the August 2, 1961,

South Bend Tribune, shortly after Harper's death. "Yet Jesse always insisted that 'Rock was a natural for the job.' Even in those early days, a change of coaches created controversy at Notre Dame.

"Some of the priests weren't exactly sold on Rock as an assistant coach," Harper remembered, "though anyone close to football knew that he had an exceptionally sharp mind. Finally, it got me mad and I told one of the objectors, 'If you hire anyone else, you'll be making the biggest mistake Notre Dame ever made.'"

"Maybe, they were only leading me on," Harper reminisced, "to a better endorsement of Rock, but it got my dander up a little bit." When Father Cavanaugh, the president of Notre Dame, finally asked Harper why he was so insistent on the university hiring Rockne, Harper explained that in 1916 he had promised Rockne the job, if he would stay, for Rockne's talents were being noticed by others, and he was being solicited by other schools. Father Cavanaugh's response was that if that was the case, that Harper had promised Rockne the job, then Rockne would be hired. Years later Harper told Joe Doyle, "If Father Matt [Walsh] had been around, he would have picked Rockne in a second." In the 1918 edition of the *Dome,* the writers congratulated Rockne: "Learned, liked, capable, inspiring, courageous, and resourceful, no one can see anything but undiluted success for the great 1913 football captain. . . . His popularity is in its infancy." Joe Doyle observes that securing Rockne as the new head football coach at Notre Dame in 1918 was the most important move Harper ever made on Notre Dame's behalf.

On December 1, 1917, in the wake of Harper's announcement, the *Scholastic* wrote: "Harper was a great man in 1913 when he flashed across the athletic horizon with an unbeatable team of veterans; he was a far greater man during 1917 when he molded a team from the greenest of material and battered his way through the heaviest schedule in the history of Notre Dame with just one defeat." Harper had worked with the faculty in setting high academic standards for his players, relentlessly enforced all rules of amateurism, and as the *Scholastic* noted, he had "countenanced nothing but the highest grade of sportsmanship."

The following year, the writers of the *Dome* paid tribute to Harper. Under a headline that read, The King Is Dead! Long Live The King! they wrote:

Five years ago there came to Notre Dame a man who enjoyed a local reputation in the vicinity of Crawfordsville, Indiana, as a developer of more or less successful athletic teams. Today that man is known throughout the length and breadth of this land as one of the foremost coaches and directors intercollegiate athletics have ever produced. That man is Jesse C. Harper, the astute generalissimo of the Notre Dame athletic department, who has raised up the Gold and Blue athletics till they now rest on a plane unsurpassed by any school East or West.

Harper has been such a success at Notre Dame because he is possessed of a vision that is tempered with good judgment and with a courage to do big things that admits of no obstacles. Before he had set foot on Notre Dame soil in the fall of 1913 he had arranged the most pretentious schedule the football world had ever known. Critics gasped, but they soon gasped again when he paraded his phantom-like eleven from the Hudson to the Rio

Grande always in step with a victory march. Year-in and year-out he has done wonders with Notre Dame teams. . . . Persistent, resourceful, and game to the core, Coach Harper stands for all that is good in athletics. Sportsmanship first, then victory or defeat second, has always been the way of Harper. Heads of athletic departments at other institutions have come to know Harper and Notre Dame, and to realize what the two stand for. No longer is Notre Dame knocking at the gate for desirable opponents. Now she is welcome in the best athletic company because her athletes and her ideas of sportsmanship cannot be surpassed.

12

Jesse Harper and Knute Rockne, 1918–1931

The Ranch

In the spring of 1918, Harper departed from the manicured lawns and thge gentle academic ambience of the University of Notre Dame to become a cattle rancher in Kansas. Harper was employed by his father-in-law as the ranch manager at a salary approximating his final salary at Notre Dame. The Ranch of the Alamos was a hardscrabble, working cattle ranch manned by real cowboys—this was not gentleman ranching or "hobby" ranching. The 20,000-acre, egg-shaped parcel of land was 10 miles in length and 5 miles in width, and located in Sitka, Clark County, Kansas. Farmland took up 2,500 acres of the ranch, while the remaining 17,500 or so acres were used to graze the cattle. M. C. Campbell,

Harper's father-in-law, was a true pioneer in the American West, having first come to that part of the country in 1874, at the age of twenty-five. Campbell took his first claim in Barton County, Kansas. Then in 1890, he started "blocking up" his ranch in Clark County, the land that would eventually become the Ranch of the Alamos. To raise the money to start accumulating land for his ranch, Campbell, for three years, drove cattle from Texas to Kansas. In those days, they called it "trailing" cattle. Some of the herds he drove were as large as five thousand head of cattle.

The morning after Harper arrived at the ranch, Campbell left on an extended vacation. Life on the ranch being as harsh as it was, Harper insisted that his wife and children live in Wichita, some 175 miles to the east. For the next several years, Harper would travel between the two places, spending ten days or so working at the ranch, then returning to Wichita for three or four days, before heading back to the ranch for another seven-to-ten-day stretch.

Harper's son Jim remembered the "primitive conditions" at the ranch well: "There was no running water, an outhouse, an iron wood burning stove in the kitchen which the cook would cook on. At the side of the stove was a tank holding about 5 gallons of water. The cooking would keep the water hot for bathing in a large tub."

The original portion of the ranch house was made up of two abandoned schoolhouses purchased by Campbell in 1891. In 1938 an addition was made, and the house was veneered with six inches of native rock.

The ranch had "over 100 miles of fence to keep up, 19 windmills to keep pumping, crops to put out, marketing to do, and books to keep." The land also featured two dirt pasture dams, three creeks, and one spring. In addition, an eight-mile stretch of the Cimarron River ran through the property. The two dirt pasture dams were installed in 1938 with the help of government water conservation funds. Harper would say with pride that on the 20,000 acres, there was no place where the cattle could be more than one mile from water. The cattle, usually over 1,800 head, were dipped twice a year for lice. When help was available, Harper had up to twelve hired hands to assist him. That was in the 1920s, when business was good. As the Depression hit, the number of hired hands decreased, and during World War II, when help was hard to come by, Harper ran the ranch with his son Mell and two hired men.

Though life on the Ranch of the Alamos was hard, Harper made sure there was always time for a little fun. Harper's son Jim has warm memories of his dad, on late summer afternoons, going out to the bunkhouse lot and hitting fungoes to him, his older brother Mell, and four or five of the ranch hands. It was during those sessions that Harper, ever the coach, taught Jim some of the finer points of baseball, particularly the art of the bunt—all of which served Jim well when he went on to play center field on his high school baseball team.

Staying in Touch with "Rock"

When Harper took over at Notre Dame in 1913, he was twenty-nine years old; Rockne was twenty-five. By the time of Harper's departure from Notre Dame, the two had become more than professional associates; they had also become friends. As Jim Harper recalls, "I have never seen two brothers any closer than Dad and Uncle Rock." The friendship would last the rest of Rockne's life, as they stayed in close contact through mail and personal visits throughout Rockne's years at Notre Dame.

Harper and Rockne had different coaching styles, but that had no effect on their personal friendship. Judge Norm Barry, who played football under both Harper and Rockne, remembered their styles:

> Harper was very good at handling men. Rockne was a rough and tough guy, and let's not say he wasn't, because I was under him for four years and I know how he handled people. He was tough, but Harper never used those tactics. He was easygoing and they respected him. He was not a driver, he just set out the plays and then the players had the confidence in him and ran the plays.
>
> Harper's style before or during a game was completely different than Rockne's. Harper did not use the same tactics that Rockne did in trying to inspire anybody. He did not shout and go on in great details, he was just calm, cool, and collected and just laid out that this is the way we are going to do it and this is the way we are going to defend the opposition. But he did not tell a lot of big stories, just put it out plain. Rockne always had a lot of stories and he would go into great detail about how we should get in there and hit him and knock him down, and all that kind of talk. After you heard Rockne, maybe after your sophomore year, you got used to all the talk and it did not make a great deal of difference, because you knew you were going to get the same kind of inspirational talk, but it just went over your head.

Rockne and Harper had a mutual admiration, which grew as the years passed. Harper frequently would say, "Rockne is the greatest football instructor the country has ever known," while Rockne was known to return the praise: "Jesse, not myself was the reason for Notre Dame becoming famous in football. Jesse put the school on a high plane, I have tried to carry out what he started."

Through the intervening years, Harper was forever giving Rockne pep talks, encouraging and advising him through the continuing challenges of coaching Notre Dame in a rapidly changing college football environment.

An embarrassing incident for Rockne and Notre Dame occurred early in 1921, but didn't reach the attention of the public until January 1922. Several Notre Dame players had agreed to play football for pay on Thanksgiving Day, 1921. The Illinois towns of Taylorville and Carlinville had a long-standing football rivalry, marked by growing intensity and high-stakes gambling. The players were to be paid $200 each, plus expenses, an offer that did not appear to the players to be inappropriate, as playing a little "pro" ball on one's off days was considered standard procedure at the time. However, this time events got out of hand. The word spread in Carlinville that Notre Dame was coming to play on their side. Not to be outdone, Taylorville promptly went out and hired nine players from the University of Illinois. The Chicago press, great admirers of both Rockne and Bob Zuppke, the coach at Illinois, stayed silent, at least as long as they could, but the story was just too big to cover up. The number of players involved and the enormous size of the betting pool—rumored to be $100,000—finally caused the entire matter to break out into the media, to the embarrassment of Illinois and Notre Dame. All of the players involved were dismissed from their respective teams. Zuppke felt that Rockne had not taken the matter seriously enough, and bad relations developed between the two. Rockne was in an embarrassing position, but, as always, Harper was there with an encouraging word. In a letter dated January 8, 1922, Harper wrote: "I was sorry you had to drop some of your men for professional football. It will be a good lesson for the rest but I know it will hurt your team for next year."

Harper's letters to Rockne were always addressed, "Dear Rock," and Rockne's to Harper were always addressed, "Dear Jesse." On December 3, 1924, Harper wrote to Rockne: "I want to congratulate you on the wonderful season you have just had. You not only had the best team in the country, but, better than that to me, you had the best coached team. Your fine success is always of great satisfaction to me." On a personal note, Harper added, "Mell goes to intermediate school next fall and is going out for the team. I have promised him an outfit. When ever you have time I wish you would send me a small headgear, shoulder pads and jersey. Just so they get to Wichita by Xmas. Send me the bill. I thought you could save me some money. . . . Most sincerely yours, Jesse." Rockne's response on December 13 read, in part: "I shall send you the small headgear, shoulder pads and jersey in a day or so and there will be no bill. It is a real pleasure for me to do this. . . . Yours cordially, Knute Rockne."

And, what a year 1924 had been! Notre Dame, led by its legendary backfield, known as the "Four Horsemen," had gone undefeated and been awarded their first national championship. That January, Notre Dame would meet Stanford University in the Rose Bowl and Rockne's team would defeat an excellent "Pop" Warner team by a score of 27–10. It would be Notre Dame's only appearance in the Rose Bowl. It was Rockne's third undefeated season. He would have two more before he was finished.

* * *

In the fall of 1925, Rockne published his autobiography and dedicated it to Harper. Harper was highly flattered, and wrote to Rockne on September 20, 1925: "A few days ago I received a copy of your football book from the publishers which you so kindly dedicated to me. I want to thank you for honoring me so highly and assure you I greatly appreciate it. I have read the book carefully, and I want to tell you it is by far the best book on football I have ever read. It is well written and I can see you have given a great deal of thought to it. . . . Sincerely, Jesse."

By the mid-1920s, after Rockne had established himself as the premier football coach in the country and Notre Dame had become "America's" team, the heartfelt admiration, pride, and support from Harper continued. "I must congratulate you on your wonderful season so far. . . . Your teams each year show to me your extraordinary ability as a coach and a handler of men. I know I appreciate your ability more than anyone else because you and I were so close together for so long. You are at the head of them all at present and hard work will keep you there for many years. Next to your wife and Mother [refers to Harper's wife], your great success means more to me than to anyone else."

Their correspondence through those years covered everything from requests for football tickets and football equipment for Harper's young son Mell, to analysis of football plays and consultation on Notre Dame's continuing discussions with the Big Ten, to personal advice about financial matters, employment, and health. And it always included consistent encouragement and confidence-building advice from Harper. In Harper's eyes, Rockne could do no wrong, and Harper told his friend so at every turn.

For Christmas in 1921, Rockne had sent a football to Harper's young son Mell. In his thank-you note, Harper noted, "I am glad to see you were not tempted to go to Northwestern. Perhaps it would be better to say you did not yield to temptation. I received a letter from them a few days ago wanting to know if I would like the job. While their pay is good enough it is a bad place to throw out your anchor."

Rockne's career included more than one flirtation with another school. The Chicago Tribune, on March 23, 1924, ran a headline speculating that Rockne was going to the University of Iowa. Rockne denied this and quickly signed a ten-year extension to stay at Notre Dame. Based on the underlying facts, it appears Rockne and his friend, Dr. Paul Belting, the athletic director at Iowa, may have reached a deal in principle for Rockne to come to Iowa, with Rockne insisting that the media not be informed. When the Tribune ran its headline, Rockne backed out and signed his extension with Notre Dame. The insinuation was that Rockne had reached two separate deals with Belting to go to Iowa.

The most serious and widely publicized incident involved Rockne and Columbia University in New York City. Rockne's affair with Columbia University was public and blatant. The Sunday *New York Times* on December 13, 1925, ran a front-page headline reading, COLUMBIA BAD FAITH CHARGED BY ROCKNE: OFFICIALS KNEW NEGOTIATIONS WERE OFF BEFORE ANNOUNCING HIS ENGAGEMENT AS COACH. In the article, Columbia charged that Rockne had signed a three-year coaching contract with them on December 1, calling for an annual salary of $25,000. Rockne vehemently denied everything and boarded the train in New York to return to South Bend, saying, "I hope my job is waiting for me when I get back." It was, of course, but the record indicates that some well-deserved "lecturing" was handed out by Father Matthew Walsh before the matter was closed.

Father Matthew Walsh, the president at Notre Dame, said, "it was a regrettable incident, but above all things, get Rockne out of New York and back home." The *New York Times* reported that there seemed to have been "deception" on both sides.

Father Walsh diplomatically and privately handled the matter, but he never forgot it. It was only one of Rockne's many machinations that perplexed Father Walsh. An accompanying article in the *New York Times* noted that Rockne would sail to Southern France the following January for a ten-day vacation. He was to be accompanied by "a few" Notre Dame alumni.

On February 19, 1925, Jesse dropped a personal financial bombshell on his protégé. "Dear Rock, You not doubt will be surprised at this letter after you have read it. On account of the poor cattle business and also on account of some trouble with Mr. Campbell I am looking for a job so I am writing you to see if you know of any vacancies that I might be able to fill. I know some mighty good places have been filled within the last month or two but there may be others. Anything you can do to help me will be greatly appreciated. I will ask you to say nothing about this to any of my friends in South Bend. Very truly yours, Jesse." Rockne responded immediately, suggesting openings at Northwestern and Duke. The correspondence on this subject ended in March of 1925, however, and never resurfaced.

The close of the 1925 football season saw a flurry of activity and meetings between the two young friends. Harper made plans to travel to

Lincoln, Nebraska, for the Notre Dame–Nebraska game. Rockne responded on October 2, noting, "I want you to sit on the bench with me and make a talk to the team and all that sort of thing and kinda bring yourself back to the old days."

That November 3, Rockne wrote to Jesse: "I will make reservations for you to stop with us and I want you to come along and go through all the details just as though you were a member of the coaching staff. I cannot tell you how tickled I am and I know you will enjoy getting back in your old environment." On November 28, after the trip, Harper wrote: "I sure had a wonderful time at Lincoln. While it would have been fine to have won the game yet that point is only incidental to the great value of football. Without doubt it was the two best days I ever had."

Rockne and his family were scheduled to spend the Christmas of 1925 in Kansas with the Harpers. Instead, Rockne was in New York City negotiating with Columbia. But after that became a fiasco, Harper, on December 31, 1925, wrote an encouraging note to Rockne, "You will soon be starting on your trip. I know you will have a wonderful time. I want you to forget yourself completely so you will have a real rest. Forget you have ever been nervous or tired and don't let anyone say anything to you about it. Forget the Columbia episode and don't talk about it anymore. Just interest yourself in your trip, the new sights you will see and the people around you." Rockne responded: "I am leaving Monday. Many thanks for your very kind letter."

In the spring of 1926, the Notre Dame administration decided to once again apply for membership in the Big Ten. Rockne was to play a key role in the effort, and he immediately consulted Harper. On March 17, 1926, he wrote: "There is one thing I want to ask you about, Jesse, and that is, the authorities here are thinking of applying for admission in the Big Ten in June. What do you think is the best method of going around and seeing these faculty men individually before a meeting and who should go. Also, who should make the formal application when the Big Ten have a meeting in May in Iowa City. I should appreciate your keeping this confidential and also the benefit of your advice."

After some communication, Rockne sent Harper a telegram on March 23: "Can you come to Notre Dame to consult on question I wrote about. Will pay expenses. Wire. Knute Rockne." Harper made the trip, and consulted with Rockne on the strategy to be employed for the proposed Big Ten application.

Harper advised that Rockne first make an exploratory trip to select Big Ten schools to "find out your possibilities. No one can do that as well as you. I think your trip would be well worth while even though you find it unwise to apply for admission. The different schools would understand you better and see your position and I believe will hesitate more in criticizing."

Rockne made the rounds and in the end the Big Ten determined not to expand. On that basis a formal application by Notre Dame was not submitted. In the process, however, Notre Dame invited the Big Ten committee to investigate Notre Dame from "top to bottom." It was clear that Michigan would be against admitting Notre Dame, but in the Big Ten's refusal to investigate Notre Dame, Rockne concluded, "I think this silences Michigan and they certainly cannot tell any stories when they very strongly refused to investigate. I believe there is some political intriguing in the Big Ten that we don't understand but one thing is sure, it is a very divided body."

In 1926, Notre Dame was scheduled to play a game at Southern California. On October 11, Harper wrote, "Dear Rock, I sure am going to try to make the Calif. Trip with you. Nothing would give me so much pleasure. Let me know your itinerary as soon as you have time."

Rockne responded on October 19, "Dear Jesse: Our present plans are to go out to California on the Rock Island & Southern Pacific. We plan on leaving Chicago Monday, November 29 at 8:00 PM, which will bring us around through your country some time the next day. . . . With kindest regards to yourself and family, I am Yours cordially, K. K. Rockne, Director of Athletics."

Jesse responded on October 31: "Dear Rock; I received your letter giving that date you would leave Chicago on the Rock Island for Calif. I am going to try my best to make the trip with you. I receive 1000 cattle at Quervo, N.M. on the 22nd and if everything goes alright believe I will meet you at Hutchinson. You sure are having a fine season. It looks like you have another tough game with the Army next week. Lots of good luck to you. . . . Sincerely, Jesse."

Rockne responded on November 5: "We leave Chicago at 8:00 PM on the Rock Island and Southern Pacific, Monday November 29—sincerely hope you can join us at Hutchinson. . . . The Army looks like the greatest team in its history according to everyone who has seen them and though I have a fair team I don't see how we can do much with them."

On November 15, Jesse replied: "Dear Rock; First I want to congratulate you on the wonderful victory last Sat. against Army. . . . No matter what happens the rest of the season I believe you have done the best job of coaching you have ever done. You have had a hard schedule and you have handled it marvelously. . . . Please send me the number of the train and whether I can get reservation in your own cars or had I better get one separately. You have no idea how badly I want to make this trip and I am working night and day to get ready to go. Remember me to Bonnie and the kiddies."

On November 18, Rockne wrote back: "What I would suggest doing is, when you let me know definitely whether or not you will be with us or not, to let me handle your ticket for you, in fact, all the details so that you will have nothing to worry about."

The trip came off just as Jesse and Rockne had hoped. Jesse traveled with the team and worked the sideline with his friend and protégé. Prior to the trip, the headline in the *Wichita Times* read: WICHITAN WILL HELP ROCKNE IN BIG COAST GAME: JESSE HARPER DEPARTS TO ADVISE MICKS IN THEIR CLASH IN CALIFORNIA.

Much of their communication during these years consisted of the usual personal exchanges between close friends so situated. Jesse needed four tickets for the Northwestern game in Chicago and sixteen tickets in the Notre Dame section for the Southern California game in Los Angeles, for a special friend of his in Los Angeles, and Rockne complied. Jesse needed four tickets for the Army–Navy game, but this one was "tough" for Rockne.

And there was football talk. The Rules Committee was cracking down on Notre Dame's famous shift. On March 21, 1927, Jesse observed, "I was thinking you could use your shift and also the one man in motion to good advantage. The man in motion could start as soon as the shift hit the ground and by the time he had moved a yard or two the play could start." Rockne liked the idea, and on May 20, he wrote: "all looking forward to seeing what we can do with the shift somewhat curtailed. I have a couple of lateral pass plays which I like and am diagramming them here for you. What do you think of them?" Rockne wrote again on October 20: "Slowing up the shift has helped us rather than hurt us and our offense looked better than ever."

Rockne is given credit for Notre Dame's shift, but actually, the strategy had been devised by Stagg years earlier at the University of Chicago and was brought to Notre Dame by Harper. Rockne, true to his own genius, elevated the shift to new heights by introducing into the mix a synchronized shift of the entire backfield. His Four Horsemen backfield was the first to use Rockne's "new" shift in 1924. The story that Rockne conceived this idea after watching a chorus line in Chicago apparently contains a high degree of truth. In an interesting bit of irony, Rockne's teams were known for the speed and deception of their running games, rather than for their use of the forward pass.

As fate would have it, this wonderful relationship came to an abrupt end on March 31, 1931, when tragedy of the worst kind struck. The commercial airliner carrying Rockne to the West Coast crashed in a pasture near Bazaar, Kansas, 100 miles from Harper's cattle ranch, killing Rockne and seven others. Rockne was forty-three years old. In his thirteen years at Notre Dame, Rockne had become a legend. His teams went 105–12–5, making his .881 winning percentage the highest in NCAA history. Along the way, the shy young Norwegian who had trouble making a public speech when he was a student and football star in 1913 had become one of the best known and most popular men in America, and one of the greatest showmen. He had coached Notre Dame to a Rose Bowl victory in 1925, with a backfield that would be immortalized by sportswriter Grantland Rice in his now famous lead, "Outlined against a blue-gray October sky, the Four Horseman rode again." He had inspired his weak 1928 team to victory over highly favored Army with his "win one for the Gipper" halftime speech, which also would be planted in posterity by Grantland Rice. His teams were undefeated in five different seasons, and he was credited with three national championships. Rockne had carried Notre Dame to the top of the college football world, and his untimely death raised his already legendary status to mythological heights.

Harper's ranch house phone rang off the hook that day with newsmen from around the try wanting to know if "it" was true. Finally, Harper got into his car and drove to the crash site. He identified Rock's body, and it was true, Rock had been killed.

13

Jesse Harper Returns to Notre Dame: 1931–1933

Notre Dame officials talked business with Harper at the functions surrounding Rockne's funeral in April 1931. It was the first time Harper had returned to the Notre Dame campus since his departure thirteen years earlier. As a result of the conversation held at Rockne's funeral, and at the urging of Harper's close friend, Father Matthew Walsh, who by then had retired as the university's president, the parties reached an agreement for Harper to return to Notre Dame as athletic director.

By 1931 the problem at Notre Dame was no longer money or scheduling—it was integrity. Part of Rockne's success was due to his soliciting football players from other schools and convincing them to transfer to Notre Dame. Many schools, especially Big Ten schools, complained loudly about this practice.

One newspaper reported, "When Harper returned in 1931, he was a little surprised at some of the changes. 'I don't want to knock Rockne in any way,' said Jesse, 'But he was a football man, first and foremost. And he liked to win. And he liked to win the with the best squads of all. . . . I didn't think it was good for football, and I still don't think so,' he said strongly. 'Rock liked to win', he noted, but, 'At times Rockne was a little too eager. He'd recruit from other school's freshmen teams. Or, he would let a player sluff off on his studies just to be a better football player.'"

Harper, with the strong blessing of the Notre Dame administration, put an abrupt end to Rockne's practices by instituting a no-transfer rule, a requirement for a 77 or better average for all athletes, and a stricter scholarship policy. By the time Harper left Notre Dame in 1934, these rules were being strongly enforced.

Who would take over as head football coach in 1931 was another matter. The president of Notre Dame, Father Charles O'Donnell, C.S.C., determined that there would be, at least initially, two coaches to replace Rockne. One, Heartley "Hunk" Anderson, would be referred to as the "senior" coach, and, the other, Jack Chevigny, would be designated the "junior" coach. Both of these men had been assistant coaches under Rockne, and the thinking seemed to be that they would be able to carry on with Rockne's system better than anyone else. The times would not have been comfortable for a drastic change in coaching methods. That Harper had returned to the mix had been attributed to a group of "influential alumni from New York" and others who felt that the situation demanded a "strong, practiced hand and a man loved by the older graduates and respected by the younger ones. Ergo the call to Harper." Also, they liked the idea of having Harper around to oversee Anderson and Chevigny, and, to "hold their hands" if necessary.

Anderson was a high school friend and teammate of George Gipp in northern Michigan, and had been an outstanding offensive guard for Rockne from 1918 to 1921, teaming with Gipp. After his senior year at Notre Dame, Anderson was named as a first-team All-American. He became an assistant coach under Rockne in 1930.

Chevigny had played halfback for Rockne from 1926 to 1928 and had been present in the locker room for Rockne's famous "win one for the Gipper" halftime speech in 1928. Chevigny ended up being the star of that game; in the second half he ran for the touchdown that either tied or won the game—depending on which account you read. While crossing the goal line, he exclaimed: "That's one for the Gipper."

Chevigny soon became a minor legend in his own right. In 1952, Frank Leahy's Notre Dame team was losing 3–0 to Texas. Leahy, who had also been in the Notre Dame locker room in 1928 for Rockne's famous talk, told his team at the half how Chevigny, who had been killed in combat at Iwo Jima in 1945, had won one for the Gipper back in 1928. Leahy then implored his team—his "lads" as he called them—to win one for Chevigny. They stormed out of the locker room for the second half to take home a 14–3 victory.

Both Anderson and Chevigny accepted the roles designed for them in 1931 by the well-meaning Father O'Donnell, but the two clashed constantly during the season. As a consequence, Chevigny left Notre Dame after the season to take a coaching position with the Chicago Cardinals of the National Football League.

At the start of their respective tenures, both men were advised in explicit terms that the university was determined to "reclaim control over athletic operations" and virtually nothing was to be done or undertaken without prior approval of Father Mulcaire and/or the athletic board. Rockne, despite all efforts to the contrary by the university administration, had become a powerful force at Notre Dame—so powerful that, best intentions aside, the administration simply could not control him. At least, they could not control him to the extent they felt appropriate, for Rockne had become a substantial rainmaker.

Even in Rockne's worst year in terms of wins and losses, 1928, the team brought in a net profit for the season approaching $500,000. In 1929 and 1930 Rockne produced what many say were his two best teams, winners of back-to-back national championships, and the profits increased. In 1929, during the construction of Notre Dame Stadium, all of Notre Dame's games were played on the road, and several were played in front of record crowds in major metropolitan areas such as Baltimore and Chicago. In Chicago, in 1929, 120,000 people crowded into Soldier Field to watch Notre Dame's 13–12 victory over Southern California. In 1929, the profits from football exceeded $500,000, a figure that would not be matched again for the next fifty years

When Father O'Donnell took over as president in 1928, he had selected the Reverend Michael A. Mulcaire, C.S.C., to be his vice president and chairman of the Athletic Board of the University. Mulcaire, who was born in Ireland in 1894, was ordained in 1922 and received his doctorate in economics in 1923. Several in the university administration in 1928 felt strongly that Rockne and the athletic department needed to be brought under closer supervision, and Mulcaire was their choice to accomplish that task. As Mulcaire would tell Hunk Anderson years later, the administration wanted to "regain control over a situation that desperately needed correction." Mulcaire undertook this direction with "all the zeal, naiveté, and good intentions of inexperience." However, Rockne was not a man easily intimidated by clerical authority. Ultimately, although Fathers O'Donnell and Mulcaire were frustrated by Rockne's "all too frequent ego tantrums and whims," they fully recognized that Rockne was an "invaluable university asset." After the 1930 season they had simply resolved to do their best to keep Rockne happy, and at Notre Dame.

Harper returned in 1931 to find a very different Notre Dame. In an interview with the *Scholastic*, he expressed his surprise at the growth of the campus and the number of men out for football, and reminisced a little about his protégé and friend Rock. "I had heard and read of the immense change in Notre Dame," he said. "But it was necessary for me to see the campus itself before I could actually realize the tremendous growth of the university. The physical appearance of the campus amazed me. I was surprised and gratified to see the exceptionally large turnout for spring football practice. Such a group . . . was undreamed of thirteen years ago. I have found the students much the same. . . . The spirit of Notre Dame lives now as it always will."

The Notre Dame campus had certainly experienced a tremendous growth since Harper had last walked the grounds. Donations were pouring in, and the vision of the Fathers of the Congregation of the Holy Cross knew no limits. In 1929, the Boston architectural firm of Maginnis and Walsh was retained to design a new law building. "They submitted a design for a very beautiful, graceful structure, collegiate Gothic in character, to cost in the neighborhood of $440,000." The building was completed in the fall of 1930.

In November 1930, university president Father Charles O'Donnell received a letter from Edward Nash Hurley, chairman of the United States Shipping Board during the previous war and Laetare Medalist of 1926, donating $200,000 for a new commerce building. The building was completed and dedicated in May of 1932.

In 1931, ground was broken for Alumni Hall and Dillon Hall, again designed by Maginnis and Walsh. The two new halls were to cost $950,000 and house a total of 600 students. They were completed that fall.

Also in 1931, alumnus John F. Cushing donated $300,000 for a new engineering building to be built next to the recently completed law school. In 1905, when Cushing was a student, he had called on Father Morrissey, then president of the university, to say he would not be able to continue at Notre Dame because he lacked the funds to pay tuition. Father Morrissey told Cushing that he should return and not worry about the finances. John Cushing graduated as a civil engineer in the class of 1906. He died in an airplane crash in 1935 and was reputed to be "not a wealthy man," having left little for the support of his large family. But, as Father Arthur J. Hope, C.S.C., in his book, *Notre Dame: One Hundred Years* wrote, "the fact that he made the gift when he did, running the risk of leaving his family without great wealth, augments the generous character of the man and lends luster to his delicate conscience."

With the advent of all of these new building projects, Father

O'Donnell, in the fall of 1931, retained renowned architect Albert Kahn of Detroit to draw up plans for a new steam and water pumping plant to be located near St. Joseph's Lake, some distance from the site of the old heating plant, all at a cost of $250,000. The plant opened the day before Christmas in 1931.

In response to public curiosity about the explosion of new construction at Notre Dame, Father O'Donnell opened the university's books to the public. It was clear that the university was not getting "rich" on its football money. It was also clear that Notre Dame's "football money" was immensely needed to take care of the expenses of the university.

Shortly after being appointed head football coach in 1931, Hunk Anderson met with Harper to discuss funds for recruiting and scholarships. Harper informed Hunk, in no uncertain terms, that there would be no money for recruiting and that football scholarships would be cut from thirty-six full scholarships and sixteen partial scholarships to sixteen full scholarships and thirty-six partial scholarships. The results were devastating, and Hunk reported that he was stunned by Harper's edict. Harper put his hand on Hunk's shoulder and said "Hunk, I am under orders to tighten the drum." He then invited Hunk to go over his head, which Hunk did. The responses he received from Father Mulcaire and then Father O'Donnell were even firmer than the one he had received from Harper. Mulcaire firmly stated, "Rockne ran things pretty much the way he wanted. Now the priests are going to run things around here." In addition, Harper was instructed to completely eliminate the budget for recruiting (or proselytizing, as it was known in those days) and he did.

Harper had lived under similar rules during his coaching years at

Notre Dame. In those years, university vice president Matthew Walsh, C.S.C., who would become Notre Dame's president from 1922 to 1928, had laid down a firm rule with Harper on recruiting. "There would be no free rides." However, jobs at the university in the kitchen and otherwise would be provided.

Hunk Anderson sounded a humorous note when he reflected, "The only money spent by coaches for proselytizing in Harper's day . . . was a quarter for a shot of booze in the pool hall while the coach looked over the clientele. If he found a 200-pounder who knew how to spell and sign his name, he was recruited."

One recruit that Harper had been unable to hang on to during his early days was Earl "Curly" Lambeau. Lambeau expressed a strong interest in attending Notre Dame, but noted to Harper that he was not too well fixed financially. Harper made it clear that if Lambeau was looking for a free ride, he would have to look elsewhere. Despite these restrictions, Harper recruited Lambeau, and Lambeau later played fullback next to halfback George Gipp on Rockne's first team in 1918. Lambeau was the only freshmen to win a letter that year. He left after the 1918 season and returned to his hometown of Green Bay, Wisconsin, where he was instrumental in starting the Green Bay Packers of the National Football League.

Through the years, the restraints or lack of restraints on recruiting would continue to be a problem, not only for Notre Dame but also for all major universities that maintained serious intercollegiate football programs. If they held too strictly to arbitrary rules, they could be guilty of eliminating worthy athletes from an education; being too liberal and having too few rules, they could, and sometimes did, create an unacceptable degree of corruption. The balancing act goes on to this day.

Meanwhile, the Great Depression was afflicting the country. From 1930 to 1935, approximately 21,000 American financial institutions failed, including 10,000 banks. By 1934 unemployment was at 25 percent and the gross domestic product had declined 30 percent from its high in 1929.

The shadow of the Great Depression did not miss the Ranch of the Alamos—Harper's $12,000-a-year salary from Notre Dame as athletic director was needed to save the ranch. In 1931, the ranch was mortgaged for twice its value. In addition, Harper and his father-in-law had an outstanding wheat loan for $56,000. A Kansas City banker advised Harper to let the local banks foreclose, at which point the bank would lend Harper the funds to buy everything back at 50 cents on the dollar. Harper, true to his character, recoiled at the suggestion, noting that he would never "dishonor" his father-in-law in such a way.

Nor did the Depression miss the Golden Dome. Notre Dame was cautiously hopeful that the record crowds seen in 1929 in Chicago and in other major venues would find their way to Notre Dame's new stadium in South Bend. Initially, they did not. Home game attendance in 1930, Rockne's last year, in which Notre Dame won its second consecutive national championship, was only 42 percent of capacity. The bright spot of the 1930 season was Notre Dame's final game of the year against Southern California at the Coliseum in Los Angeles, where 73,000 fans watched Notre Dame defeat Southern California, 27 to 0.

Nonetheless, at the outset of 1931, Notre Dame found itself in a stable financial condition. Enrollment remained steady, at approximately 3,200 students, and football proceeds for the previous year were solid. But by the end of the 1931 season, Harper's first year back at the helm as athletic director, football profits declined approximately 26 percent from their 1929 level, to $400,000.

The decline in football revenue came as a shock to the university administration, and their reaction was severe. As economic conditions worsened nationwide, the university harassed lay faculty members to pay their overdue accounts in the dining hall, student jobs were limited generally to athletes and to seniors, and more lay faculty experienced a jolt when the administration advised them that their contracts would not be renewed. Enrollment at the University for 1932–1933 would drop 14 percent, with virtually the entire student body of 2,780 residing on the campus. Enrollment for the 1933–1934 school year would decline ever further, though, by 1934–1935 it was turning upward.

As he had when he first became athletic director and head football coach in 1913, Harper went right to work on scheduling. One of his first new targets was Ohio State University. One newspaper soon reported, incorrectly, that the two schools had agreed to meet each other in 1933 and 1934. Another reported that the two schools had negotiated a postseason game to be played on December 5, 1931, in Cleveland, with the proceeds going to charity. Both reports cited Harper as the source, but he denied both.

Harper would, however, manage to schedule two games between Notre Dame and Ohio State, for 1935 and 1936. Then coached by Elmer Layden, one of Rockne's Four Horsemen, Notre Dame won both of those games. The 1935 game, held at Ohio State on November 2, would be hailed as "the greatest game of the century." Ohio State entered the game unbeaten and highly favored to win. The game was to be played in Columbus in front of a partisan crowd of 81,000. Notre Dame, led by halfback Andy Pilney, scored three touchdowns in the final period, and though they missed all three extra point attempts, the final touchdown, scored with fifty seconds remaining, gave them the win, 18–13. It was one of the greatest last-ditch rallies in football history, the victory added to the growing Notre Dame legend. An "almost miraculous victory," wrote Allison Danzig in the *New York Times*.

1931: The University of Southern California Travels to South Bend

What a day—until the sun began to set! The 1931 season ended with Notre Dame winning six, losing two and tying one.

Oct. 3	Indiana	25–0	Away
Oct. 10	Northwestern	0–0	Away
Oct. 17	Drake	63–0	Home
Oct. 24	Pittsburgh	25–12	Home
Oct. 31	Carnegie Tech	19–0	Away
Nov. 7	Pennsylvania	49–0	Home
Nov. 14	Navy	20–0	Neutral
Nov. 21	Southern California	14–16	Home
Nov. 28	Army	0–12	Yankee Stadium

Indiana

The Harper-Anderson era got off to a strong start before 22,000 fans in 80-degree heat in Bloomington, Indiana. On Friday before the game, the ghosts of Notre Dame made one of their first appearances, as Jack Ledden, sports editor of the *South Bend Tribune* could not help but observe that several changes had taken place at Notre Dame. He wrote, "Knute Rockne, greatest coach of them all, will not be here to add his colorful presence to the game. He will be watching the contest from the great beyond, with Gipp, his greatest player, at his side." Led by a strong running attack, Notre Dame won by a score of 25–0.

Herbert Hoover was president of the United States in 1931 and the front page of the *South Bend Tribune* told of Japan's bombing of Chinchow, Manchuria. The United States warned that if the League of Nations did not step in, the United States might. World War II was on the horizon.

Northwestern

The following Saturday Notre Dame traveled to Soldier Field in Chicago and in front of "seventy-five thousand rabid fans" saw their three-year unbeaten streak come to an end. In a driving rain on a muddy field, Northwestern succeeded in tying Notre Dame, 0–0. It was an omen of things to come. Without Rockne, the Notre Dame football program was going to suffer.

Drake and Pittsburgh

Drake proved to be nothing more than an organized warm-up for the Pittsburgh game. A home crowd of 30,000, including 15,000 children who were guests of the athletic department, witnessed the game, which Notre Dame won, 63–0.

Pittsburgh came into South Bend on Saturday October 24, 1931, with 7,000 fans and their university band in tow. In front of a home crowd of 38,000, Notre Dame secured a solid 25–12 victory. On the same day, the University of Chicago played Indiana University, in Chicago, in front of a crowd of 6,000. The University of Chicago would soon call an end to its intercollegiate football program.

Carnegie Tech, Pennsylvania, and Navy

These three opponents all fell with comparative ease, not one of them being able to score a point against Notre Dame.

Carnegie Tech fell by a score of 19 to 0 in Pitt Stadium before a crowd of 52,000. Rockne and his sudden death were still on the minds of the football world. In a touching ceremony before the start of the game, two Carnegie Tech buglers stood beneath opposite goalposts and blew "Taps" for Knute Rockne—the game was dedicated to his memory.

November 7 saw the University of Pennsylvania come to South Bend with 300 students and a 96-piece band. In front of 20,000 spectators, Notre Dame won, 49–0.

In Baltimore on November 14, Notre Dame defeated a stubborn Navy team by a score of 20 to 0. Marchy Schwartz was the star for Notre Dame.

Southern California—a Great Day in South Bend— Until the Sun Started to Set!

On November 21, 1931, Southern California made its first trip ever to South Bend. What a grand day it would be! The game would be played in Notre Dame's beautiful new stadium in front of a capacity crowd of 55,000, on a partly cloudy, unseasonably warm day, with a game-time temperature in the low 60s. The prospect of Southern California coming to South Bend had created a party atmosphere. The city went wild with excitement, and hotels in South Bend and the surrounding area were overflowing. In some of the leading hotels, large rooms were supplied with four, five, and six beds. Traffic to the stadium was in gridlock for two hours before the game, as some 8,200 cars descended upon Notre Dame—more cars than ever before had arrived on campus.

Anticipation for the game was at such a height that, in addition to the Southern California team, "Notables of Stage, Screen and Finance" came into town for the game. The box-seat section of the stadium was said to resemble a Broadway first night with celebrities and leaders of politics, society, radio, and big business gathering for this college football classic. Mayor Jimmy Walker of New York, with a party of friends, joined Anton J. Cermak of Chicago as guest of university president O'Donnell. Coming in from New York on the New York Central were Vincent Bendix, president of Bendix Aviation; Harvey Firestone, president of Firestone Tire & Rubber Co.; Mr. and Mrs. Anthony J. Drexel Biddle of New York and Philadelphia; George P. Marshall of Washington, D.C.; Mr. and Mrs. John Hearst of New York. Edsel Ford, of the Ford Motor Company, would attend, as would Charles Schwab, president of U.S. Steel; Paul Whiteman, the King of Jazz, and his wife, the former Mary Livingston; Freeman Gosden and Charles Coryell, the *Amos 'n Andy* radio show; motion picture magnate Jesse Lasky; radio star Morton Downey; and motion picture comedian Joe E. Brown. Also of note were R. B. Von Kleinschmidt, president of the University of Southern California, and Major John Griffith, commissioner of athletics for the Big Ten Conference. Altogether, it was a long way from the meager crowds that Harper first witnessed at Cartier Field in 1913.

What had Harper and Rockne wrought? The Notre Dame legend was in full bloom.

For the first three quarters of the game, Notre Dame halfback March-mont "Marchy" Schwartz ran the offense. The future College Football Hall of Famer from St. Stanislaus High School in New Orleans would be a unanimous first-team All-American selection at the end of the 1931 season. One writer speculated that if there had been a Heisman Trophy when Schwartz played, he would have won at least one. He would later go into coaching, first as an assistant at Notre Dame, then Chicago, and later as the head football coach at Creighton and Stanford.

Through three quarters, led by Schwartz, Notre Dame had dominated Southern California, and had broken out to a 14–0 lead. But in the fourth quarter. As Howard Jones's Southern California team mounted a comeback, Notre Dame coach Hunk Anderson, for reasons difficult to understand, made a series of fatal substitutions, pulling several of his first-string players, including Schwartz, from the game. The rules in place at that time provided that a player, once removed from the game, could not return until the next quarter of play, so pulling a player in the fourth quarter was, in effect, taking him permanently out of the game. Southern California scored twice in the fourth quarter, but missed one of their point-after attempts. As the game drew to a close, the score stood at Notre Dame 14, Southern California 13. But the depleted Notre Dame team, staffed with several of its second-string players, while many of the first-string players sat helplessly on the bench, was unable to mount any offense or sustain much if any defense against Southern California.

With the sun setting in the West and one minute left to play in the game, John Wilberforce Baker, "a big curly-headed kid" from Southern

California, kicked a twenty-four-yard field goal, making the score was Southern California 16, Notre Dame 14, and that's how the game ended.

Notre Dame's students and fans were stunned. Mayor Jimmy Walker of New York sat in the stands and cried. This loss would live in infamy, and Anderson would never be forgiven. Two years later, at the end of the 1933 season, he would be fired.

Army

A week later, in front of 80,000 fans in a "swirling snow storm" at Yankee Stadium, the U.S. Military Academy thoroughly dismantled Notre Dame. The final score, 12–0, did not reflect the complete dominance by the Army team. Army's scores came on two long plays, a fifty-eight-yard pass and a sixty-eight-yard end around. Notre Dame was never in the game. The Notre Dame team returned to South Bend at 9:30 the following Monday morning. Classes were delayed so that the entire student body could greet the team at the railway station—3,000 students, together with the university band, met the disappointed team on their return.

Edward "Moose" Krause—"Mr. Notre Dame"

For Harper, a personal highlight of 1931 was his first encounter with Edward "Moose" Krause. Krause was a 6-foot-3, 220-pound freshman tackle on Rockne's undefeated 1930 team. He would hold the position until 1934.

Krause played at De LaSalle High school in Chicago for Notre Dame grad Norm Barry, who always said Krause was the best player he'd coached and the best he'd ever sent down to Notre Dame. Krause was also an All-American basketball player three years in a row—the 1931–1932, 1932–1933, and 1933–1934 seasons—and was inducted into the College Basketball Hall of Fame in 1976. Perhaps Krause's most important contribution to Notre Dame, however, was his service as Notre Dame's athletic director from 1949 to 1981. Before his career at Notre Dame was finished, Krause had been given the title of "Mr. Notre Dame." He wore it proudly.

Harper and Krause became such close friends that Krause delivered the eulogy at Harper's funeral service in Kansas in 1961. Whenever Harper visited the Notre Dame campus in the years after his final departure from his service to Notre Dame in 1934, his first stop was always at Krause's office.

Building relationships came naturally to Krause, but the importance of those relationships in his role as athletic director was always reinforced by his friend Harper. One of the many, and perhaps surprising, ways this benefited Notre Dame was Krause's close friendship with Don Canham, who served as athletic director at the University of Michigan from 1968 to 1988. When Canham took the post in 1968, his first priority was to address the dwindling crowds at Michigan home football games. In 1967, he said, "We weren't drawing any people for football; we had 50,000 people in that damn stadium at the time." Canham quickly hired Bo Schembechler, who won games immediately. Canham then got in touch with his old friend, Moose Krause. He understood that one sure way to fill the stadium was to play Notre Dame. Notre Dame and Michigan had not met since 1943 when Notre Dame won, 35–12, and Michigan coach Fritz Crisler became so incensed at Frank Leahy's intensity that he never scheduled Notre Dame again. Krause and Canham sat down and worked out an agreement to renew the series. The series resumed in 1978 and, with brief breaks, continue to this day.

1932—Victory Over Army in New York

Oct. 8	Haskell	73–0	Home
Oct. 15	Drake	62–0	Home
Oct. 22	Carnegie Tech	42–0	Home
Oct. 29	Pittsburgh	0–12	Away
Nov. 5	Kansas	24–6	Away
Nov. 12	Northwestern	21–0	Home
Nov. 19	Navy	12–0	Cleveland
Nov. 26	Army	21–0	Yankee Stadium
Dec. 10	Southern California	0–13	Away

Haskell, Drake, and Carnegie Tech

The first three games of the 1932 season were at home and were admittedly against weak opponents. Notre Dame promptly shut out all three teams. Haskell fell 73 to 0; Drake, 62 to 0; and Carnegie Tech, 42 to 0. The next six games were against strong teams and the outcomes were dramatically different.

Pittsburgh

Notre Dame traveled to Pittsburgh for what was deemed to be the "hardest" game on the 1932 schedule. 65,000 fans witnessed a defensive struggle well into the last quarter, when, with the score tied at 0 to 0, Jock Sutherland's Pittsburgh team struck twice and came away victorious, 12–0. At game's end, the demoralized Notre Dame team was said to have had its "assurance and cohesion absolutely destroyed" by Pittsburgh's fourth-quarter surge.

Kansas, Northwestern, and Navy

Next, Notre Dame beat Kansas, 24–6, in Lawrence. In the following game, on November 12, Northwestern visited South Bend, only to be defeated, 21–0, in front of "38,000 fans who braved the bleak climatic conditions and sat in snow covered stands."

In Cleveland on November 19, in front of 70,000 fans who "braved a bitter wind and threat of snow" the Midshipmen of Navy put up a strong defense and held a highly favored Notre Dame squad to two scores in the second period, with the game ending in Notre Dame's favor, 12 to 0. The crowd was said to be the largest crowd to view a game in the Midwest that season.

The next morning, the report on the Navy game shared the front page of the *South Bend Tribune* with a story about a young German corporal named Adolf Hitler, who was engaged in a series of meetings with Field Marshall Paul Von Hindenburg, the president of Germany, to discuss how the two men might achieve a "better understanding."

Army and Southern California

Army at Yankee Stadium and Southern California in Los Angles would close out the 1932 season for Notre Dame.

On November 26, 1932, Notre Dame traveled to New York's Yankee Stadium to once again meet Army. Both teams came into the game with only one defeat, and for both that defeat had come at the hands of the University of Pittsburgh, who had defeated Army, 18–13, and Notre Dame, 12–0.

But November 26, 1932, was Notre Dame's day. Playing their best game of the season, in front of 80,000 spectators, who paid a total of close to $360,000 to sit in a "cold, raw November wind," the Notre Dame squad rolled over Army by a score of 21 to 0.

Next on the schedule, the final game of the season, would be nemesis Southern California, in Los Angeles. By 1932, the game had already "developed into one of the biggest drawing cards in intercollegiate sports."

On the Friday before the game, at a dinner for the coaches and athletic directors, it was announced that Jesse Harper had come to Los Angeles the previous day to sign an agreement extending the series between the two schools through the 1935 season.

Though Southern California had been generally "unimpressive throughout the season" they completely outplayed Notre Dame. Arch Ward's lead paragraph in the *South Bend Tribune* said it all: "Southern California today demonstrated to the satisfaction of 100,000 spectators that it has one of the finest football teams in the land. Capitalizing on their only two scoring opportunities, the Trojans defeated Notre Dame 13 to 0." It was Southern Cal's nineteenth win in a row, and a disappointing end to the season for Notre Dame, Anderson, and Harper.

1933—Disaster in the Form of Six Shutouts

Entering the 1933 season, Notre Dame was expected, according to preseason evaluations, to have one of the finest teams in the country. They won three games, lost five, and tied one. All five losses, as well as the tie, were shutouts. Someone would have to pay.

| Oct. 7 | Kansas | 0–0 | Home |
| Oct. 14 | Indiana | 12–2 | Away |

Oct. 21	Carnegie Tech	0–7	Away
Oct. 28	Pittsburgh	0–14	Home
Nov. 4	Navy	0–7	Baltimore
Nov.11	Purdue	0–19	Home
Nov. 18	Northwestern	7–0	Away
Nov. 25	Southern California	0–19	Home
Dec. 2	Army	13–12	Yankee Stadium

Kansas, Indiana

The University of Kansas traveled to South Bend on October 7, 1933, and for the first time in thirty-two years, Notre Dame failed to win the opening game. It ended in a scoreless tie. The game-day reporter observed Notre Dame to be "sluggish," "out fought and out played."

The next weekend, traveling to Bloomington, Notre Dame defeated Indiana, 12–2. 20,000 spectators viewed the game. It was the largest crowd in Bloomington since the Ohio State game of 1930.

Carnegie Tech, Pittsburgh, Navy, Purdue

Following the Indiana victory, the bottom fell out. Notre Dame was shut out in its next four games, losing to Carnegie Tech, 7–0; to Pittsburgh, 14–0; to Navy, 7–0; and finally to Purdue, 19–0. Though there were three games remaining on the schedule, it was clear that Hunk Anderson had a debacle on his hands.

Against Carnegie Tech, Notre Dame fumbled on the first play of the game. On the very next play, Carnegie Tech threw a twenty-seven-yard pass for a touchdown. After that, the game was reported as fairly even. But, the damage had been done and the loss secured.

Pittsburgh traveled to South Bend the following weekend along with 7,000 fans. It was the official student trip, and the train that carried the Pittsburgh students to South Bend also carried the Pittsburgh cheerleaders. The day before the game, Notre Dame's coach inexplicably said to the gathered sportswriters that Notre Dame would lose by two touchdowns. And, in front of a crowd of 38,000, that is exactly what they did. The final was 14–0. Jack Ledden, sports editor of the *South Bend Tribune,* wondered in his column about Notre Dame's "failure to display an offense."

Navy was next on the schedule, in a game to be played in Baltimore. This time coach Anderson wisely had "no comment to make on the outcome of the game." The Associated Press described Navy's 7–0 victory: "tonight there flashed the word to America's fighting ships and seamen everywhere that a six-year humiliation had been avenged, the Navy's honor satisfied." Accompanying the article on Navy's win was an article speculating on a successor to Anderson.

On Saturday, November 11, Purdue traveled to South Bend, and in front of 35,000 fans, thrashed the Irish 19 to 0. Their primary offensive scoring weapon was the forward pass. Purdue's coach was Noble Kizer, one of the "Seven Mules" who had opened holes for the Four Horsemen of Notre Dame in 1924. It was the fifth time during the 1933 season that Notre Dame had been held scoreless.

Northwestern, Southern California, Army

In an evenly fought contest in front of 40,000 spectators at Dyche Stadium in Evanston, Illinois, Notre Dame eked out a 7–0 win over Northwestern. The winning score came on an eleven-yard run late in the second period by sophomore sensation Andy Pilney. The play was set up when Moose Krause broke through the Northwestern line and blocked a punt.

Next up for Notre Dame was Southern California. It would be Southern California's second trip to South Bend, and the game was being billed as "one of the bitterest feuds of modern football history," a seemingly fair description. Southern California walked off with its third victory in a row over Notre Dame, winning by a score of 19 to 0. The *South Bend Tribune* sports editor remarked that: "Notre Dame was vastly out classed and never made a serious threat to score."

The finale to the 1933 season would pit Notre Dame against an undefeated Army team in Yankee Stadium, under cloudy skies and moderate temperatures, in front of 78,000 fans. Army was strong in 1933 and a heavy favorite in the game, which would be the nineteenth in the series. As the final quarter started, Notre Dame was trailing by a score of 12 to 0. Moose Krause blocked an Army punt, and Notre Dame exploded. Notre Dame took over possession at midfield, and Nichols Lukats made two successful runs, the second of which scored Notre Dame's first touchdown. A missed extra point made the score Army 12 to Notre Dame 6. Late in the fourth quarter, Notre Dame's Wayne Milner fell on a blocked punt in the end zone and the extra point made the score Notre Dame 13, Army 12. Sportswriters hailed the victory as the biggest upset of the 1933 season.

The Army win was an exciting and melodramatic victory for Notre Dame, but it was not enough to save jobs. With the 3–5–1 record, and the six shutouts, 1933 was promptly deemed the "most disastrous season" in the modern history of Notre Dame. A week later, both

Anderson and Harper turned in their resignations. Harper's long formal service to Notre Dame had come to an end.

"Harper formerly coached the Notre Dame football teams and was instrumental in making the Fighting Irish nationally known," *South Bend Tribune* sports editor Jack Ledden wrote. "It was under Harper's coaching that Rockne learned the game and he succeeded his teacher when Harper decided to retire. Upon Rockne's death, Harper was recalled."

During his term as athletic director from 1931 to 1933 Harper was credited with renewing and cementing Notre Dame's football contacts as well as making new contacts. He was referred to as the head of the Notre Dame diplomatic corps by Alan Gould, the sports editor for the Associated Press in New York. In an article written at some point in the middle of the 1933 football season, Gould noted that, with Harper's presence as athletic director, "It is fair to say that Notre Dame's relationships from coast to coast within the past three years have been strengthened and extended. Harper was instrumental, for example, in averting a threatened rupture between Army and Notre Dame growing out of some roughness in the game won by the Irish at Yankee Stadium last season, there were a few reverberations, but only those on the inside realized at the time how much feeling existed and how close these famous rivals were to going their separate ways." The athletic director at West Point told Gould in response, "We have every confidence in Harper. Our relations with Notre Dame have always been in the highest plane."

After his departure, Harper wrote to his friend Father John Cavanaugh, "I feel that some of the younger men do not realize that you laid the real foundation that made Notre Dame the great school it is today. You and Rockne made Notre Dame and very few people appreciate it as much as I do. Someday I hope to have a nice visit with you."

To replace Anderson and Harper, Notre Dame hired one of Harper's favorite people, the popular and talented Elmer Layden. Layden would serve in the dual capacity of athletic director and head football coach until 1940, when he would become commissioner of the National Football League. Some years later Harper remarked that: "Elmer Layden was a wonderful man. He was completely honest and extremely well liked by almost everybody in sports."

At 5-foot-11, 162 pounds, Layden was the outstanding fullback for Rockne's famous backfield, the Four Horsemen, the biggest and the fastest of the quartet. Yet Layden's greatest talent was his diplomacy, evidenced by his winning over three of Notre Dame's longtime, hard-line detractors. Layden succeeded in arranging for Stagg to bring his College of the Pacific football team to South Bend to play Notre Dame in the 1940 opener; Layden convinced coach Bob Zuppke of the University of Illinois to play a home and home series with Notre Dame beginning in 1937; and most amazingly, Layden wooed Michigan's Fielding Yost. Yost, a Notre Dame antagonist throughout his historic coaching career at Michigan, visited the Notre Dame campus in 1939 at Layden's invitation, and agreed to the scheduling of a home and home series to start in 1942—thus ending the hostilities between Michigan and Notre Dame that had begun in 1909.

14

Reflections

Harper was faced with several unique challenges when he served at Notre Dame. During his initial tenure, from 1913 to 1918, he was charged with bringing financial stability to a floundering football program. Accomplishing this required major changes in scheduling, which was a problem for Notre Dame in those years. There was a general bias against Notre Dame as a result of its strong showings in Midwest football—teams were not interested in adding Notre Dame to their schedule if it likely meant losing. Furthermore, Notre Dame's early scheduling efforts were hampered, to a degree, by latent anti-Catholicism. In the background were World War I and the historic influenza pandemic of 1917 and 1918—it was a tumultuous time.

When Harper returned to Notre Dame as athletic director in 1931, his term of service was marked by a new set of extraordinary challenges. First, Harper had to replace Knute Rockne, who by virtue of his success on the football field and his charismatic personality had become, by the time of his death, one of the most popular figures in America. Harper was not simply replacing a man who had moved on, he was replacing a legend. Harper understood full well the shoes he was being asked to step into. "I know I cannot take Rock's place," Harper said in an interview with the *Wichita Star* soon after his agreement to return to Notre Dame was announced. "No hundred men could do that and there can be no argument along that line, but I'm going back to do the best I can to carry on for Rock, to work out his plans, work out his visions." As Harper was returning to Notre Dame, America was starting to cope with the Great Depression. Harper was now faced with the dual tasks of keeping the Notre Dame football program and his family's cattle ranch financially afloat.

But Harper had a way with problems. He had faced them all of his life and always overcame them with his strong character and patience. "Jesse had a special gift for working out difficult problems," his wife, Melville, wrote after Harper's death in 1961. "He had shown this ability while associated with Notre Dame. It took a good many years of patience, persistence, integrity and wise planning. It was a happy day for the Harper family when the 'Mortgages' were burned and all indebtedness was cleared." She knew her husband well.

Scheduling and Finances at Notre Dame

When Harper took over in 1913, Notre Dame's football program had been operating in the red. Though the team went undefeated during the

1911 and 1912 season, Notre Dame's list of available opponents was lean, and as a result the financial outlook was bleak—the team lost $2,400 and $500, respectively, in those seasons. Those losses are not large by today's standards, but they were daunting to a small Catholic men's school that was struggling financially in the early years of the twentieth century. The Notre Dame administration was taking a hard look at the school's continued participation in big-time college football.

The primary reason for Notre Dame's scheduling difficulties was that Notre Dame had been blackballed by the Big Nine schools, the major football-playing institutions in the Midwest, and had been forced to schedule minor opponents such as Saint Viator and Adrian. These opponents brought with them two related problems: they were unable to offer rewarding competition on the football field, and the lack of fair competition failed to attract the interest of paying customers. The resulting financial losses were inevitable. It was evident to Harper that successful economics were tied directly to a strong schedule of opponents. The goal for Harper was clear, and he pursued it relentlessly.

Despite Harper's efforts to crack into the Big Nine, only once during his coaching years, 1913–1918, were Harper's efforts successful—when he was able to schedule a game with Wisconsin in 1917.

As early as 1908, Notre Dame had applied for membership in the Big Nine, only to have its application denied. Harper tried again at the end of his first year at Notre Dame. At the 1913 annual conference, the Big Nine, led by the University of Chicago and the University of Minnesota, rejected Notre Dame's application. At the time, the University of Michigan was not a member of the Big Nine, having withdrawn in 1907 over a dispute concerning eligibility. But Michigan would join the conference again in 1918, when, led by head football coach Fielding Yost, they promptly spearheaded the conference's opposition to Notre Dame's membership. The Big Nine charged that Notre Dame lacked faculty control and systematically cheated in academics, but many sportswriters perceived the Big Nine's charges to be dishonest. "In fact, Notre Dame ran a cleaner athletic program than most of their schools." Several writers of that day attributed the turndown to Notre Dame's athletic success. Father Matthew Walsh, C.S.C., soon to be Notre Dame's president, attributed the rejection to "religious prejudice."

Murray Sperber believes that the Big Nine's repudiation in 1913 was the most significant event in Notre Dame's early development as a football power. He writes, "Again, at a crucial juncture in the creation of Notre Dame football, a rejection by the Western Conference forced the Catholic institution to remain independent and to look beyond its geographic region. In 1913, the veto by the Big Nine determined the future national character of Notre Dame football and was more significant than the victory at West Point."

In 1926, Rockne, with Harper's advice and counseling, made a major effort to join the Big Nine conference. He toured various Big Nine institutions and spoke with well-placed representatives in each school. In order to countermand the prevailing negative attitude toward their program, Notre Dame offered to open its records to the Big Nine, formally requesting that the Big Nine send a committee to investigate Notre Dame's academic and athletic programs. The Big Nine officials declined and again turned Notre Dame's application aside. Their decision was based on "misperception, not reality." "They chose to believe the rumors," Sperber wrote. "Their acceptance of anti–Notre Dame gossip was reprehensible."

Nevertheless, over Harper's five years as head coach, Notre Dame took gross receipts from football from the $3,800 range in 1913 to a high of $16,600 in 1916. After the restrictions of World War I set in, profits for 1917 fell somewhat, but a profit was still made. More importantly, Harper's efforts had laid out a winning financial road map for his successor, Knute Rockne—if Notre Dame could field a competitive football team, there was money to be made in games against major opponents in major metropolitan areas. In 1925 the Notre Dame–Army game in Yankee Stadium drew 70,000 fans, with gate receipts estimated to have exceeded $250,000. Notre Dame's share was approximately $72,000. Things had come a long way from the $154.50 that Harper brought home to the university after the 1913 game, just as Harper had predicted they eventually would. Of course, one of the key ingredients in the formula was a "competitive football team," and Rockne, as the greatest coach of his era and arguably the greatest of any era, supplied that essential ingredient.

Anti-Catholicism Seeps into the Picture

The issue of anti-Catholicism during Harper's years at Notre Dame was real, and it was well understood by the fathers of the Holy Cross who ran Notre Dame. The existence of anti-Catholicism can reasonably be assumed to have been one of the reasons that Notre Dame selected Harper, a well-connected Protestant, to head their fledging football program. They were dealing in a Protestant environment, and it was reasonable for them to speculate that a Protestant would be more acceptable and better able to navigate such an environment than a Roman Catholic.

Though unpleasant, the anti-Catholic sentiment in the early years of the twentieth century was, in a way of speaking, a logical extension of our nation's roots. America's founders were predominantly Protestants, from Great Britain, and they brought with them to this new nation the legacy of the Protestant Reformation, which began in England and Europe in the early 1500s. As one historian notes, a "universal anti-Catholic bias was brought to Jamestown in 1607 and vigorously culti-vated in all the thirteen colonies." Nothing in the early days of our country, it was noted, could bring Anglican ministers and Puritan divines together faster than their common hatred of the Church of Rome. The author Andrew Greeley has said that anti-Catholicism remains as one of the ugly little secrets of American history.

Also at work on the American psyche during the early twentieth cen-tury was the specter of new immigrants flooding into the United States. Between 1900 and 1920, some 14 million immigrants entered the United States, and the great majority were Irish, Italian, Polish, Hungarian, Czech, Slovak, and Croatian—most of them Catholic. Notre Dame's vic-tory over Army on November 1, 1913, brought Notre Dame to the atten-tion of the entire country, especially to the attention of the nation's new immigrant population. Bursting with ethnic and religious pride, many adopted Notre Dame as their school. As the author and Notre Dame his-torian Robert E. Burns put it, "The university had achieved an enormous public relations triumph. Everyone in the country would know about the football heroics of the team from Notre Dame. Most important of all, American Catholic pride in this single athletic victory was unbounded. In an afternoon the university had acquired intense emotional commitments from a whole generation of Catholic working-class supporters and defenders that would endure for years."

Though prejudice in any form is repugnant, it is not difficult to imagine how the coming of these immigrant groups sparked a resurgence of anti-Catholicism in the United States. In 1915, the Ku Klux Klan was resurrected. The heart of the Ku Klux Klan may have been in the South, but the Klan was strong in Indiana. In the mid-1920s, in an environment described by the historian and author Todd Tucker in *Notre Dame vs. The Klan,* students from the University of Notre Dame actually engaged in a pitched battle with the Klan on the streets of South Bend, Indiana.

Harper has not left us with a clear statement of his personal view of anti-Catholicism, but we can surmise that he had absolutely no tolerance for such thinking. While Harper was coaching the Wabash baseball team, facing Notre Dame, a Wabash baseball player, R. B. "Ted" Williams, as Williams himself recalled years later, yelled to the Wabash pitcher, "Put the Holy Water on it, Harry." Harper walked up to his young player and said firmly, "Do not say that again." That was the end of that line of heckling.

"Dad was not a particularly religious man," Harper's son Jim remembered. But Jim also noted that his father, without fail, accompanied his Notre Dame team to their traditional Catholic Mass before every Notre Dame football game.

One of Harper's favorite memories of Notre Dame was the attitude toward religion that prevailed among the men on campus, both the students and the administrators. "I was head coach there five years," Harper told a sportswriter for the *Topeka Daily Capital* in a July 1955 interview, "and four of my football captains, elected by the squad, were Protestants. The religious belief of a man never was important. It never was an issue, or even a point of discussion. At Notre Dame, they take a man for what he is." Interestingly enough, despite the fact that Notre Dame is a deeply Catholic institution, it has always had an ecumenical inclination. As Joe Doyle likes to point out, the great Ohio State victory of 1935 was sealed in the last minute of play by a Protestant, Bill Shakespeare, throwing the winning pass to his Jewish teammate, Wayne Milner.

Harper's Honors

Though Harper's career in football has been relatively unsung, he did garner a number of impressive honors during his lifetime, related both to his athletic and coaching activities and his business activities.

While a student at the University of Chicago, Harper was elected captain of the school's baseball team. Harper's next commendations came from his ranching activities. In 1931, he was elected as president of the Kansas Livestock Association; later, he was inducted into the Kansas Cattlemen's Hall of Fame. During the 1930s, he was elected as a member of the Executive Committee of the American National Cattlemen's Association; Harper and his friend Cal Floyd were the first members on that Executive Committee from Kansas. Harper was elected to the National Cowboy Hall of Fame and Western Heritage Center in Oklahoma City in 1964.

Finally, in 1958, Harper's achievements in football began to be recognized. He received the Helms Award at Notre Dame in 1958 and was honored at halftime of the 1958 Notre Dame–Army game in South Bend. The night before the game, in the old Notre Dame Field House, Harper was made an honorary member of the Notre Dame Monogram Club. Harper's son Jim accompanied his father and recalls that it was only the second time he had ever seen his Dad cry. The first time, Jim recalls, was when Harper was waving good-bye to Jim as Jim's troop train pulled out of the station in Denver, carrying Jim to duty in the Air Force shortly after the United States had entered World War II. Harper was also elected to the Wabash College Athletic Hall of Fame and named an honorary member of the Wabash College Class of 1913. In 1971, Harper was elected to the College Football Hall of Fame.

Taking into account only their years spent coaching at the University of Notre Dame, Harper has the second best win-loss record in Notre Dame history. His record is surpassed only by the mark set by his protégé, Knute Rockne. Six of Harper's players have been inducted into the College Football Hall of Fame as coaches: Edward "Slip" Madigan, Jim Phelan, Charlie Bachman, Gus Dorais, Harry Baujan, and Knute Rockne. Along the way, Harper mentored Knute Rockne and almost was single-handedly responsible for Rockne becoming the head football coach at Notre Dame in 1918.

Through all the years, Harper was held in high esteem by the Notre Dame administration. Father J. Hugh O'Donnell, C.S.C., who, as a young student at Notre Dame had played center for Harper on the 1915 Notre Dame football team, wrote to Harper years later: "Let me hear from you, Jesse, when you find time. I would appreciate also having your frank opinion on any matter relating to the athletic side of the University. I value your opinion just as high now as I always did in the past. Your stay here has left an indelible impression for good on the University. As a pioneer, you contributed greatly to the stabilizing of athletics at Notre Dame, and you builded [sic] well for the future. Always remember that Notre Dame cherishes you as one of its most loyal friends and benefactors. Yours as ever."

Harper left Notre Dame in 1934, and received a letter dated February 7, 1934, from his old friend Father John Cavanaugh thanking him for "the great service you rendered Notre Dame all the years of your life here . . . you and Mrs. Harper will always have your secure place in my remembrance and affection. Your devoted friend."

Army 1913

The high-water mark in Harper's career was, without a doubt, Notre Dame's victory at West Point on November 1, 1913. It was truly the game that changed football. It set the stage for all of Notre Dame's multiple and future successes, both on the football field and off. The author and Notre Dame football historian Ken Rappoport said it well: "With all of Harper's innovations, it is quite possible that Notre Dame would never have gained its present euphorious status without the 1913 Army game. Without a doubt, getting the Cadets on the Notre Dame schedule was Harper's most strategic move. And beating them was his greatest triumph."

In 2000, to celebrate the turn of the millennium, ESPN prepared a ranking entitled the "Greatest Coaching Decisions of the Twentieth Century." The ranking covered all sports, collegiate and professional. Harper's decision to use the forward pass against Army in 1913 was selected as the sixth-greatest coaching decision of the twentieth century, in any sport, and the number-one coaching decision of the twentieth century in college football. Years later Harper himself recalled his decision that day: "We played a helluva game. At the half we were ahead by 14 to 13, but I was afraid it couldn't last. We had thrown only a couple of passes, and they weren't worth much. I told Gus to start throwing and keep throwing. We figured it was the best chance we had. . . . He went out in the second half and threw thirteen straight passes, most of 'em to Rockne. . . . We just kicked hell out of 'em."

As the years passed, football historians reflected on the importance of the 1913 victory over Army. In 1992, Wiley Lee Umphlett, an author and historian, placed the 1913 Notre Dame–Army game in perspective with the following words: "The most startling achievement of 1913 . . . was produced by a then little-known college in Indiana called Notre Dame. When it went east and defeated Army, 35–13, for the Cadets' only loss that year, the little Catholic school demonstrated the devastating potential of the forward pass, which even by this time was still a little-used weapon. . . . To be sure, the modern day of the forward pass had now arrived."

The University of Notre Dame—100 Years Later

Despite its austere birth; despite the great fire of 1879; despite the constant lack of finances and despite the existence of institutional and religious prejudice, Notre Dame flourished. Almost a century after Harper first stepped on to the campus of the University of "Our Lady," Notre Dame stands at the pinnacle of college football.

In 2005, ESPN published a tome titled *The Comprehensive History of College Football.* The Notre Dame section begins: "Every sport needs its kings. Kings define excellence and provide a standard for everyone else in the sport to measure themselves against. They are loved and hated, respected and feared, revered and reviled. They are royalty, regardless of the year, regardless of the era. Baseball has the Yankees, pro basketball the Celtics, pro hockey the Canadiens. And college football has Notre Dame."

A headline in the sports section of the *New York Times* in November of 2006 read: "In College Football, the Pinstripes Belong to Notre Dame." After reviewing the origins of the "Notre Dame mystique" the writer quoted the commissioner of the Big East Conference: "They are the New York Yankees of college football, and you either love them or hate them, but everyone cares." There are other storied programs in college football, but none has matched the sheer drawing power of Notre Dame. In 1990, NBC signed an agreement to nationally broadcast all Notre Dame home games—an agreement that pays Notre Dame $9 million a year through 2010. In 1998, when the Bowl Championship Series was implemented, Notre Dame was given the same weight as a major conference school. Of the 250 college athletic sites in the CSTV fold, Notre Dame set a record in the fall of 2006 with 7.8 million page views in one month, 42 percent higher than the second-place site.

In the years since Harper first arrived at the university, the Notre Dame football team has won eleven national championships and has produced seven Heisman Trophy winners. No other school has more. In addition, they have produced 178 All-Americans and thirty-one unanimous first-team All-Americans, both more than any other school. Five former Notre Dame coaches, including Harper, have been elected to the College Football Hall of Fame. The lifetime winning percentages of Rockne (.881) and Frank Leahy (.855) remain the two highest in Division I college football history. In recent years, Notre Dame has traded places with the University of Michigan on an almost weekly basis during the football season, as the team with the highest winning percentage in the history of college football—the two teams on any given game-day Saturday are within hundredths of a percentage point of each other.

Through all of its accomplishments on the football field, the University of Notre Dame has, more than any other institution of higher learning, recognized and confronted the classic challenge of balancing athletic achievement with academic excellence. Their quest is unending, but their current overall graduation rate of 98.7 percent among their football players, based on those who enter on scholarship and remain at least four years, is a manifestation of the success of their efforts in this regard.

To say that Harper was the man responsible for Notre Dame's many successes in football through the past century would be an overstatement. However, to say that Harper was there at the beginning and that he had a strong influence on Notre Dame's successes and the development of its athletic character would seem fair. As one Notre Dame historian put it, "It was Jesse Harper who set the table for Knute Rockne and the creation of America's most famous and legendary team." And, years after Harper had left Notre Dame in 1918, Rockne himself said of Harper, "When I'm gone I hope this will be remembered. It's Jesse Harper's system—what he began at Notre Dame, I have only followed."

Harper's Funeral in Kansas

Harper passed away on July 31, 1961, at his ranch in Sitka, Kansas, at age seventy-seven. The cause was heart failure. One of Harper's obituaries noted that he was descended, on his father's side, from the Scots families of Kirk and Irwin and on his mother's side from the Congraves of Leicestershire, England. In closing, the obituary noted that Harper was "a Republican" and "a member of the Rotary Club and the Wichita Country Club. His favorite sport is football."

He was survived by his widow, Melville, two sons, Mell and Jim, and a daughter, Katherine. Harper was buried in Ashland Cemetery, three miles east of Ashland, Kansas. The cemetery is described by Harper's son Jim as being akin to an unkempt horse pasture. Today, Jesse's wife, Melville, and his son Mell and his daughter Katherine are buried there with him.

There were no services. That was Harper's request. At the grave site, however, just as her husband was to be lowered into the earth, Mrs. Harper stepped forward and said: "As most of you know, Jesse was not a man of religion. He didn't want any formal funeral service, but in his lifetime, he dearly loved a very religious school, Notre Dame, where we twice spent some enjoyable years.

"Notre Dame has sent two representatives, Mr. [Ed Moose] Krause and Mr. [Herb] Jones, [Notre Dame business manager], to his funeral. And even though Jesse may not have wanted it, I would ask Mr. Krause if he would say a few words." Also present was Joe La Fortune, of Tulsa, Oklahoma, the chairman of Notre Dame's Board of Regents.

Moose spoke: "He was a person who played hard. He wanted to win, but when he did, he never gloated, and when he lost, he never whined. He just went back the next week and played harder." Moose then recited the following poem:

Let me live, O Mighty Master, such a life as I should know.
Testing triumph and disaster, joy and not too much of woe.
Let me run the gamut over, let me live and love and laugh,
And when I am beneath the clover, let this be my epitaph:
Here lies one who took his chances in a busy world of men.

Battled life and circumstances, fought and fell and fought again
Won some times but did not wail, lost some times but did not fail
Took his beating, but kept on going, never let his courage sail.
He was fallible and human, therefore loved and understood
Both his fellow men and women, whether good or not so good
Kept his spirit undiminished, never laid down on a friend
Played the game 'til it was finished, lived a Spartan to the end.

Jim Harper recalls the day well and remembers Moose shedding tears as he delivered his eulogy to his longtime friend. "It was heartrending to see that big man standing there with tears streaming down his face. They were very, very close. Dad had some tremendous friends at Notre Dame."

Shortly after he returned to Notre Dame after Harper's funeral, Krause wrote to Harper's widow, Melville, sending her the words to the poem he had recited at Harper's funeral service and concluding his letter with the following lines:

"As I tried to say in my faltering way at the services, Jesse has become a great part of the history of our fine University. He had a plan in developing Notre Dame in the years when Notre Dame needed the courage and foresight of pioneers. . . . Notre Dame became nationally known because of Jesse's strong desire to 'put Notre Dame on the map,' as he so often said. His return to Notre Dame after the tragic death of Knute Rockne, his protégé, will never be forgotten too. It was then again when we needed guidance to go over the rough spots."

There is an inscription on the Edmund P. Joyce Athletic and Convocation Center at the University of Notre Dame that reads: "So much owed to so many." It's an insightful inscription and Jesse Claire Harper certainly qualifies to be included in the group of the many to whom Notre Dame owes so much.

Afterword

Notre Dame football historians, or those who dabble in Irish trivia, cite Jesse Claire Harper as Notre Dame's only full-time coach to start his career with a perfect season.

They will tell you, too, that Harper brought Notre Dame in "the big time" when he arranged the Army game of 1913. And that his team's passing attack to win that game forever changed the impressions of the sport.

Of the thirteen full-time successors (and two listed as interim), not one can match the 7–0–0 record of Harper's 1913 opening year. Only Frank Leahy in 1941 (8–0–1) comes close. And only Rockne (.881) exceeds the winning percentage (.863) of the 1913–1917 career of Harper.

The accomplishments of Jesse Harper at Notre Dame are much more than the football victories.

Notre Dame sought him out when he was the Wabash coach for several reasons. At a speech in Indianapolis one time, a very interested Notre Dame alumnus heard Harper say "college football should pay its own way with gate receipts from its fans."

At the time, a sign outside the Notre Dame ticket booth read "admission 25 cents." The school was playing mostly home games, and as a result, football was a costly and losing proposition. (That was ninety-five years ago, and things have changed since then. Notre Dame took a page from Harper's book, and now the face value of home tickets is $62.)

When I first met Jesse on the Notre Dame practice field early in the 1950s, I was impressed, not as much with his interest and knowledge of a game he had coached for almost forty years, but with his candor and friendliness to a writer he had just met.

I was instantly taken with his pointed observations of the formations and players working with various coaches at all areas of the field. And when I accompanied him to visit some old acquaintances on campus, I sensed that Harper may have left Notre Dame in 1918 and again in 1934, but he was still very aware of what went on at the university he loved.

One of the acquaintances he always sought out was Reverend Matthew Walsh, C.S.C., who had been his supervisor and confidant in his early years, and later president of Notre Dame. And each time he visited the campus, he met with Father Walsh, a strange but sincere relationship between a Catholic priest and a man who professed no religion.

Father Walsh was the administration's "point man" over athletics in Harper's days. At the time Harper was ready to leave Notre Dame to help manage his father-in-law's vast ranch in Kansas, Father Walsh was preparing to enter military service as a chaplain, but wanted to take part in the decision to hire a new football coach.

Father Walsh, and Harper, too, wanted Rockne to take over. After a little persuasion, the university agreed. And now you know the rest of the story.

Jesse Harper was no ordinary man. In his early life and then again in his last three decades, he was a man of the soil, a farmer and rancher, who became enamored of the game of football. And through that sport, he became known, not only at schools where he coached, but across the wide spectrum of college football.

Harper, perhaps better in baseball than in football, eagerly learned the sport from the greatest of all teachers, Amos Alonzo Stagg, generally referred to as "the Grand Old Man of Football." Harper himself, and surely his famed successor Knute Rockne, many times insisted that almost everything in football originated with Stagg.

Lon Stagg cut such a long swath across the game that he was still coaching at the age of ninety-six, more than twenty years after he was cast aside by the University of Chicago as "being too old for the game."

Harper followed football across his lifetime, but was directly involved as a coach for less than a dozen years. But what a career it was!

The game had progressed from its brutish and brutal running game to a more wide-open game that would feature the pass. And Harper was one of the instigators and innovators who changed the game.

You can read all this in this book, and the College Football Hall of Fame named Harper as one of the honored coaches.

Harper left more than a football legacy for Notre Dame teams of the ages. His lasting legacy reflected many great accomplishments, some of them vital to college football's outstanding program:

- He recommended (some administrators said that he demanded) that Knute Rockne become the new coach and athletic director in 1918.
- When he returned as athletic director on the death of Rockne, he immediately insisted that (1) all athletes be full-time students in good academic standing with a percentile average of 77, (2) no transfer athletes would be permitted, and (3) money used to recruit athletes away from campus would be ended.
- He made sure that academics always would be emphasized over athletics.
- He resolved that athletic opponents would be considered friendly rivals, and not the enemy, as many coaches, players, and particularly supporters seemed to insist.
- And, of course, he insisted that the sport pay its own way.

His greatest move might have been when he hired a graduate chemistry geek to become his assistant coach. Harper never regretted that move and neither did Notre Dame. It formed a relationship that has produced college football's greatest program.

—Joe Doyle
Sports Editor, *South Bend Tribune*

Notes

Introduction
For an excellent discussion of the origin of the "Fighting Irish" nickname, see, Sperber, *Shake Down the Thunder*, 79–83.

1 | A University Is Born on the Frontier
14   In 1680: Hope, *Notre Dame: One Hundred Years*, 37. This book is used as a source for background material throughout Chapter 1.

14   *At some future date:* ibid., 50–52.

15   In 1842: ibid., 50–52.

15   That winter: ibid., 55.

15   Alexis Coquillard: ibid., 1.

17   Construction of: ibid., 216–218.

17   Notre Dame was growing: ibid., 183–188, re: the fire of 1879.

18   Within three hours: ibid., 184.

2 | A History of the Early Game, 1869–1905
23   *During these first years:* Bernstein, *Football: The Ivy League Origins of an American Obsession*, Preface.

23   *The first recorded:* ibid., 6–8.
24   *In 1874:* Danzig, *The History of American Football,* 9–10; and Umphlett, *Creating the Big Game,* 5–7.
27   *Camp was born:* Watterson, College Football, 20.
27   In 1880: Source and background on Camp and Yale during these years: Danzig, *The History of American Football,* 14–17; Watterson, *College Football,* 18–23; and Bernstein, *Football: The Ivy League Origins of an American Obsession,* 12–23.
28   *As dramatic as:* Umphlett, *Creating the Big Game,* 14.
29   *"We had no helmets":* ibid., 21.
29   *To facilitate this:* ibid., 23.
29   *The line play:* ibid., 22–23.
31   *Football had always:* Source and background material from the following histories of the game of football: Kaye, *Good Clean Violence;* Danzig, *The History of American Football;* Watterson, *College Football;* Bernstein, *Football: The Ivy League Origins of an American Obsession;* Danzig, *Oh, How they Played the Game;* and Umphlett, *Creating the Big Game.*
32   *During these early years:* Hope, *Notre Dame: One Hundred Years,* 176.
32   *Father Corby:* ibid., 192.
32   *Football at the University:* ibid., 241–248 and Rappoport, *Wake up the Echoes,* 11–14.
35   *Notre Dame's 1908:* Source and background material for the early history of Notre Dame football: Rappoport, *Wake up the Echoes,* 11–33; and Grant, *Before Rockne at Notre Dame.*
35   *By the start of:* Source and background for the 1909 Michigan game and the 1910 Michigan cancellation: Rappoport, *Wake up the Echoes,* 34–37; Grant, *Before Rockne at Notre Dame,* 127–167; and Sperber, *Shake Down the Thunder,* 30–33.
38   *Notre Dame's student newspaper: The Notre Dame Scholastic,* December 13, 1913, 373–375.
39   *$500.00 in 1912:* Sperber, *Shake Down the Thunder,* 34–35.

3 | Injuries and Death Lead to a Crisis, 1906–1913

41   *Michael Burke:* The list of names is long. The ones selected above for purposes of example were all reported in the New York Times as follows: Moore, November 29, 1905; Saussy, November 12, 1893; and O'Brien, November 24, 1893.
42   *"The number of deaths":* New York Times, November 29, 1905.
44   *Roosevelt's conference:* Kelley, "Evolution of the Rules of Intercollegiate Football," 203–220
46   *At the time of the New York:* The negotiations between the group led by Camp and the Harvard group and Harvard's ultimate leadership on resolving the issues then facing football are detailed in Smith, "Harvard and Columbia and a Reconsideration of the 1905–1906 Football Crisis."
49   *In April 1906:* Camp, *Spalding's Official Football Guide:* 1906.
50   *"the opposing forwards":* New York Times, September 30, 1906; and Camp, Collier's Magazine, October 20, 1906.
50   *Notwithstanding Camp's:* New York Times, August 12, 1906.

50   *ignored the pass: New York Times,* September 30, 1906; and Camp, *Collier's Magazine,* October 20, 1906.

51   *The Forward Pass:* Source and background material for Chapter 1: Danzig, *The History of American Football;* Danzig, *Oh, How they Played the Game;* and Umphlett, *Creating the Big Game.*

52   *Heisman never forgot:* Danzig, *The History of American Football,* 33.

53   *Carroll College:* Brian Kunderman, "Football's Forward Pass Turns 100 Years Old," SLU Newslink: The Inside Guide to Saint Louis University: September 1, 2006, http://www.slu.edu/readstory/newslink/7166, (accessed September 25, 2006).

53   *Knute Rockne credits:* Danzig, *The History of American Football,* 35.

56   *"At that time the ball":* ibid., 40–41.

57   *Two weeks later: New York Times,* October 31, 1909.

57   *The deaths of:* Cadet Byrne's injuries were reported in the *New York Times* on October 31, 1909, and his death in the *New York Times* on November 1, 1909. Midshipman Wilson's injuries were reported in the *New York Times* on October 18, 1909, and his death in the *New York Times* on April 7, 1910.

57   *Nineteen-year-old: New York Times,* November 14, 1910.

59   *The results were:* Camp, *Spalding's Official Football Guide: 1910.*

61   *Perhaps the most important:* Kelley, "Evolution of the Rules of Intercollegiate Football," 321–323; and Camp, *Spalding's Official Football Guide: 1912.*

4 | Jesse Harper Before Notre Dame

65   *"We lived in Iowa": Chicago Tribune,* article on Harper, November 16, 1913; Dick Snider, "On Sports," *Topeka Daily Capital,* July 6, 1955; and Melville H. Harper, handwritten biography of Jesse C. Harper, 1961, Jim Harper private collection.

66   *Chicago's 1905 gridiron:* Lester, *Stagg's University: The Rise, Decline and Fall of Big-Time Football at Chicago,* 67–69; *The University of Chicago Magazine,* October 1995; and "Art of Football," Bentley Historical Library, University of Michigan Athletics History, September 1, 2001, http://bentley.umich.edu/athdept/football/fbart/aofchic.htm, (accessed October 29, 2006).

67   *At Chicago, Harper: Chicago Tribune,* article on Harper, November 16, 1913.

70   *After leaving College:* Power, *Story of Amos Alonzo Stagg: Grand Old Man of Football,* 6–8.

70   *Years later, Rockne said:* Danzig, *The History of American Football,* 61.

71   *"great character builder":* Dick Snider, "On Sports," *Topeka Daily Capital,* July 5, 1955.

71   *Stagg had nothing:* Amos Alonzo Stagg, to J. C. Hardy, president of Mississippi Agricultural and Mechanical College, (now Mississippi State University), 8 January 1906, University of Chicago Library.

71   *Mr. Harper is:* Amos Alonzo Stagg, to J. C. Hardy, president of Mississippi Agricultural and Mechanical College (now Mississippi State University), April 7, 1907, University of Chicago Library.

72   *After graduating:* Amos Alonzo Stagg to Professor H. B. Patton, Colorado School of Mines, March 16, 1909, University of Chicago Library.

72   *Reflecting on Harper's: The Almanian,* October 1906.

72   *Young Harper:* In Harper's day Michigan State was known as Michigan Agricultural College. The school went through several name changes until 1964, when it became Michigan State University.

72   *Hillsdale and Olivet: The Almanian,* December 1906.

72   *Two close games lost: The Almanian,* September 1907.

73   *The game, which ended: The Alma Record,* November 27, 1907.

73   *"instilled a spirit": The Almanian,* June 1907.

74   *Stagg wrote:* Amos Alonzo Stagg to Professor H. B. Patton, Colorado School of Mines, March 16, 1909, University of Chicago Library.

74   *Wabash College: The Wabash,* January 1910.

75   *The highlight of the: The Wabash,* November 1909.

75   *Wabash finished:* ibid.

75   *"sanguine dreams": The Bachelor,* December 15, 1909.

76   *"Wabash was fortunate":* The Bachelor, December 2, 1909.

76   *"The hard Purdue":* ibid.

76   *Harper's first year:* The quote and the entire paragraph are found at *The Bachelor,* December 2, 1909.

76   *Harper's 1910: The Wabash,* November 1910.

77   *The year 1911:* quote from *The Wabash,* April 1911; also facts from *The Bachelor,* September 28, 1911.

79   *"dozen full teams": The Wabash,* October 1911 and November 1911.

79   *Harper certainly had: The Wabash,* November 1911.

79   *The game was billed: The Bachelor,* October 23, 1912.

80   *"had an exceptionally strong": The Bachelor,* October 23, 191.

80   *"far superior to us": The Wabash,* December 1912.

80   *"Too much cannot be said": The Wabash,* November 1912.

80   *In a 1911 article:* Leland L. Rowe, Wabash Class of 1915, letter to the editor, *The Wabash College Magazine,* Spring 1979.

81   Harper showed: The Wabash, December 1911.

81   At the end of his article: ibid.

5 | Jesse Harper's First Year at Notre Dame, 1913

85   *By the time he arrived:* ibid., 86–88.

86   *NCAA: Blue & Gold Illustrated,* October 9, 2006, citing September 27, 2006 NCAA report on graduation rates.

87   *Dan I. Sultan:* Lt. General Dan I. Sultan, interview by Staff Sgt. Art Heenan, as reported in his column "Sports Roundup," publication unknown, 1946.

88   *$154.50 from the game:* Harper expense report for the 1913 Army game, Hesburgh Library.

89   *totaling $4,311.00:* Harper expense reports for 1914 season, Hesburgh Library.

89   *"Jesse Harper":* Kent Stephens (historian and archivist, College Football Hall of Fame), letter to author, February 27, 2006.

90   *Combination: The Wichita Beacon–Town Crier,* Sunday Magazine Section, (undated, circa 1928).

90   *Rockne a coach:* ibid.

92   *Notre Dame's first game:* All quotes from the *South Bend Tribune,* October 3, 4, and 6, 1913.

94   *In a hard-fought:* All quotes from the *South Bend Tribune,* October 17, 18, and 20, 1913.

94   *Penn State and Army: South Bend Tribune,* October 24, 1913.

95   *Dimick's grave: South Bend Tribune,* October 28, 1913.

6 | The Game That Changed Football: Notre Dame vs. Army, November 1, 1913

97   *Schultz: South Bend News-Times,* November 1, 1913.

98   *"No prospects": South Bend Tribune,* October 29, 1913.

98   *fighting spirit:* ibid.

98   *Life and death:* ibid.

102   *"We are going": South Bend Tribune,* October 30, 1913.

102   *Military Academy: The Notre Dame Scholastic,* November 1, 1913, 95.

103   *$500,000.00 in ticket:* Francis Stann, "Win Lose or Draw," *Evening Star Sports,* January 4, 1954.

104   *"We were permitted":* Rappoport, *Wake Up the Echoes,* 49.

105   *Rockne's quick loyalty:* Jesse Harper, interview by the Sports Editor, *Wichita Star,* April 25, 1931. Stagg had nothing on Harper when it came to discipline. Harper tolerated little, e.g., on October 21, 1914, Harper wrote to Supt. Glassock at the Culver Military academy:

"I am very sorry to learn that the Freshmen took three spoons from your mess hall when they dined there last Saturday. I assure you I will take the matter up at once. . . . I want you to understand that we do not approve of such conduct on the part of our students and that things of this nature seldom happen. . . ."

107   *"It was in":* All of the quotes from Baird are taken from Rappoport, *Wake up the Echoes,* 49–51.

111   *Six passes:* Jim Beach and Daniel Moore, *Army vs. Notre Dame: The Big Game.* As they noted, the feature of the game that most amazed the sports fans in the East was the length of Dorais's passes and that some of the spiral throws traveled thirty-five to forty yards to the receiver, an unheard-of distance in those days.

116   *Notre Dame 35:* All of the quotes from the New York Times, November 2, 1913.

116   *In 1956, Danzig:* Danzig, *The History of American Football,* 41.

7 | The Final Games of 1913

123   *five years: South Bend Tribune,* November 8, 1913.

124   *"the season": South Bend Tribune,* November 4, 1913.

124   *As one paper:* ibid.

124   *State College: South Bend Tribune,* November 8, 1913.

125   *14–7 victory: South Bend Tribune,* November 10, 1913.

127   *a bridge too far: South Bend Tribune,* November 11, 1913.

127   *had been planted: South Bend Tribune,* November 25, 1913.

127   *higher plane: South Bend Tribune,* November 14, 1913.

127   *blue system:* ibid.

128   *Dorais: South Bend Tribune,* November 11, 1913.

128   *Western man:* ibid.

128   *east or west: South Bend Tribune,* November 14, 1913.

128   *in the country: South Bend Tribune,* November 19, 1913.

128   *Christian Brothers: South Bend Tribune,* November 17, 1913.

128   *St. Louis: South Bend Tribune,* November 17, 1913.

130   *Thanksgiving ball: South Bend Tribune,* November 26, 1913.

130   *strong advocate:* ibid.

130   *water supply: South Bend Tribune,* November 29, 1913.

130   *Austin: South Bend Tribune,* November 26, 1913.

130   *Longhorns: South Bend Tribune,* November 28, 1913.

130   *game's end: South Bend News-Times,* November 28, 1913.

131   "Harper's calibre": South Bend Tribune, November 28, 1913.

8 | 1914: Mighty Yale Is on the Schedule

134   *Greatest football: The Notre Dame Scholastic,* October 3, 1914, 46.

134   *Chicago Examiner:* ibid., 16.

135   *Under wraps: The Notre Dame Scholastic,* October 10, 1914, 61–62.

136   *University of Virginia: South Bend Tribune,* October 5, 1914.

136   *unprecedented: South Bend News-Times,* October 14, 1914.

136   *freshmen run: South Bend News-Times,* October 8, 1914.

136   *battle with: South Bend News-Times,* October 14, 1914.

137   *No passes: South Bend Tribune,* October 12, 1914.

137   *15,000:* ibid.

137   *thousand were looking: South Bend News-Times,* October 7, 1914.

137   *Speculation: South Bend Tribune,* October 12, 1914.

137   *student speaker: South Bend News-Times,* October 17, 1914.

138   *Belgium: South Bend Tribune,* October 17, 1914.

138   *no excuses:* ibid.

138   *forty yard: South Bend Tribune,* October 18, 1914.

139   *two more: South Bend News-Times,* October 18, 1914; and *South Bend Tribune,* October 20, 1914.

139   *little solace: South Bend Tribune,* October 21, 1914.

139   *two-yard: South Bend Tribune,* October 19, 1914.

140   *worn the blue:* ibid.

140   *Yale showed:* Mark Keller, "What-Nots," *Los Angeles Examiner,* Sunday December 9, 1928.

140   *all eyes: South Bend Tribune,* October 19, 1914.

140   *star fullback: South Bend News-Times,* October 21, 1914.

141   *spectacular run: South Bend Tribune,* October 20, 1914.

141   *intense: South Bend Tribune,* October 22, 1914.

141   *University of Minnesota: South Bend News-Times,* October 24, 1914.

141   *exploded: South Bend News-Times,* October 25, 1914.

141   *key players: South Bend News-Times,* October 31, 1914.

141   *practice: South Bend News-Times,* October 29, 1914.

141   *Bergman: South Bend News-Times,* November 1, 1914.

142   *five undefeated: South Bend Tribune,* October 15, 1914.

142   *1913 invasion:* South Bend News-Times, November 2, 1914.

142   *Finegan: South Bend News-Times,* November 5, 1914.

142   *four: South Bend Tribune,* November 5, 1914.

142   *Hodgson: South Bend Tribune,* November 8, 1914.

142   *Pliska: South Bend Tribune,* November 10, 1914.

144   *innovator:* Kaye, *Good Clean Violence,* 56.

145   *Eisenhower:* Dineen, *The Illustrated History of Sports at the United States Military Academy,* 38; Adams, "More Than a Game: The Carlisle Indians Take to the Gridiron." There seems to be a consensus among the authorities that Eisenhower did suffer a knee injury, but not while attempting to tackle Thorpe. Dineen explains that Eisenhower sprained his knee the week after the Carlisle game when Army played Tufts, then reinjured it while vaulting a horse in the riding hall. The Thorpe injury is a better story, but perhaps a myth.

145   *gold medals:* Adams, "More than a Game: The Carlisle Indians Take to the Gridiron."

146   *"Paid to Glenn":* Sperber, *Shake Down the Thunder,* 46.

146   *Chicago alumni: South Bend News-Times,* November 12, 1914.

146   *report to: South Bend News-Times,* November 13, 1914.

146   *Rockne took: South Bend News-Times,* November 15, 1914.

146   *Indians:* ibid.

147   *twelve thousand:* Sperber, *Shake Down the Thunder,* 44–46.

147   *Syracuse: South Bend News-Times,* November 15, 1914.

147   *three stars: South Bend News-Times,* November 19, 1914.

147   *school spirit: South Bend News-Times,* November 17 and November 19, 1914.

147   *wet field: South Bend News-Times,* November 23, 1914.

147   *football history: South Bend News-Times,* November 25, 1914.

148   *Michigan: South Bend News-Times,* November 26, 1914.

148   *To the delight: South Bend News-Times,* November 27, 1914.

148   *senior fullback: South Bend Tribune,* November 27, 1914.

148   *Welch–Brown boxing: South Bend Tribune,* November 29, 1914.

148   *equal claim: South Bend Tribune,* November 27 and November 29, 1914.

149   *Paris: The Notre Dame Scholastic,* November 28, 1914, 171.

149   *tremendous amount: The Notre Dame Scholastic,* November 28, 1914, 190 and 214.

9 | 1915: The University of Nebraska Makes Its Notre Dame Debut

152   *since 1912: The Notre Dame Scholastic,* October 30, 1915, 124.

152   *supremacy: South Bend News-Times,* September 30, 1915.

153   *menial task:* Sperber, *Shake Down the Thunder,* 200–202.

154   *secret: South Bend Tribune,* October 8, 1915.

154   *school spirit: South Bend Tribune,* October 7, 1915.

154   *automobiles: South Bend Tribune,* October 8, 1915.

155   *Yell Master: South Bend Tribune,* October 10, 1915.

155   *"Dutch": South Bend News-Times,* ibid.

155   *trademarks: South Bend News-Times,* October 22, 1915.

155   *husky: South Bend Tribune,* October 12, 1915.

155   *Nebraska:* ibid.

155   *gloom: South Bend Tribune,* October 20, 1915.

156   *kicker: South Bend Tribune,* October 16, 1915.

156   *Cartier field: South Bend Tribune,* October 5, 1915.

156   *newsmen: South Bend Tribune,* October 22, 1915.

156   *eleven pounds: The Notre Dame Scholastic,* October 30, 1915, 125.

156   *cheering: South Bend News-Times,* October 21, 1915.

157   *15 points: South Bend News-Times,* October 21, 1915.

157   *keener:* ibid.

157   *music: South Bend News-Times,* October 24, 1915.

157   *Goats: South Bend News-Times,* October 23, 1915.

157   *Chamberlain: South Bend News-Times,* October 24, 1915.

157   *Cornhuskers: South Bend News-Times,* October 25, 1915.

157   *Lincoln: South Bend Tribune,* October 25, 1915.

158   *so good: The Notre Dame Scholastic,* October 30, 1915, 125.

158   *first team: South Bend News-Times,* October 27, 1915.

158   *South Dakota: South Bend Tribune,* October 26, 27, and 29, 1915.

159   *The final: South Bend News-Times,* October 31, 1915; and *South Bend Tribune,*
        November 1, 1915.

159   *football classic: The Dome,* 1916, 204.

159   *hard fight: South Bend News-Times,* November 5, 1915.

159   *workout: South Bend News-Times,* November 6, 1915.

160   *"West Pointers":* ibid.

160   *play-by-play: South Bend Tribune,* November 5, 1915.

160   *crossbar: The Notre Dame Scholastic,* November 13, 1915, 158.

160   *1913 game: South Bend News-Times,* November 7, 1915.

160   *day of rest: South Bend Tribune,* November 8, 1915.

161   *Southwest: South Bend Tribune,* November 11, 1915.

161   *another matter:* ibid.

162   *pepper and spirit: South Bend News-Times,* November 17, 1915.

162   *all season: South Bend News-Times,* November 20, 1915.

162   *typhoid fever: South Bend Tribune,* November 26, 1915.

162   *most of the game: South Bend Tribune,* November 29, 1915.

163   *South and West: The Dome,* 1916, 192.

10 | 1916: Undefeated and Never Scored Upon Until Army Turns the Tables

166   *were bright: South Bend Tribune,* November 27, 1915.

166   *ninety-five yards: South Bend News-Times,* October 1, 1916.

167   *sans anything: South Bend Tribune,* October 14, 1916.

167   *racist terms: South Bend News-Times,* October 15, 1916.

168   *Trinity College: South Bend Tribune,* October 20, 1916.

168   *Academy: South Bend Tribune,* October 28, 19.

168   *Iowa: South Bend Tribune,* October 30, 1916.

168   *South Bend: South Bend News-Times,* October 29, 1916.

169   *Oliphant:* ibid.

169   *best of the east: South Bend Tribune,* November 4, 1916.
169   *Army held: South Bend Tribune,* November 6, 1916.
169   *new rules: South Bend News-Times,* November 15, 1916.
169   *the ruling:* ibid.
169   *last quarter: South Bend Tribune,* November 6, 1916.
170   *out of reach: South Bend News-Times,* November 6, 1916.
170   *passing attack: South Bend Tribune,* November 13, 1916.
171   *school's history: South Bend News-Times,* November 18, 1916.
171   *Grant: South Bend News-Times,* November 19, 1916.
171   *46 to 0: South Bend News-Times,* November 25, 1916.
171   *Nebraska field: South Bend Tribune,* November 28, 1916.
171   *the game: South Bend News-Times,* November 29, 1916.
171   *display of speed: South Bend News-Times,* December 1, 1916.
171   *Miller to Bergman: South Bend Tribune,* December 1, 1916.
172   *want me:* Sperber, *Shake Down the Thunder,* 51.
172   *of the university: The Notre Dame Scholastic,* December 9, 1916, 190.

11 | 1917: Harper's Final Season

174   *into the service: South Bend Tribune,* October 5, 1917.
174   *Wisconsin: South Bend Tribune,* October 12, 1917.
174   *since 1908: The Notre Dame Scholastic,* October 20, 62.
175   *its history:* ibid.
175   *all year: South Bend Tribune,* October 22, 1917.
175   *"in victory": The Notre Dame Scholastic,* October 27, 1917, 78.
175   *George Gipp: South Bend Tribune,* October 19, 1917.
178   *upsetting Army:* Bacon, John, "The Gipper," *Michigan History Magazine,* November–December Issue, 2001, 48–55. There are numerous sources for background on George Gipp. See especially, Rappoport, *Wake up the Echoes;* Sperber, *Shake Down the Thunder;* and *Blue & Gold Illustrated,* "The George Gipp Collection," circa 2004.
178   *Missouri: The Notre Dame Scholastic,* November 10, 1917, 79.
178   *to the team: The Notre Dame Scholastic,* December 1, 1917, 162.
179   *for the game: South Bend Tribune,* October 26, 1917.
179   *forty yards: South Bend Tribune,* October 29, 1917.
179   *school gymnasium: South Bend Tribune,* November 12, 1917.
179   *contest of the season: South Bend Tribune,* November 2, 1917.
179   *all time:* ibid.
180   *on the ground: South Bend Tribune,* November 5, 1917.
180   *desired: The Notre Dame Scholastic,* November 10, 1917, 109.
180   *other way:* Rappoport, *Wake up the Echoes,* 67.
180   *a kick:* ibid.
180   *in years: The Notre Dame Scholastic,* November 10, 1917, 109.
181   *the men of Notre Dame: The Notre Dame Scholastic,* November 11, 1917, 161.
182   *near the ankle: South Bend Tribune,* November 12, 1917.
183   *50 yards: South Bend Tribune,* November 19, 1917.
183   *in the country: South Bend Tribune,* November 23, 1917.

184   *3 to 0 victory: The Dome,* 1918, 192.
184   *be surpassed: The Dome,* 1918, 184.

12 | Jesse Harper and Knute Rockne, 1918–1931

191   *on his high school baseball team:* Jim Harper, Jesse's son, in discussion with the author about life at the ranch; and "Ranching Shorthand," *Kansas Farmer Magazine,* April 20, 1946.
192   *"over your head":* Judge Norman J. Barry (played for both Jesse Harper and Knute Rockne) in discussion with author in Judge Barry's law office in Chicago in 1987. The Judge had just two pictures on his office walls, both small, about 8 by 10, and in black and white. One was the Judge standing as a player with Gipp, the other was of the 1920 Notre Dame team.
193   *An embarassing incident:* Sperber, *Shake Down the Thunder,* 120–121.
195   *more to me:* Jesse Harper to Knute Rockne, November 5, 1927, Hesburgh Library.

13 | Jesse Harper Returns to Notre Dame: 1931–1933

206   *football player:* Joe Doyle, *South Bend Tribune,* article describing an interview with Harper, August 2, 1961.
207   *if necessary:* Daniel Staff, *World-Telegram Sports,* April 6, 1931.
207   *14–3 victory:* Dick Snider, "On Sports," *Topeka Daily Capital,* March 31, 1954.
209   *"as it always will":* The Notre Dame Scholastic, May 8, 1931, 823.
210   *delicate conscience:* Hope, *Notre Dame: One Hundred Years,* 406–407.
211   *Christmas in 1931:* ibid., 404–409.
211   *"around here":* Heartley "Hunk" W. Anderson, with Emil Klosinski, *Notre Dame, Chicago Bears, and Hunk: Football Memoirs in Highlight,* 101.
212   *"he was recruited":* Sperber, *Shake Down the Thunder,* 51.
212   *Football League:* Sperber, *Shake Down the Thunder,* 50–51; and Marder, Keith, Mark Spellen, and Jim Donovan, *The Notre Dame Football Encyclopedia,* 117.
216   *"player at his side":* South Bend Tribune, October 4, 1931.
216   *going to suffer: South Bend Tribune,* October 11, 1931.
217   *football program: South Bend Tribune,* October 23 and 24, 1931.
217   *to his memory: South Bend Tribune,* November 1, 1931.
217   *Notre Dame won: South Bend Tribune,* November 7, 1931.
217   *star for Notre Dame: South Bend Tribune,* November 15, 1931.
218   *55,000: South Bend Tribune,* November 19, 1931.
218   *on campus: South Bend Tribune,* November 19, 21, and 22, 1931.
219   *Big Ten Conference: South Bend Tribune,* November 21, 1931.
220   *the contest ended: South Bend Tribune,* November 22, 1931.
220   *on their return: South Bend Tribune,* November 29, 1931.
223   *fourth-quarter surge: South Bend Tribune,* October 30, 1932.
223   *covered stands: South Bend Tribune,* November 13, 1932.
223   *that season: South Bend Tribune,* November 20, 1932.
224   *defeated Army: South Bend Tribune,* November 25, 1932.
224   *1935 Season: South Bend Tribune,* December 9, 1932.

225   *13 to 0: South Bend Tribune,* December 11, 1932.
225   *"out played": South Bend Tribune,* October 8, 1933.
226   *1930: South Bend Tribune,* October 15, 1933.
226   *loss secured: South Bend Tribune,* October 22, 1933.
226   *"an offense": South Bend Tribune,* October 27, 1933.
226   *"of the game": South Bend Tribune,* November 3, 1933.
227   *"honor satisfied": South Bend Tribune,* November 5, 1933.
227   *Noble Kizer: South Bend Tribune,* November 12, 1933.
227   *in 1924: South Bend Tribune,* November 2, 1933.
227   *blocked a punt: South Bend Tribune,* November 19, 1933.
227   *"threat to score": South Bend Tribune,* November 26, 1933.
227   *1933 season: South Bend Tribune,* December 1, 1933.
228   *resignations: South Bend Tribune,* December 8, 1933.
228   *"Harper was recalled":* ibid.

14 | Reflections

232   *"his visions": Wichita Star,* April 25, 1931. The reporter rode half a day by train to interview Harper at his ranch.
233   *membership:* Sperber, *Shake Down the Thunder,* 62.
234   *"of their schools":* Sperber, *Shake Down the Thunder,* 42.
234   *he spoke:* ibid.
234   *"more significant":* ibid.
235   *"reprehensible":* Sperber, Shake Down the Thunder, 211.
235   *$72,000:* ibid., 197–198.
236   *"colonies":* James Martin, S.J., "The Last Acceptable Prejudice?" America, March 25, 2000.
236   *Rome:* ibid.
236   *Catholic:* Robert Burns, *Being Catholic, Being American: The Notre Dame Story,* 1842–1934, 266–267.
237   *"endure for years":* ibid., 83.
238   *"for what he is":* Jesse C. Harper, interview by Dick Snider at the Harper ranch, Sitka, Kansas, "On Sports," *Topeka Daily Capital,* July 3, 5, 6, 7, 8, and 9, 1955.
240   *"greatest triumph":* Rappoport, *Wake up the Echoes,* 60.
240   "Greatest Coaching Decisions": "Greatest Coaching Decisions," ESPN.com, December 23, 1999, http://poll.espn.go.com/endofcentury/s/other/coaches.html, (accessed April 7, 2007).
241   *"kicked hell out of 'em":* Dick Snider, "On Sports," *Topeka Daily Capital,* see note above.
242   *ESPN published:* MacCambridge, *ESPN College Football Encyclopedia,* 634.
243   *"legendary team":* "The Man Who Set the Table," *Blue & Gold Illustrated,* "1988 Yearbook," 8.
243   *"I have only followed":* ibid., 12.
244   *"a few words":* ibid., 9.
245   *"played harder": Chicago Sun-Times,* August 4, 1961.

Bibliography

Archival Sources
Alma College Library, Alma College, Alma, Michigan
College Football Hall of Fame, South Bend, Indiana
Hesburgh Library, University of Notre Dame
Lilly Library, Wabash College, Crawfordsville, Indiana
University of Chicago Library
U.S. Military Academy Library, United States Military Academy, West Point, New York

Newspapers
The Bachelor (Wabash College Newspaper)
Chicago Sun-Times
Chicago Tribune
New York Times
South Bend News-Times
South Bend Tribune
Topeka Daily Capital
Wichita Beacon–Town Crier
Wichita Star
World Telegram Sports

Magazines

The Alma Record
The Almanian (Alma College Library)
Collier's Magazine
The Dome (University of Notre Dame yearbook, Hesburgh Library, University of Notre Dame, South Bend, Indiana)
Michigan History Magazine
The Notre Dame Scholastic (Hesburgh Library, University of Notre Dame)
University of Chicago Magazine
The Wabash (Lilly Library, Wabash College)
The Wabash College Magazine

Books

Anderson, Heartley W. "Hunk," with Emil Klosinski. *Notre Dame, Chicago Bears, and Hunk: Football Memoirs in Highlight.* Oviedo, FL: Florida Sun–Gator Publishing Co, 1976.

Beach, Jim. *Notre Dame Football.* New York: Macfadden-Bartell Books, 1962.

Beach, Jim, and Daniel Moore. *Army vs. Notre Dame: The Big Game, 1913–1947.* New York: Random House, Inc., 1948.

Bernstein, Mark F. *Football: The Ivy League Origins of an American Obsession.* Philadelphia: University of Pennsylvania Press, 2001.

Brondfield, Jerry. *100 Years of Football.* New York: Four Winds Press, 1969.

Burns, Robert E. *Being Catholic, Being American: The Notre Dame Story, 1842–1934.* Notre Dame, IN: University of Notre Dame Press, 1999.

Camp, Walter, ed. *Spalding's Official Football Guide.* New York: American Sports Publishing Company, 1906. A complete collection of *Spalding's Official Football Guide* can be found in Rare Books and Special Collections, Hesburgh Library, University of Notre Dame and the archives of the College Football Hall of Fame, South Bend, Indiana.

Danzig, Allison. *Oh, How They Played the Game: The Early Days of Football and the Heroes Who Made It Great.* New York: The Macmillan Company, 1971.

———. *The History of American Football: Its Great Teams, Players, and Coaches.* Englewood Cliffs, NJ: Prentice Hall, Inc., 1956.

Dineen, Joseph E. *The Illustrated History of Sports at the United States Military Academy.* Norfolk, VA: The Donning Company, 1988.

Grant, Chet. Before *Rockne at Notre Dame: Impression and Reminiscence.* Notre Dame, IN: Dujarie Press, 1968.

Heisler, John, ed. *Echoes of Notre Dame Football: The Greatest Stories Ever Told.* Chicago: Triumph Books, 2005.

Higham, John, *Strangers in the Land, Patterns of American Nativism, 1860–1925.* Rutgers University Press, 2004.

Hope, Arthur J., C.S.C, *Notre Dame: One Hundred Years.* South Bend, IN: Icarus Press, Inc. / The University of Notre Dame Press, 1943.

Kaye, Ivan N., *Good Clean Violence.* New York: J. B. Lippincott Company, 1973.

Kelley, James Daniel. "Evolution of the Rules of Intercollegiate Football." Master's Thesis, Springfield College, June 1950. A copy of this impressive work can be found in the archives of the College Football Hall of Fame in South Bend, Indiana.

Layden, Joe. *Notre Dame Football A–Z*. Dallas: Taylor Publishing Company, 1997.

Lester, Robin. *Stagg's University, The Rise, Decline and Fall of Big-Time Football at Chicago*. Urbana: University of Illinois Press, 1995.

Lucia, Ellis. *Mr. Football: Amos Alonzo Stagg*, South Brunswick, NJ: A. S. Barnes and Company, 1970.

MacCambridge, Michael, ed. *ESPN College Football Encyclopedia: The Complete History of the Game*. New York: ESPN Books, 2005

Marder, Keith, Mark Spellen, and Jim Donovan. *Notre Dame Football Encyclopedia*. New York: Citadel Press/Kensington Publishing Corp., 2001.

Oriard, Michael. *Reading Football: How the Popular Press Created an American Spectacle*. Chapel Hill: University of North Carolina Press, 1993.

Power, Francis J. *Life Story of Amos Alonzo Stagg: Grand Old Man of Football*. St. Louis, MO: C.C. Spink & Sons, 1946.

Rappoport, Ken. *Wake up the Echoes: Special 100th Anniversary Edition*. Tomball, TX: Strode Publishers, a division of Circle Book Service, 1988.

Robinson, Ray. *Rockne of Notre Dame: The Making of a Football Legend*. New York: Oxford University Press, 1999.

Schoor, Gene, ed. *A Treasury of Notre Dame Football*. New York: Funk & Wagnalls Company, Inc., 1962.

Sperber, Murray. *Shake Down the Thunder: The Creation Of Notre Dame Football*. New York: Henry Holt and Company, 1993.

Tucker, Todd. *Notre Dame vs. The Klan: How the Fighting Irish Defeated the Klan*. Chicago: Loyola Press, 2004.

Umphlett, Wiley Lee. *Creating the Big Game: John W. Heisman and the Invention of American Football*. Westport, CT: Greenwood Press, 1992.

Wallace, Francis. *The Notre Dame Story*. New York: Rinehart & Company, Inc., 1949.

Walters, John. *Notre Dame Golden Moments: 20 Memorable Events That Shaped Notre Dame Football*. Nashville: Rutledge Hill Press/Thomas Nelson Publishers, Inc., 2004.

Watterson, John Sayle. *College Football: History, Spectacle, Controversy*. Baltimore: The Johns Hopkins University Press, 2000.

Periodicals

Adams, David Wallace. "More Than a Game: The Carlisle Indians Take to the Gridiron," *Western Historical Quarterly*, vol. 32, no. 1, Spring 2001.

Keller, Mark. "What-Nots," *Los Angeles Examiner*, Sunday, December 9, 1928.

Kunderman, Brian. "Football's Forward Pass Turns 100 Years Old," *SLU Newslink: The Inside Guide to Saint Louis University*, September 1, 2006.

"The Man Who Set the Table." *Blue & Gold Illustrated*, Yearbook, 1988.

Martin, James, S. J. "The Last Acceptable Prejudice?" *America*, March 25, 2000.

"Ranching Shorthand," *Kansas Farmer Magazine*, April 20, 1946.

Robins, Lester. "Legends of the Fall," *The University of Chicago Magazine*. October 1995.

Smith, Ronald A. "Harvard and Columbia and a Reconsideration of the 1905–1906 Football Crisis," *Journal of Sport History*, vol. 8, no. 3, 1981.

Stann, Francis. "Win Lose or Draw," *Evening Star Sports*, January 4, 1954.

Index